AF372086

The story of
Veteran & Vintage Cars

by Cyril Posthumus

Hamlyn

LONDON · NEW YORK · SYDNEY · TORONTO

in association with Phoebus

CONTENTS

Illustrated by J. W. Wood and Associates
Edited by Gillian Harvey
Designed by Sarah Reynolds

Radio Times Hulton

Cyril Posthumus entered the field of professional motoring journalism in 1950 when he joined the weekly magazine *Autosport*. He then took on the editorship of *Motoring News* in 1957 and has worked subsequently for various British magazines including *Motor* and *Motor Racing*, and the American magazine *Road and Track*. Currently working as a freelance, he is the author of several books including *World Sports Car Championship*, *Sir Henry Segrave*, *Vintage Cars* and *The German Grand Prix* (published in English and German). He was also co-author with Denis Jenkinson and Cecil Clutton of *The Racing Car—Development and Design*.

John Wood was an aircraft designer for a major British aircraft company for 20 years. Today, he and his team of artists have built up a considerable reputation in the field of technical illustration, and have produced more than 100 books which have been sold in many different countries including America, France, Germany, Spain, Italy, Sweden and Japan. The specially commissioned illustrations in this book pay particular attention to the authentic colouring and detail of cars of the period.

Published 1977 by
The Hamlyn Publishing Group Limited
London · New York · Sydney · Toronto
Astronaut House, Feltham, Middlesex, England

ISBN 0 600 39155 8

This edition © 1977
Phoebus Publishing Company
BPC Publishing Limited
169 Wardour Street
London W1A 2JX
This material first appeared in *First Cars* © 1976
Phoebus Publishing Company

Made and printed in Great Britain by
Waterlow (Dunstable) Limited

ABOUT THIS BOOK

When Karl Benz travelled those few hesitant yards in the world's first petrol-driven car in October 1885, who could have foreseen the tremendous impact this strange machine was to make on the 20th century way of life? Yet within thirty years there were four million motor cars in existence: the prototype horseless carriage had been transformed into a practical, essential means of transport.

Well-known motor historian Cyril Posthumus gives a vivid account of the growth of the motor car during the Veteran and Vintage eras, in the perspective of the social and economic conditions of the time. After a slow start, with pioneering efforts exclusive to Germany and France, 'the new locomotion' caught on, and by the mid-1890s most Western European countries and the USA had produced their first designs. Famous names like Ford, Mercedes, Renault and Fiat began to emerge, and by 1914 practically all the important basic features of the modern car had been developed.

The First World War saw the motor car in an entirely new role. Thousands of people came in contact with motor vehicles in the war effort, and peace brought with it an unprecedented demand for cars from all levels of society. The Twenties witnessed the car at a peak in individual character, with a quality of workmanship unequalled in later years when mass production dominated. The variety in design was astonishing, ranging from the utilitarian Austin Seven to the magnificent super-luxe models from the *grandes marques* such as Rolls-Royce, Hispano-Suiza, Cadillac and others. It was at once a period of great classics and the decade when the car became a way of life in the Western world and was also making its influence felt in the tradition-bound East and Far East.

Lavishly illustrated with excellent colour drawings by J. W. Wood and many contemporary photographs, this very readable and informative book recaptures an exciting and unforgettable era.

GOTHAM
VISIBLES
KNITTING MILLS

FATHERS OF

The history of the automobile really begins with two Germans, Karl Benz of Mannheim and Gottlieb Daimler of Cannstatt. Both engineers were working towards the same goal at the same time, although neither knew the other. In each case their achievement was the culmination of long years of hard work and untiring experimentation, and was to be followed by more of both before the motorcar could really be said to have 'arrived'.

The pioneer Benz and Daimler vehicles were remarkably different in their methods of self-propulsion. Karl Benz, at that time partner in the Rheinische Gasmotorenfabrik, gas engine manufacturers of Mannheim, adapted gas engine principles, using liquid hydrocarbons for his fuel source, and installed the power unit in a specially designed tubular steel chassis with three wheels only. Gottlieb Daimler, on the other hand, developed his own liquid fuel-burning, fast-running four-stroke engine, which he fitted to the most readily available chassis, a four-seater horse-type carriage with the shafts cut short.

If Benz's 1885 creation looked spidery and precarious, Daimler's of 1886 looked ponderous and archaic, but both inventors were far too busy perfecting their devices to worry about appearance. The first stage, that of constructing the cars, had been reached and these vehicles worked after a fashion, but much modifying and refinement lay ahead before it could be claimed that the horse had been superseded.

Gottlieb Daimler (top), builder in 1886 of the world's first four-wheeled, petrol-driven car (above). It was virtually a coach minus the horse and shafts, with the watercooled 1.1hp single-cylinder 4-stroke engine fitted between the front and rear seats. A surface carburettor and platinum 'hot tube' ignition were employed, the rear wheels were driven by belts and ring gears, and the tires were solid.

INVENTION

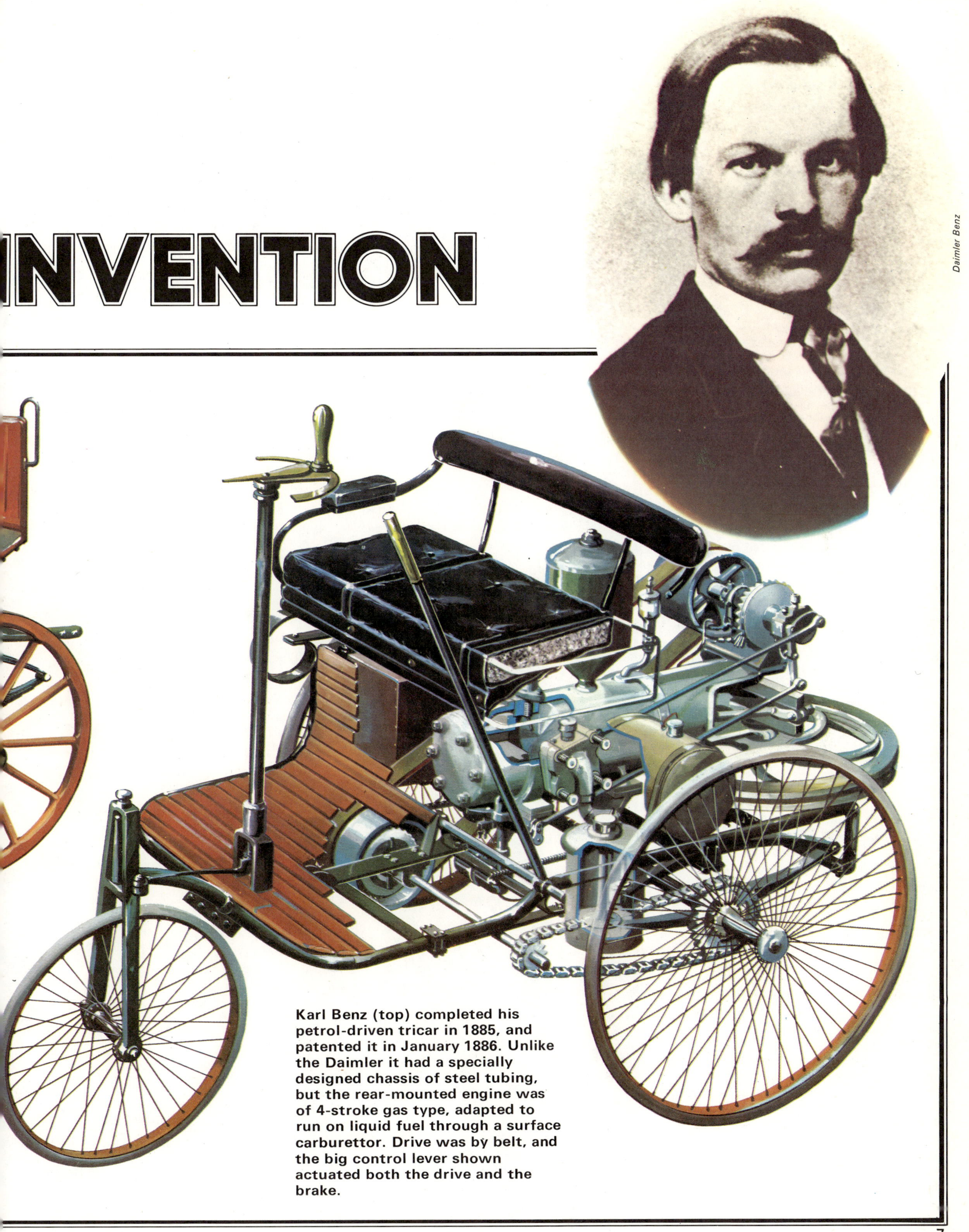

Karl Benz (top) completed his petrol-driven tricar in 1885, and patented it in January 1886. Unlike the Daimler it had a specially designed chassis of steel tubing, but the rear-mounted engine was of 4-stroke gas type, adapted to run on liquid fuel through a surface carburettor. Drive was by belt, and the big control lever shown actuated both the drive and the brake.

A great deal of romantic nonsense has been spoken and written about the peaceful, unpolluted days of horse transport. For although 'Dobbin' the horse had served man long and faithfully, it was not realized how limited his role was. The constant pounding of hooves and iron-shod cart wheels on unmetalled roads meant bumpy centres and rutted gutters, which filled with water in winter, or churned to dust in summer.

Horse traffic in towns was rarely the gay, colourful affair depicted by so many artists. Their cheerful pictures tactfully omitted the unsavoury manure heaps along the way and at every stop, or the teams of boys kept to clean up after each coach's visit. Urine-soaked roads in towns and cities were a distinct menace to health, contributing largely to fly-borne diseases such as botulism, which killed off so many children. The summer sun on city roads drew out an unbearable stench from the soaked wood blocks, while the dust, kicked up so picturesquely in the paintings, was composed more of dried manure than of powdered soil or sand.

Limitations of steam

There was the further, commercial factor that the horse was a very wasteful 'engine'. Whether working in the shafts or resting in the stable or paddock, he still consumed food; he could not be 'switched off', but had to be left 'ticking over' and burning fuel. Moreover, long journeys meant relays of fresh horses, all requiring to be fed and maintained, and when one considers the duration of some of England's fastest coach services — five hours from London to Brighton (50 miles), twenty hours from London to York (197 miles) — it is easy to understand why imaginative men sought progress.

Steam power had seemed to be the answer, but here, too, were limitations: the need to carry coal and take on water frequently, and the excessive weight inherent in early steam machinery. Coal gas, another source of power, had its drawbacks, for although it worked well in slow-turning stationary engines, it was of little use in mobile carriages, where the limited capacity of the gas cylinder inhibited the length and speed of a journey.

Pre-petrol power sources ranged from the comic (extreme left) proposing two dogs in a 'tread-wheel' (1870), to many successful steam cars, including (left) the Rickett, sold as a private 3-seater in 1860. Below: Charing Cross, in London before the motor age — a confusion of cabs, horses and people.

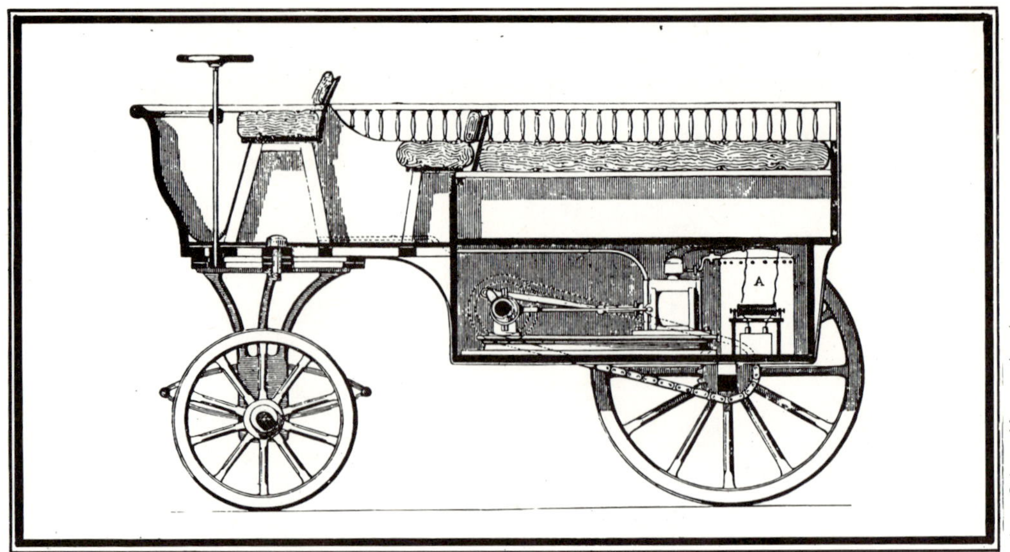

Lenoir (left) claimed to have driven this 'break' several times in 1862–63 from Paris to Joinville, a distance of 6 miles, in 3 hours, using a gas-type engine.

It was Etienne Lenoir's modified gas engine of 1863 which he claimed could run on liquid fuel of petroleum base, that pointed the way to both Benz and Daimler. Petroleum – from *petra* (rock) and *oleum* (oil) – could be refined to produce a variety of liquid fuels, such as paraffin (kerosene), benzine, gasoline, naphtha, etc. These could be gasified by being sprayed through a fine jet, or drawn through a wick, and the more volatile of them, such as benzine or gasoline, were to prove all-important in developing the car.

For years the world's sources of petroleum had been tapped only to refine lamp oil, with at least 50 per cent being burned as waste by-products! The coming of the automobile, however, led to greater demand and precipitated the oil boom which is still in progress. A mere gallon of petroleum fuel could propel a horseless carriage for 25, 30 or more miles, so that an ample quantity could easily be carried in a tank on the vehicle.

The four-stroke cycle

Lenoir's experimental carriage was invaluable in another way; it proved the total inadequacy of the early gas-type engine for driving a car. The Lenoir 'break' took nearly three hours for a six-mile journey, its engine revolving at only 100rpm yet consuming wasteful quantities of fuel. Clearly a new kind of internal combustion engine was required. This was met by the 'Otto' four-stroke cycle, patented in 1876 for gas engines by Nicolaus Otto of the gas engine manufacturing firm of Otto & Langen at Deutz. Although intended for gas combustion, this principle was ideal for use with liquid fuels.

The four piston strokes – downward for the sucking-in of gas/air mixture, upward for compression of mixture, downward under explosion of the mixture, and upward to force out the burnt gases – remain the basic principle of the modern petrol (gasoline) engine; only cylinder head design, valves and valve gear, ignition, bearings, etc., changing with time. The 'Otto' cycle

was actually anticipated, although the original inventor, a French scientist named Beau de Rochas, simply laid down his theories on paper in 1862, rather than in the metal. However, his specification was enough to negate the 'Otto' patent rights, thus enabling Daimler (who had greatly assisted Otto in perfecting his 'cycle') and Benz to employ the principle without licence complications.

Both Benz and Daimler have been called 'the father of the automobile', and considering their respective work they can justly be accorded joint parenthood. Karl Benz completed his first car in 1885. After a grounding in engineering he founded a small works in 1874 to manufacture two-stroke stationary engines running on coal gas. Not long after, Benz became acquainted with a new design of a velocipede – a treadle-and-lever operated three-wheeler constructed as lightly as possible, on which a strong young man in the single basket seat could propel himself at an exhilarating 10–12mph in favourable conditions.

Benz then turned his thoughts to the possibilities of driving such a machine with an engine, thus dispensing with muscle power. From there, ideas of a horseless carriage able to carry two or more persons followed, and with financial help from Mannheim businessmen, Max Rose and Friedrich Esslinger, he began serious work in 1883 to develop a suitable source of power. It would have to be light, much lighter than steam, and it would have to be totally mobile, which meant carrying one's own fuel. He chose benzine, a variant of what we know today as petrol or gasoline, purchasable at that time from pharmacists, and erroneously thought by many to be a Benz speciality because of its name.

The Benz engine recipe was simple to the point of crudity. It was a single-cylinder, water-cooled, four-stroke, 'Otto'-type unit with 91.4×150mm bore and stroke, giving 985cc and perhaps ¾ horsepower at approximately 250 rpm. Although it largely followed the pattern of the stationary gas engines made by Benz & Co., the petrol unit was

installed horizontally between the rear wheels of the three-wheeled chassis, with the crankshaft disposed vertically and fully exposed, and a spoked iron flywheel mounted horizontally below it. To convert the liquid benzine into gas he devised a surface vaporizer (carburettor), and to ignite it he employed a battery and trembler coil ignition and a sparking plug which he made himself.

First forays

Mixture intake was via a slide valve, and a 'mushroom' type exhaust valve was used, both mechanically operated, and the engine drove a countershaft by belt. The 'clutch' to transmit the power to the wheels was a forked lever which slid the belt across from a loose to a fast pulley. The countershaft embodied a differential – a device first evolved by medieval watchmakers and adapted to a steam wagon in 1828 – to compensate for the different rotating speeds of the inner and outer wheels when cornering.

From the countershaft, side chains drove both rear wheels. These wheels were large-diameter spoked type, built for Benz by cycle maker Heinrich Kleyer (who later founded the Adler car company), and they carried solid rubber tires. The smaller single front wheel ran unsprung in a fork, steered by a wheel and handle at the top of a vertical column, with a rack and pinion working a forward arm at its lower end. One of the more striking features of the Benz was its frame, a special structure of steel boiler tubing with brazed lugs and mounting points, and supported by carriage-style fully-elliptic leaf springs at the rear.

Controls on this single-speed vehicle were very basic; a long side lever pushed forward moved the belt onto the drive pulley, while if moved back it 'declutched' and also worked a brake on the fixed pulley. The hand or foot throttle had yet to come, and Benz controlled his engine speed somewhat haphazardly by governing the lift of the exhaust valve.

This, then, was the machine for which Karl Benz was granted German patent number

10

Dr Nicolaus Otto (right) of the Gasmotorenfabrik Deutz, originally patented the modern 4-stroke principle for use on his firm's gas engines (above).

37/435 on January 29, 1886. It worked, but only just. On his first trial run in October of the previous year, Benz lost control of his new 'baby' within a few yards, struck a wall, and broke the front forks. On his next run he managed about 100 yards, but, gradually improving and taming his creation, he extended this to nearly a mile, then more, increasing the distance with each journey he made.

In Baden province, where Benz was working, speeds of over 4mph in towns or 8mph on open roads were against the law, so he resorted to making most of his test runs in the late evening. For a rather timid, law-abiding citizen, Benz tackled the problem enterprisingly. He arranged for an interview with the Provincial chief of police, collecting him from Mannheim railway station in his tricar. They were persistently obstructed by a horse-drawn milk wagon, and the police chief, enjoying the ride and entering into the spirit of things, urged the wagon to pull over. Benz chose this moment to emphasize the value of a self-propelled car "if it isn't hobbled to a horse's pace"; the official took the point, and soon the speed limits were eased. Only later did Benz admit that he had deliberately planned the milk wagon episode.

The first motor tour

Benz's car was first shown at the Paris Exhibition in 1887, attracting much attention, but meanwhile he was building a second car with two-speed planetary transmission. This proved unsuccessful, so on a third car he substituted a two-speed belt drive and also fitted a bigger 116×160mm engine, giving 1½ to 2hp. The whole car was sturdier and carried four-seater *dos-à-dos* bodywork in which the back passengers faced the rear. In 1888 this improved Benz vehicle was offered for sale in Germany, but no buyers came forward. Then a Frenchman named Emile Roger, who had sold Benz stationary engines and was much taken by the car shown in Paris, ordered one and obtained the sole agency for France. He made arrangements to assemble Benz cars

in Paris from parts sent from Mannheim, calling them the Roger-Benz, but again no customers materialized.

In September 1888 a Benz car was displayed at the Munich Power Machinery Exhibition, Benz driving it through the city streets and creating great excitement. His car was awarded the Grand Gold Medal for special merit, but that same year had already seen a further, and totally unexpected demonstration of the potential of the horseless carriage.

Karl Benz's wife, Berta, was a staunch believer in her husband's cars, but was annoyed by his reluctance to give them a really extended test (his trial runs seldom exceeded about six miles.) She resolved to take action. Her sons Eugen and Richard were fully familiar with the working of their father's cars, so Berta Benz planned that the three should drive the third tricar from Mannheim to Pforzheim, a distance of 100 kilometres (62¼ miles), spend a week's holiday there, and then return.

Confident that Karl was fully absorbed in building his next car, she casually told him that she and the boys were off in a day or so to Pforzheim 'by the first train'. The trio quietly prepared and left very early, pushing the tricar until well beyond earshot of the house and the still-sleeping Karl, then set off. All went well at first, Berta, Eugen and Richard, their baggage, spare batteries, water cans, etc. travelling at some 10 to 12mph through Weinheim and Heidelberg to Wiesloch, where they ran out of 'ligroin' — a chemical name for benzine, and had to buy more from a pharmacist's shop.

Beyond Bruchsal and Bretten the road became decidedly hilly so that one or other was obliged to jump off and push. Then came the Bauschlott, a really steep hill, where both Berta and Eugen had to dismount and push, with 13-year-old Richard driving the Benz at little more than walking pace. Relief in reaching the summit at last was offset when, on descending into the village, they found the brakes were virtually worn out, but they persuaded a shoemaker to reline them by nailing on some more

leather. After buying some more 'ligroin' they detoured through Wilferdingen rather than face more hills, only to encounter trouble with the trembler coil, which was breaking apart. After investigation, Berta bade her sons look the other way, removed one of her garters, and cured the trouble by doubling it around the casing!

Pforzheim was getting nearer, but they were now entering the hilly Black Forest; ahead was a forbidding mountain and darkness was falling. Again the heavier members of the party jumped off and pushed while little Richard steered the Benz, until at last they topped the rise, to see the welcome lights of Pforzheim far down below. Without lights but with their engine giving ample audible warning, the adventurous trio on their horseless carriage finally entered the town, dusty, oily, weary but triumphant.

Safe arrival

Berta telegraphed the news of their safe arrival to 'Papa' Benz, who replied tersely "Send driving chains by express", for he needed them for the Munich exhibition car, then nearing completion. He soon sent them a replacement pair, and after holiday joy-riding with friends, the Benz trio made the return journey to Mannheim without major troubles. The world's first extended motor journey had been completed.

With Emile Roger holding the French agency, and planning to offer the Roger-Benz on the British and U.S.A. markets in the near future, the Benz & Co. factory in Mannheim's Waldhofstrasse with its staff of five workmen, prepared to go into small-scale car production — the very first in the world. Orders, however, were desperately slow in coming. By 1891 Roger had sold his first cars, but production amounted to a mere handful. The Frenchman blamed sales resistance on the fact that the Benz had only three wheels, which meant a rough ride and limited stability on bumpy roads. Accordingly Karl Benz agreed to build a four-wheeler in 1892, but by then things had happened elsewhere.

Berta Benz (left), wife of Karl Benz, who, with her teenage sons, made the world's first extended motor drive of 125 miles in 1888 (pictured below). Wilhelm Maybach (right), Daimler's right-hand man in helping him with development of his first cars and engines.
Next page, top left: Daimler's second car, the V-twin cylinder-engined 'Stahlrad' of 1889. Top right: The platinum 'hot tube' ignition system on the Stahlrad's engine. Below: Early Daimler publicity shows that Daimler foresaw many other uses for his engines besides in cars.

By 1886 Gottlieb Daimler knew fully about Benz's activities and his patents, and was himself deeply involved in similar trial-and-error experimentation to prove his principles. He was much more preoccupied with perfecting his engine than developing a car, foreseeing the possibility of its use in boats, railcars and bicycles. His first single-cylinder petrol engine, a compact 264cc unit of only half a horsepower which he built in his garden workshop at Cannstatt, with his faithful partner Wilhelm Maybach, was first placed in a bicycle — the world's first motorcycle — in 1885. It was called the *Einspur* ('one-track'), and for reasons of secrecy they made it themselves, using wood for the frame at a time when quite sophisticated bicycles with steel tube frames were already being made.

The Einspur seemed to satisfy the inventor that his engine would work, and he concentrated on designing a larger one. Like Karl Benz, Daimler took advantage of the invalidity of Otto's patent by adopting the four-stroke principle. Unlike Benz's cautious 250rpm, however, Daimler designed his motor to turn over at a daring 750rpm, thereby aiming for more power and flexibility. His was the true ancestor of the modern car engine.

Daimler sets the pace

In his first 'car', the 1886 four-wheeler carriage minus horse and shafts which he bought for 795 marks, he fitted an engine similar to that in the motorcycle but of larger capacity giving 1.1hp. Its single-cylinder was mounted vertically on a round aluminium crankcase, and the inlet valve, operated by suction of the piston, was located above the mechanically operated exhaust valve — a system that became known simply as *i.o.e.* or inlet-over-exhaust, and which remained popular for many years. For ignition at such high engine speeds Daimler eschewed electricity, then still something of a mystery force of dubious reliability, and devised what was called a *glow tube* or *hot tube*, which projected into the combustion chamber and was permanently heated by a Bunsen-type burner.

In search of a material able to withstand constant heat for prolonged periods he tried steel, ceramics and nickel before finally

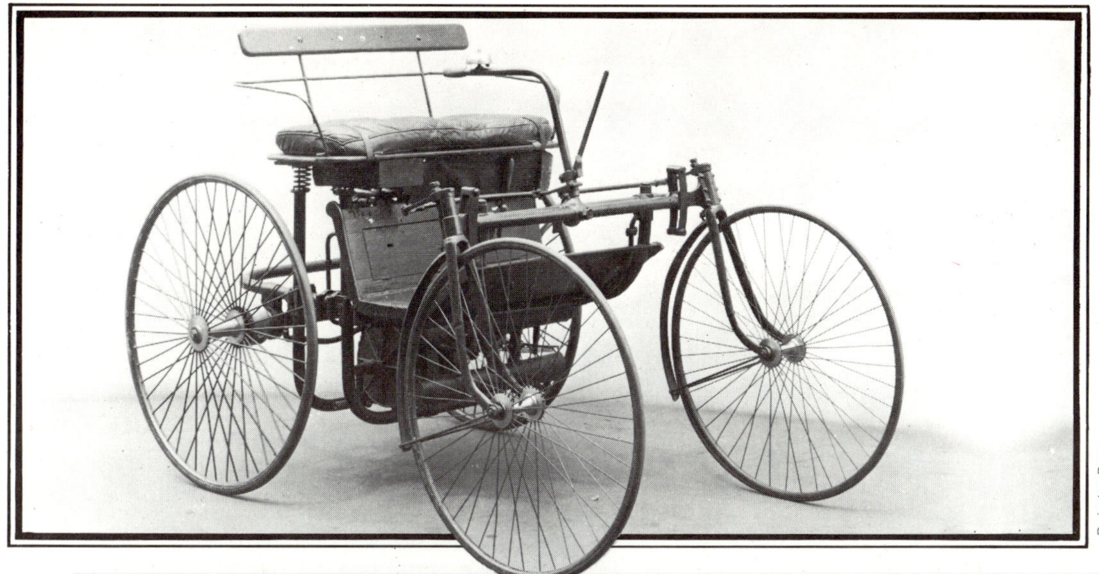

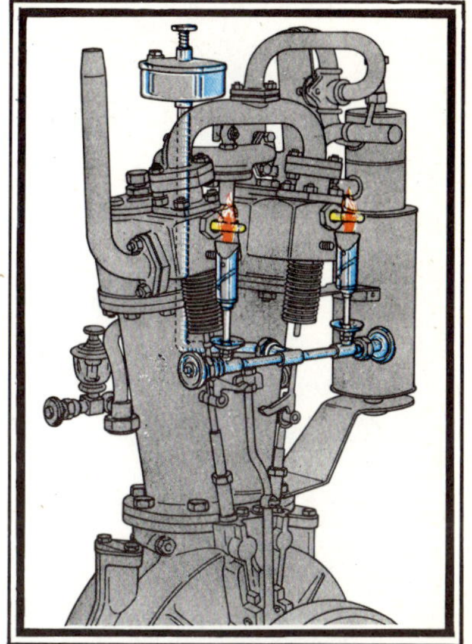
Daimler Benz

Daimler Benz

hitting on platinum, and this, too, became standard in many early motor engines. A surface carburettor was used, and the cylinder was water-cooled in a thin surrounding metal jacket, pump-circulated to a rear-mounted radiator. This engine occupied the space between the front and rear seats where the nearside rear passenger's legs would have been; it drove the rear wheels through two belts and exposed gearwheels giving two speeds, and embodying a 'poor man's' differential formed from leather pads relying on slip.

Daimler's 1886 car was as crude as his engine was advanced, but once satisfied that the latter functioned well, he offered all his patents taken out between 1883 and 1886 to his former employees, the Gas-motorenfabrik Deutz, emphasizing the engine's versatility for propulsion on land, water, rails and even in the air. The Deutz concern, well content with the success of their stationary engine business, turned his offer down flat, so Daimler continued alone, independent but under-financed.

He continued to concentrate on improving his engines rather than the car as a whole, with the result that his next vehicle, known as the *Stahlrad*, was almost as primitive in chassis as the first, amounting broadly to two bicycles joined together to make a quadricycle. But the engine, now fitted lower, in front of the rear axle, had progressed to become a narrow vee-twin with cylinders at 20°, and giving an estimated 1.6hp at 700rpm. Moreover, it drove the rear wheels by sliding spur wheels, which provided four forward speeds. The tubular steel frame was built for Daimler by the Neckarsulmer Stahlfabriken, cycle-building ancestors of the modern NSU company.

Like Benz, Daimler had business associates in France through gas engines — the Otto & Langen products which he had largely developed for the Deutz factory — and when their French agent, Edouard Sarazin, saw Daimler's 1-cylinder petrol engine of 1886 he was intrigued. He became the French licensee, and persuaded the Paris firm of Panhard et Levassor to take up manufacture of the Daimler engine.

FRANCE, THE

France at the end of the nineteenth century was a vigorous and progressive nation, ahead in artistic, scientific and technical affairs as epitomized by the great World's Fair held in Paris between May and October 1889. Overlooking the site of the Fair loomed that latest 'wonder of the world', the Eiffel Tower, but down below, little noticed among the massed exhibits, lay the first seeds of 'automobilism', destined to grow into something infinitely more mighty and influential than an inanimate steel structure 1000 feet high.

Relations between France and Germany were still strained as a result of the Franco-Prussian war of 1870, so much so that Germany was not represented officially at the Fair, yet amid a welter of steam and gas stationary engines in the *Machines et Moteurs* section, examples of both Benz's and Daimler's four-stroke petrol engines contrived to be present, imported by French agents. Indeed, one particular Daimler unit drew the public like moths to a candle, for it drove a dynamo which lit a dazzling cluster of 30 electric light bulbs, or *incandescent lamps* as they termed them then. Elsewhere, in the *Charronage* display among elegant landaus, berlines, broughams and other horse-drawn vehicles stood two curious *voitures à pétrole*, one the latest three-wheeler by Karl Benz as supplied to his French agent Emile Roger, the other Daimler's second car, the ungainly wire-wheeled *Stahlrad* quadricycle with 1.6hp twin-cylinder engine.

The enterprising widow

This had arrived at a late stage in the six-month Fair, but not too late for some convincing demonstrations that were firmly to cement the next two major developments in automobile history. Gottlieb Daimler, making the most of the occasion, had also sent along two motorboats with Daimler petrol engines, which were demonstrated from a special dock on the Seine. Among those who rode in these boats with Daimler himself were a couple seemingly more absorbed in talking business than in the pleasures of water travel without oars or sails. They were Mme Louise Sarazin, the widow of Edouard Sarazin who had been the Paris agent for

Otto & Langen and a close friend of Daimler's until his death in 1887, and Emile Levassor of the Paris engineering concern, Panhard et Levassor.

For years Panhard-Levassor, formerly Périn et Pauwels, had made wood and metal bandsaws, but when Sarazin approached Emile Levassor, told him he held the French rights to Daimler's patents, and wanted Panhard-Levassor to build engines to Daimler designs for him, Levassor was extremely interested. Sarazin's death the following year was thus a severe setback to him, but fortunately the widow proved a worthy successor to her husband in business. During his last hours, on Christmas Day 1887, Sarazin had urged his wife: ''Keep working with Daimler — nobody today has any conception of the enormous potential of his patents,'' and once again a woman was to play a vital role in the coming of the car.

In 1888, some months after her husband's death, Mme Sarazin went to Cannstatt to negotiate personally with Gottlieb Daimler. No written agreement had ever been drawn up with her late husband, but Daimler cordially accepted the widow as his new French representative. She returned to Paris with the French and Belgian patent rights to the Daimler motor, and in addition, she actually managed to bring back one of the engines, which she passed on to Panhard-Levassor as a master pattern. That firm dismantled it, studied the engineering problems, and forthwith embarked on the manufacture of similar units, undertaking to sell them for use in horseless carriages, boats or railcars, or else as stationary power units.

Panhard-Levassor planned also to build their own car around the Daimler engine, but in the meantime supplied three of their first production units to another French manufacturer, Armand Peugeot, who had also decided to try his hand at producing a petrol car. Peugeot was an old French concern dating back to the fifteenth century, which became famous as early exponents of cold rolling of steel, using steam presses. They turned out an intriguing variety of products, including clock springs, saws, shears, farm implements, steel strip, domestic hardware, spectacle frames, crinolines, umbrella ribs and coffee grinders.

FORCING HOUSE

Mme Louise Sarazin (far left), who secured Daimler engine patent rights for Panhard-Levassor of Paris. Armand Peugeot (right), French industrialist and cycle manufacturer, whose company installed a Panhard-built Daimler engine in their 1890 car (below), the first to be built in France.

René Panhard and Emile Levassor (far left & left) were partners in the great French pioneer marque which set the pace and the fashion in the first 15 years of motoring. Below: An early example of the front-engined Panhard-Levassor which first appeared in 1891, and established the traditional design order known as the 'système Panhard'. Right: The same system, with engine in front driving the rear wheels via gears, propellor shaft and chains, was in fact anticipated on Amédée Bollée's famous 1878 steam car, 'La Mancelle'.

When the cycle craze began they joined in, becoming pre-eminent among the countless manufacturers, and then Armand Peugeot built an experimental steam car with Serpollet engine and boiler, exhibiting it at the same Paris Fair that included displays of Benz and Daimler products. The limitations of steam dissatisfied Peugeot, however, and in discussion with Emile Levassor, whom he knew well and whose company were good customers for Peugeot steel, he heard about the Daimler petrol motor. A demonstration run with Daimler and Maybach on the *Stahlrad* during the 1889 Fair amply convinced him, and suddenly the world's car manufacturers had increased in number from two to four: Benz, Daimler, Panhard and Peugeot. Events were now really moving, and were to snowball sensationally in the next few years.

The first Peugeot

Apart from their common use of the Daimler engine, the Peugeot and Panhard-Levassor cars differed widely. The first Peugeot, largely evolved by the firm's chief engineer Rigoulot, was a much refined edition of the tubular-framed Daimler *Stahlrad* four-wheeler. The duplicated bicycle-type forks were replaced by an axle suspended on a transverse leaf spring, steered on the so-called *Ackermann* system which compensated for the tighter radius taken by the inner wheel in turning. This had been devised in 1816 by Eugen Lankensperger for use on horse-drawn carriages, but the conservative, tradition-bound coachbuilders of the day dismissed this progressive idea as valueless, preferring their archaic and dangerous centre-pivot steering. The coming of the car gave the system an opportunity of being exploited but under the name of its English patentee, Rudolf Ackermann, and not that of its inventor.

As cycle makers, Peugeot were familiar with working steel tube for the frame, with lugs brazed in at crucial points, and as on the *Stahlrad* they made the tubes serve as water pipes between the engine and the cooling tank. The Daimler narrow-angle vee-twin engine was installed vertically ahead of the rear wheels, but Rigoulot's system of mounting allowed the entire engine/final drive unit to flex. It was also fully enclosed,

while wire wheels of smaller diameter than on the *Stahlrad* were fitted, running in ball bearings instead of plain bushes.

Peugeot developed this experimental vehicle remarkably quickly, and put it through its first tests early in 1890. Preoccupied with getting the Daimler single and two-cylinder engines into production, René Panhard and Emile Levassor were slower in producing their first car. It followed horse carriage lines much more closely than the Peugeot, having a wooden chassis with the front axle turning on a centrally-pivoted turntable, and iron-shod wooden wheels. It was also larger and more robust, partially compensated for by having a bigger 2hp two-cylinder motor.

This, again, was set ahead of the rear axle, enclosed in a neat *dos-à-dos* — i.e. back-to-back — four-seater body. The most significant feature of the design lay in its transmission; Levassor disliked belt drive and was sceptical of Daimler's huge sliding pinions. He set the engine transversely, that is with cylinders crosswise rather than lengthwise as on the Peugeot, the drive passing from the fore-end of the crankshaft through an open pinion gear cage giving two speeds to a countershaft and thence by side chains to each rear wheel.

The year 1891 was decisive. Both Peugeot and Panhard had encountered the abundant 'teething troubles' that earlier had assailed Benz and Daimler, but both persevered throughout 1890. Emile Levassor had set himself and his car a firm target: to reach a point $6\frac{1}{4}$ miles from the workshops and return. Repeated *pannes* (breakdowns) foiled him, but doggedly he overcame one trouble after another until, one splendid day late in January 1891, he accomplished the return journey. There was much rejoicing at the factory when he triumphantly entered the yard.

Achievements and competition

Two weeks later, Levassor motored as far as Versailles and back, some 34 miles, and on July 31–August 1, 1891, motoring took another great stride with a 140-mile journey accomplished by Levassor and his new wife, the former Mme Sarazin whom he had married the previous year. On a second improved two-seater Panhard they travelled

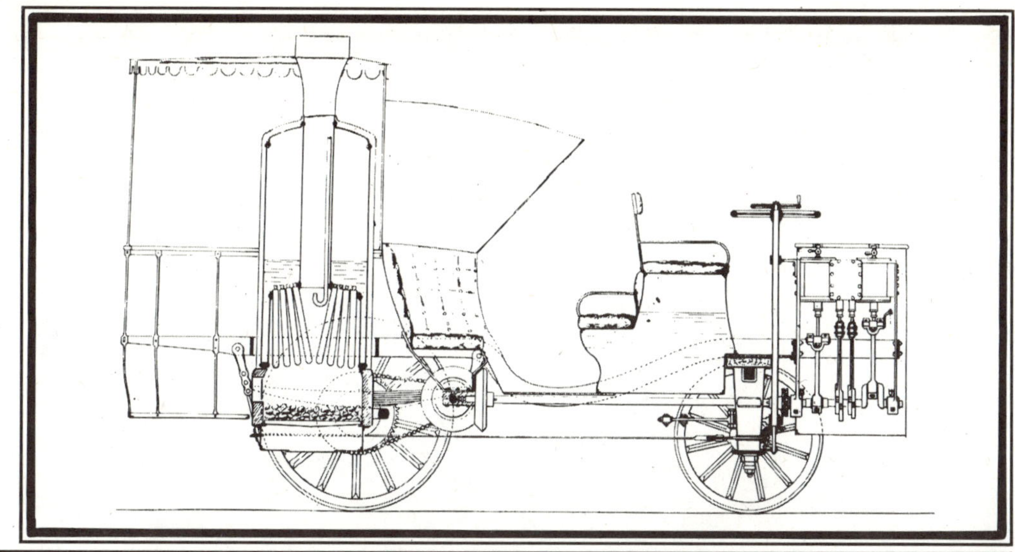

from Paris to the Normandy seaside resort of Etretat in two days, including an overnight stop at Rouen and breaks for meals, averaging around 6mph despite poor roads, heavy rain on the first day, and some problems with the hot tube ignition due to poor fuel. Levassor was delighted at the car's performance, declaring that with better conditions they could have averaged 10mph without undue haste.

Peugeot were to cap this feat in a most astonishing way. They had now built three cars, each embodying improvements over the last, they had already sold two to private customers and were busy on a fourth destined to shake both Panhard-Levassor and France itself. Peugeot No. 4 differed in having larger front wheels, almost equal in size to those at the rear, with solid rubber tires, semi-elliptic rear springs, a 2½hp twin-cylinder Panhard-built Daimler engine now set tranversely amidships and driving the rear wheels through four speeds and a differential. Moreover it could carry four passengers while weighing considerably less than the Panhard with only two, and Rigoulot had already achieved over 12mph in early tests.

Gruelling test

In September 1891 the French newspaper *Le Petit Journal* promoted a big cycle race from Paris to Brest and back, a distance of 1200 kilometres (745 miles). Peugeot, as builders of many of the bicycles competing, found this ample excuse to follow the race with their latest car. Before embarking on this gruelling test, however, they drove the car the 268 miles from their own works to those of Panhard, where they prepared the vehicle for its much tougher test to come. Clearly Peugeot and Panhard were good friends rather than rivals at that time.

When the Peugeot completed the long, arduous journey to Brest and back behind the cyclists at an overall average of over 9mph, despite a day lost through a broken differential, Emile Levassor — who had, after all, supplied the engine — put on a good face and congratulated the drivers. But when the car went on to complete the journey all the way back to the Peugeot factory without further trouble, this was really rubbing salt into the wound, and Levassor's admiration was tempered by a firm resolve that Panhard-Levassor must do better still.

It is difficult today to understand how slow the public was in reacting to pioneer motoring feats such as these. Life was more leisurely then, people were more parochial, and news travelled slowly. There was no transport revolution, nor an overwhelming rush of customers to Peugeot's door; in fact just four cars were sold that year. But without question the petrol carriage had arrived. Granted it made a lot of noise and gave out unpleasant fumes, it frightened horses and upset other livestock. But it was faster than horse or man, and could carry goods as well as people from door to door.

As Sarazin said on his deathbed, its potential was enormous, but in the late nineteenth century the message was slow to spread. Over six years had elapsed since the first horseless carriages had appeared, and

Daimler Benz

yet less than a dozen cars had been bought by the public.

After building four experimental cars, and finding passenger space and comfort a problem on each, Levassor renounced his earlier contention that the engine's place was behind, where its noise and fumes affected the occupants less, and fitted it at the front, under what came to be called the *bonnet* in Britain and the *hood* in the United States. He thereby created the pattern for the conventional car of today, with engine, gearbox and final drive in a line from front to rear, but his layout was naturally cruder. The engine was no smooth short-stroke overhead valve four, six- or eight-cylinder such as we know today, but the faithful Daimler narrow-angle twin in 72×106mm, 885cc form, driving a short cardan shaft to a 'gearbox' which as such had no box; the gear sets, giving three speeds, were open beneath the driver's floorboards, and lubricated by a periodic handful of grease.

The Panhard's twin side chains no longer featured; instead a countershaft carrying a single sprocket drove a central chain to the rear axle. The 'wire bristle' clutch, leather disc 'differential', wooden chassis, iron-shod wooden wheels and tiller steering all remained, and this basic model, albeit with periodic detail improvements, was to be built for a period of five years.

The front-engined Panhard has long been acclaimed as establishing the definitive automobile format, and yet the basic principle had already been seen back in 1878 when Amédée Bollée was exercising his *La Mancelle* steam vehicle, on which the twin-cylinder in-line power unit projected well ahead of the front axle. With typical historic illogic, however, front engine location on a car became known as the *système Panhard,* and was widely copied in years to come.

Trouble on the Alps

Between October and December 1891 five of these cars were built, each of which was sold. One of them changed hands three years later and the new owner ran his Panhard for no less than 30 years, covering over 100 000 miles. The makers then offered to buy it from him and he reluctantly agreed, but insisted on driving his beloved car the 90 miles to Paris to deliver it, the gallant old Daimler hot tube ignition engine still performing lustily in a staggering testimony to the toughness of the early Panhards. Called *L'Ancestre* by its makers, it became a proud exhibit at their works for many years.

All this, however, was in the future, and back in the 1890s Panhard-Levassor had to establish their reputation the hard way. In 1893 René Panhard gave his son Hippolyte a 3½hp Panhard as a 20th birthday gift. Hippolyte promptly set off on an ambitious 485-mile drive from Paris to Marseilles, and completed the journey in six days, averaging about 12mph. Emboldened by his success, he rashly planned his return route over the French Alps. The mountains quickly revealed the shortcomings of Panhard's peculiar 'wire bristle' clutch, which lost all its grip and obliged both driver and car to finish their journey by train. Within a few months Levassor had replaced the offending component on all models with a pedal-operated double cone-type clutch.

Across the Rhine

With France seemingly forging ahead, what of the Germans who had initiated the revolutionary motoring movement? Karl Benz fortunately found two new financial backers who saved him from probable bankruptcy in 1890, but was relying heavily on Emile Roger's French agency for sales of his tricar. The model had changed little since its 1885 precursor, apart from the provision of two speeds. The three-wheeled layout was much criticized by Roger for its instability and uncomfortable ride, caused by the single, central front wheel contacting the road just where it was churned up by horses' hooves. Benz accordingly set about developing a four-wheeler with Ackermann-type steering by double rack-and-pinion, and the new model, larger and more substantial, appeared early in 1893 as the Viktoria.

It retained Benz's slow-turning single-cylinder engine at the rear, but now 'on its side' with the crankshaft horizontal instead of vertical; bore and stroke were 130× 150mm (2000cc) giving a sturdy 3hp at 470rpm, some welcome extra flexibility and a maximum of 11mph. The Viktoria proved a great success, no less than 45 being sold

Above: Karl Benz with his family, friend Theodor von Liebig and two Benz Viktoria four-wheelers. Liebig drove his from Bohemia to Reims, in France, and back. **Below:** The 1893 Viktoria, Benz's first production four-wheeler. **Right:** Commemorative issue of 'Le Petit Journal', sponsors of the 1894 Paris-Rouen Concours.

18

in 1893; a 130×130mm, 1725cc version was also built, and in 1894 Benz supplemented it by a smaller, 'economy' 1.5hp, 1700cc model called the Velo. This became even more popular, some 1200 being manufactured between 1894 and 1902, so that Karl Benz's genius and hard work was at last rewarded.

Gottlieb Daimler, too, had run into company troubles. His engines were going well enough in Panhard and Peugeot chassis, but policy differences arose in the Daimler Motoren Gesellschaft which had been formed in 1890 to build cars. Daimler, a better engineer than company tactician, found himself outmanoeuvred into a minority position on the DMG board in 1891, and was denied the services of the invaluable Wilhelm Maybach. He had to accept the situation for the time, but quietly employed Maybach independently on further design development in a private workshop, biding his time.

Meanwhile, DMG produced a modified *Stahlrad* with a new 2hp parallel twin-cylinder engine; several were made but were not a success. By 1893 Daimler himself had left the company, and he and Maybach worked quietly away in his own workshop, first developing a new constant-level float feed carburettor to replace Daimler's old surface type, while a longer term project was the design of an all-new engine. The carburettor proved its worth in the world's first organized motoring event, the Paris-Rouen *Concours* — a kind of pioneer rally — held on July 22, 1894 with sponsorship by *Le Petit Journal,* the newspaper that was responsible for the Paris-Brest cycle race of 1891.

New carburettor

The new Maybach carburettor was fitted to the $3\frac{1}{2}$hp Panhard driven in the *Concours* by Emile Levassor, who found his engine ran far more flexibly and as well as this used less fuel; basically the same float-type instrument, with refinements, is still used today. Five Panhards and five Peugeots reached the finish, so the first prize was jointly awarded to the two companies, their cars being declared as the best in meeting the required conditions of safety, easy handling and low running cost.

It is generally accepted that Gottlieb Daimler and Karl Benz never met. Had they done so at the unique Concours of 1894 they might well have chuckled at the remarkable number of weird and wonderful would-be entrants. There were no less than 102 indicating that many minds were now being applied to the new form of locomotion, albeit often arriving at optimistic solutions. They included cars driven by gravity, compressed air, weight of the passengers, levers, pendulums, 'combined liquids', electricity, high pressure gas, electro-pneumatic power, hydraulic power, and vague systems such as 'automatic' and 'self-acting'. Yet the actual starters totalled 21, all either petrol- or steam-propelled. Emile Roger drove the only Benz entered, a Viktoria four-wheeler, reaching Rouen at a serene but sure 7.9mph, last of the 13 petrol cars entered, all of which successfully completed the course — a firm pointer for the future.

Daimler Benz

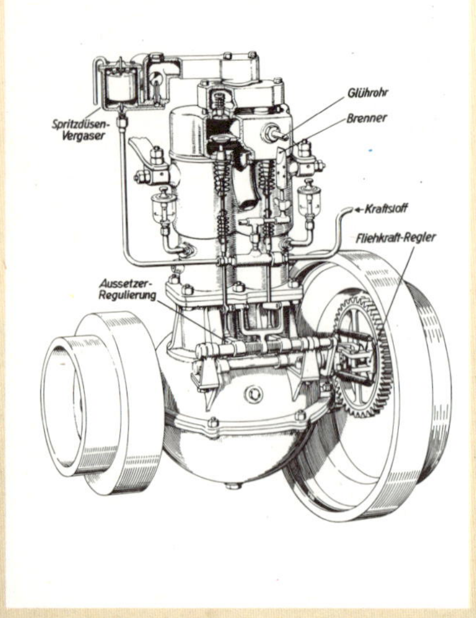

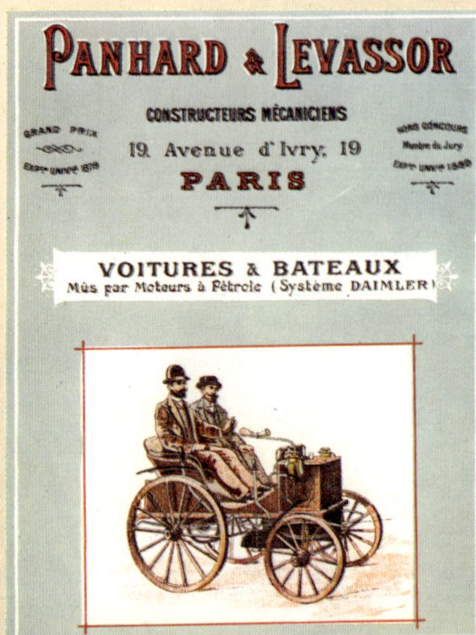

The Daimler 'Phénix' in-line twin-cylinder engine (far left) developed for Panhard-Levassor, which made a magnificent debut in 1895 when Emile Levassor finished first in the world's first motor race, the gruelling 732-mile Paris-Bordeaux-Paris. Below: The successful car at the Versailles starting control. Left: One of the world's first car catalogues, issued by Panhard-Levassor in 1892.

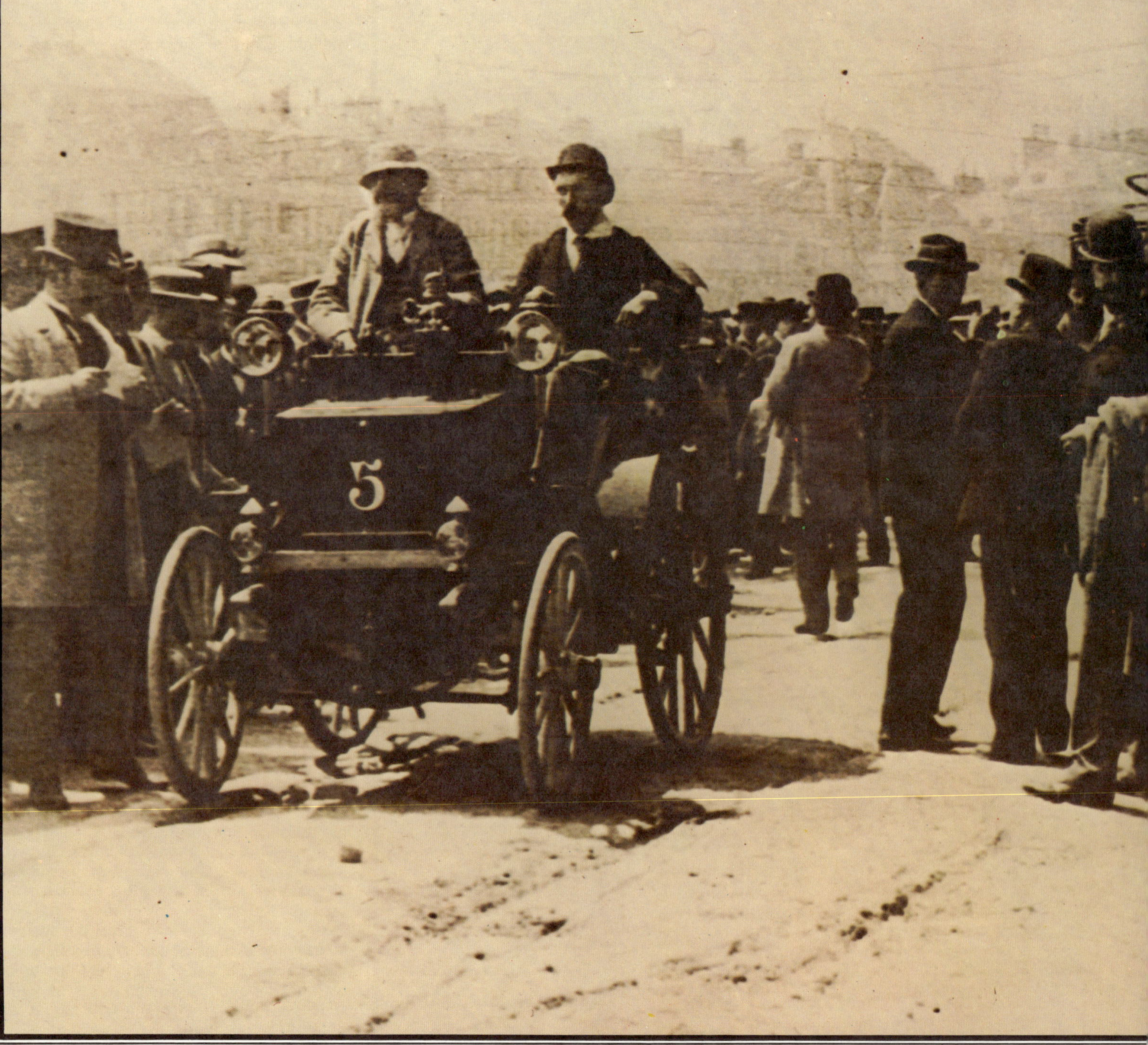

A French paper, *Le Génie Civil,* put things in a nutshell when it said of Paris-Rouen *Concours* that it drew "wide public attention to the petroleum vehicle, the general use of which will result in a thorough change of our locomotion habits and of the transportation industry." The *Concours* didn't exactly send the horse-and-carriage and allied industries into a panic, but it emphasized that the automobile had come to stay.

After the world's first rally-type event came the world's first motor race, and racing came to play an important part in maturing design by improving performance, road-holding and handling, and teaching designers to blend strength with lightness. A single race, with cars driven at maximum stress for several hours, could bring to light defects which would go unnoticed in a month of ordinary road running, and although many makers disliked racing as an expensive digression from production, they found it almost obligatory in the early days, in order both to prove and advertise the stamina of their products.

The world's first motor race, held on June 11–13, 1895, was of staggering severity considering that the car was still in its infancy, entailing a 732-mile journey from Paris to Bordeaux and back! Today the world's longest race is the classic Le Mans 24 hours, while a modern Grand Prix covers less than 200 miles. Yet that unique Paris-Bordeaux-Paris marathon produced 46 entries, 22 starters and 9 finishers, first home being Emile Levassor in a 4hp Panhard-Levassor after a truly epic drive lasting 48 hours 47½ minutes. He was at the tiller for the entire 732 miles, although a relief driver was available, and despite a 22-minute loss through a defective valve governor he averaged 15mph and beat Rigoulot's second place Peugeot by over five hours.

Apart from this personal success for Levassor, the race was important for other factors. The winning Panhard had the new Daimler engine on which Maybach had worked for nearly two years, an 80×120mm 1206cc unit with two in-line cylinders cast in one block, like one half of a modern 'four'. This unit, called the Phénix, was a great advance over the old narrow-angle vee, turning at 800rpm and weighing little more than half its predecessor. Naturally it employed Maybach's latest spray-type carburettor, and a further vital advance was the first use of an enclosed gearbox containing four speeds and its own lubricant; an enclosed differential on the countershaft was employed, and for the final drive Levassor reverted to twin side chains.

Riding on air

A further novelty of immeasurable significance in this race was the appearance of a car running on pneumatic tires. One major reason for the instability and discomfort of the earliest cars was the fact that their narrow, solid rubber or iron-rimmed wheels had to run on nineteenth-century roads, cobbled and steeply cambered in towns, and unmade in the country.

Rubber had been discovered by Europeans back in the sixteenth century. Charles Goodyear of Connecticut had discovered how to vulcanize it in 1839, R. M. Thompson had patented a pneumatic tire for coach wheels in 1845, and J. B. Dunlop had re-patented the principle with improved technology and made it work for bicycles in 1888. In France the Michelin brothers André and Edouard of Clermont-Ferrand had followed suit, and a bicycle running on their pneumatics won the Paris-Brest race of 1891 which was followed so successfully by an early Peugeot car.

To design pneumatic tires able to withstand both the weight of a car and the erratic power thrust through the driving wheels was a more formidable problem, but the Michelins, undaunted, experimented first with air tires on horse-drawn carriages, and finally produced a test car of their own, comprising an old Daimler boat engine fitted into an early Peugeot chassis, the wire-spoked wheels of which bore their plump white pneumatic tires. With some irony they called the car *L'Eclair* ('The Flash of Lightning') and entered it for the marathon Paris-Bordeaux-Paris race of 1895. They had interminable troubles with punctures from the rough roads and the heavy load, changing tires 22 times and mending countless punctures, but while on the move they were more comfortable than any of the other competitors on their solid, unyielding *bandes*. Their repeated halts cost the brothers so much time that they exceeded the time limit and had to retire from the race on the return leg. But they had proved that air-cushioned tires could largely alleviate the appalling vibration experienced in so many pioneer cars. Defiantly they issued a press notice predicting that "In ten years all cars will have pneumatic tires." They were wrong; it took only five years . . .

A profitable partnership

If Panhard and Peugeot lorded it in France as the great pioneers — and indeed, further successes by Panhard-Levassor earned it the title *Le Roi des Automobiles* ('The King of Cars') — two other concerns were soon to offer their contributions to motoring history. One was De Dion-Bouton of Paris, the other Léon-Bollée of Le Mans, and like Benz, both made their debuts on three wheels.

Count Albert De Dion, later to become a marquis, was a Parisian nobleman of impressive stature and aristocratic airs with a penchant for mechanical devices. Georges Bouton was a humble artisan, over a foot shorter than the Count, but a shrewd and talented mechanic, and the pair formed an unlikely but immensely profitable partnership. Like so many others, they began with steam and built a series of experimental three- and four-wheelers, finally marketing a highly successful steam 'tri' with two or four seats, this was exhibited at the same 1889 Paris World's Fair where Daimler and Benz displayed their petrol motors.

De Dion was much impressed by these, and decided to follow the same track, although in fact De Dion and Bouton did not wholly desert steam, developing diverse wagons, buses, etc., and leading the cavalcade into Rouen on the famous 1894

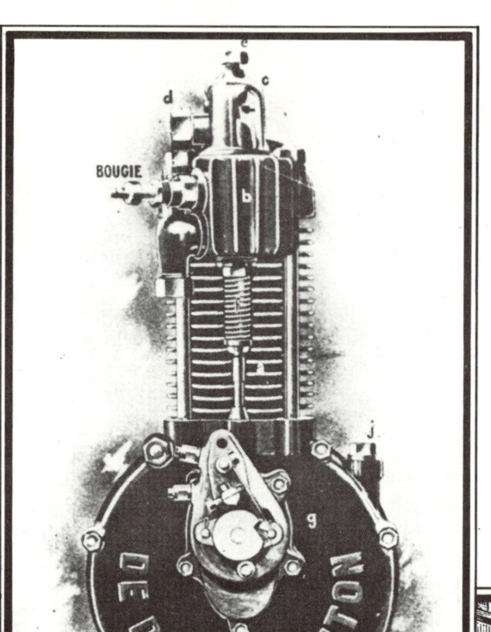

BOUGIE
DE DION BOUTON

Leon Bollée

Count Albert de Dion (top far left) and Georges Bouton (top near left), founders of the De Dion-Bouton enterprise. Top middle left: Their light high-speed, single-cylinder 1¾hp petrol engine.
Below left: One of steam's 'last kicks' – the De Dion-Bouton tractor-cum-carriage driven by Count de Dion in the 1894 Paris-Rouen Concours. Bottom left: The remarkable 1896 Léon-Bollée tricar, which with its 6hp engine gave a sporting if erratic performance. The Michelin brothers, André (right) and Edouard (far right), produced the first pneumatic tires to be fitted to a car. Below: The brothers competing in the Paris-Bordeaux race in 1895 in their Peugeot 'L'Eclair'.

Concours with one of their 'tractors'. A year later, however, they surprised the motoring world with a remarkable lightweight aircooled single-cylinder engine able to reach the unheard-of crankshaft speed of 1500rpm.

This engine, furthermore, was positively diminutive, with a bore and stroke of 50×70mm, giving only 137cc; yet so efficient was it that it developed almost 1hp, making it ideal for fitting to light tricycles. It employed one of the first low tension coil ignition systems, having advance and retard ignition control, and so well did it run that they put it into production that same year. In 1896 they built a 62×70mm, 250cc version which gave 1¾hp while still larger units gained fame as the world's first proprietary engines, available for sale to other manufacturers to fit into their own chassis. The tremendous impact this made was to be seen in the next few years.

The name of Amédée Bollée Snr was well known as one of the most advanced constructors in the steam age before the internal combustion engine was invented. His sons, Amédée and Léon, switched from steam to petrol (gasoline) in the 1890s, and while Amédée Jnr evolved some remarkably advanced experimental engines by 1895, Léon that same year put a strange new conception of a small, light car into production.

He called it a *voiturette,* a term that came to be applied to any small car. It had three wheels only, two at the front and all three with pneumatic tires; twin lever steering and tandem seating for two were also features, with the passenger sitting in front. The 3hp, 650cc aircooled single-cylinder engine with hot tube ignition was mounted horizontally on the nearside, driving the rear wheel through three speeds and a belt. The Léon-Bollée was, indeed, midway between a motorcycle and a car, and an overall weight of only 450lb gave it a vigorous if fractious performance. But it was, after all, only 1895, and like the De Dion tricycle this machine sold at a modest price and gave hundreds of adventurous people their first experience of sporting motoring.

THE WORLD

y 1895, ten years after Mannheimers had witnessed Karl Benz's spidery tricar stuttering along, and five years after Panhard-Levassor and Peugeot had pioneered the way in France, other firms and countries were getting in on the act. Despite Germany's cool reception of the new locomotion, Benz found a compatriot keen enough to build cars to his pattern in 1893. This was Friedrich Lutzmann of Dessau, whose four-wheelers, though short-lived, gained fame as the forebears of the Opel. Adam Opel of Russelsheim began making sewing machines in an old cowshed in 1862; soon he and his brother were making bicycles, becoming one of Germany's largest manufacturers. Then Benz and Daimler ushered in the motor age, and the brothers Opel, biding their time, avoided much experimentation by buying the Lutzmann production rights in 1898. Today they rank as one of the biggest German car manufacturers.

Other continental pioneers

In France, not only De Dion-Bouton and Léon-Bollée, but marques such as Delahaye, Rochet-Schneider, Berliet and Mors (an offshoot of a famous electrical company) now figured in the list, most of them Benz-inspired, some destined to early obscurity, others for wide fame. Countries bordering either Germany or France were also swiftly infected with the automobile virus. Belgium's first car came in 1894, when a Verviers engineer, Gérard Dasse, constructed a small three-wheeler with a single wheel at the front. The usual Benz-style single-cylinder engine figured at the rear, and a long tiller for steering heightened the bathchair effect. But Dasse turned his tricar round the following year, and by 1896 had built a twin-cylinder four-wheeler which was the first all-Belgian car on the market. A year earlier, however, a Belgian-built Benz had been offered for sale by the Malines coachbuilding firm of Vincke & Delmer, who exhibited it at the first Paris Motor Show in 1895.

For a nation not involved in motor manufacture on a large scale today, Switzerland began production surprisingly early; Fritz Henriod of Bienne made an experimental petrol-powered car in 1893. With rear-

JOINS IN

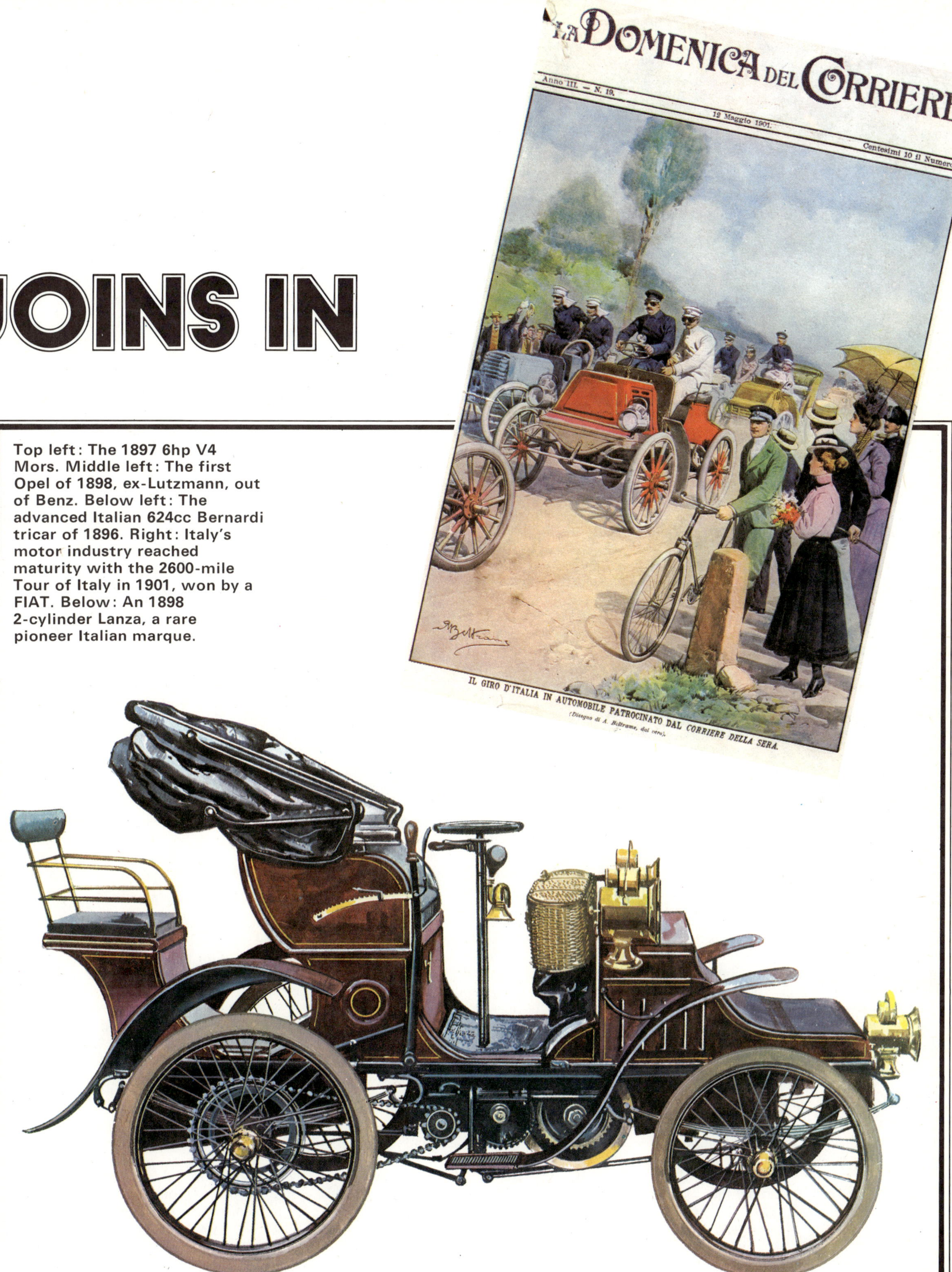

Top left: The 1897 6hp V4 Mors. Middle left: The first Opel of 1898, ex-Lutzmann, out of Benz. Below left: The advanced Italian 624cc Bernardi tricar of 1896. Right: Italy's motor industry reached maturity with the 2600-mile Tour of Italy in 1901, won by a FIAT. Below: An 1898 2-cylinder Lanza, a rare pioneer Italian marque.

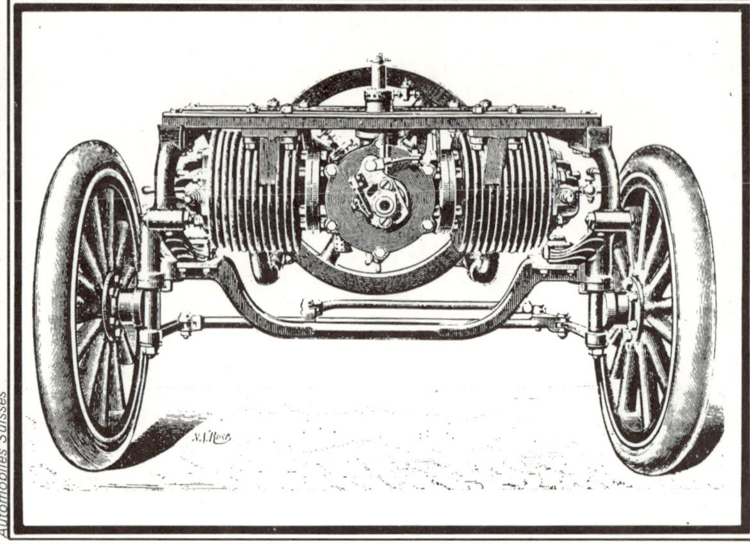

mounted one-cylinder motor and large sliding pinion transmission, it borrowed both from Benz and Daimler. Despite teething troubles, Henriod and his young brother Charles-Edouard persevered, spurred on by the remarkable feat of one Count Cognard, who successfully crossed Switzerland's St Gotthard pass with a Peugeot car in 1894.

Accompanied by his wife, a mechanic, a dog and 165lbs of baggage, the Count motored to Andermatt, then crossed the 6867ft-pass and entered Ticino, the Italian sector of Switzerland. Their only difficulty occurred when the Peugeot frightened the horse of a Swiss guards officer, who was so annoyed at being pitched into the snow that he telephoned officials in Airolo to apprehend the *automobilistes* and impose a fine on them. Such were the vagaries of the early telephone that the word *amende*, meaning 'fine', emerged as *chambres* or 'rooms', and the Count's party found themselves escorted as honoured guests to the best hotel !

Experimental race

A contemporary of Henriod was Rudolf Egg of Zürich. After building an experimental tricar in 1893, he evolved an extraordinary four-wheeler with rear-mounted 3hp Benz engine driving through an infinitely variable transmission. This ancestor of the modern DAF Variomatic used twin expanding conical pulleys connected by belt, with gear final drive. Egg cars of diverse types were made for some years, mainly for domestic use, but the Henriod faded out after Fritz's ambitious young brother left to make cars in France.

Italy had her pioneers too. On paper, Professor Enrico Bernardi of Padua University had designed a simple belt-driven three-wheeler in 1884, to be powered by a Bernardi 'Pia' two-stroke gas engine converted to run on liquid fuel. In 1889 he also patented a constant level atomizing carburettor which featured on the first Bernardi *triciclo* of 1895–96. This was driven by a 624cc single-cylinder engine, very advanced in that it had overhead valves, automatic lubrication (by olive oil!) full enclosure and a primitive form of honeycomb radiator, a type later adopted generally.

A few Benz and Daimler vehicles had in-filtrated into Italy since 1891, inspiring the Piedmontese to promote a local version of the famous 1894 Paris-Rouen run. They chose a hilly route from Turin to the village of Asti and back, a distance of $57\frac{1}{2}$ miles, and it was planned to take place on 29 May, 1895. Despite only five assorted entries, they called the event 'an experimental race'. The runners comprised a big four-seater Daimler, a Benz, a six-seater steam car and two early motorcycles. The Benz driver retired at Asti from fatigue, and the winner, Simone Federmann in the Daimler covered the course at an average speed of 9.6mph, watched by Gottlieb Daimler himself.

A disappointed non-runner because his car was not ready in time was Michele Lanza, a wealthy candle manufacturer from Turin, who was inspired by the early French cars into trying to produce one himself. The Fratelli Martina concern built his first model, purely a break minus the horse, with an engine of suspected Benz origin installed at the back, driving through three speeds and side chains. Lanza's approach was somewhat dilettante, and it fell to others to put Italy seriously on the motoring map.

An unexpectedly early participant in the new industry was Spain, where Francisco Bonet y Dalmau of Barcelona patented a four-wheeler with mid-engine and chain drive in 1889. Bonet had visited the famous Paris World Fair that year, and figures in early Panhard-Levassor order books as a customer for French-built Daimler engines for use in his textile business. A working drawing of the car dated December 12, 1889 shows that a Daimler-type engine was fitted, but it is uncertain whether this car was in fact ever built. However, Bonet certainly constructed and ran a Daimler-Panhard powered four-seater tricar in 1890–91, this having two speeds and chain final drive, with the single rear wheel sliding fore and aft in guides.

Across the Atlantic, the young, vigorous and technically ambitious United States quickly joined the automobile race. A Daimler *Stahlrad* was sent to Chicago for the important World Columbian Exposition held from May to October 1893, and, as at the Paris World Fair, the German car gave some convincing demonstration runs. William Steinway, piano maker of New York, had already met Gottlieb Daimler in Germany, and secured American patent rights for his engines and cars. The Daimler Motor Co. of Long Island was formed in 1893, initially selling stationary and launch engines, but after the Chicago 'Expo' a special car assembly plant was built, achieving full production by 1896.

A Benz Viktoria also arrived in the U.S.A. late in 1893, the two German cars precipitating a rush of home designs in the ensuing months. Yet even before the Exposition, Americans had been at work on the horseless carriage problem. The first Duryea, built in 1893, is generally declared to be America's first domestic automobile, but there were earlier efforts. In 1891 the brothers Henry and Philip Nadig of Allentown, Pennsylvania, constructed a 'pleasure carriage' with mid-mounted one-cylinder engine, chain drive and tiller steering. Claims of 8hp and 15mph seem exorbitant for that time, but the Nadig was frequently driven in Lehigh county by the brothers. Two years later Henry Nadig's two sons modified the car, giving it a twin-cylinder engine with electric ignition, and rubber-rimmed tires in place of the iron rims.

Pioneer Americans

An American Lambert car also existed in 1891, although its constructor did not persevere with it. Even the much acclaimed Duryea of 1893 was a failure. Built by two brothers, Charles and Frank Duryea of Illinois, it was virtually a horse buggy powered by a single-cylinder engine with electric ignition and a spray-type carburettor, two speeds and friction drive. Frank, the younger brother, wrestled hard with the car but eventually started afresh in 1894. The second Duryea, with $1\frac{3}{4}$hp four-stroke two-cylinder engine, three speeds and an unsprung rear axle, performed much better, and the brothers boldly founded the Duryea Motor Waggon Co. at Peoria, Illinois, the first American automobile factory.

It was in this car, with its high wagon wheels, 'cow's tail' tiller steering, and curved metal sheet for frontal protection, that Frank Duryea won the first motor race in the United States, the 54-mile Chicago-Evanston-Chicago, run in a snowstorm on November 28, 1895. Of the six starters, only

Swiss enterprise: The brothers Fritz
and Charles-Edouard Henriod of
Bienne caught the motor virus early,
building their first car in 1893. This
1896 model (far left) seen with C-E
Henriod at the controls, had an aircooled flat-twin engine (left),
mounted at the rear.
Founders of the US motor industry:
Charles Duryea (right) and his brother
Frank (far right) built their first
experimental car (below) in 1893 with
rear-mounted single-cylinder engine
and two speeds. An improved twin-
cylinder car encouraged the pair to
establish the first American
automobile factory in 1894.

two finished; the Duryea averaged a dizzy 5.05mph, heading a 3hp Benz by over 1½ hours after Mueller, driving the German car, was overcome by exposure to the cold and had to be relieved at the tiller. On the strength of this success, the Duryeas put basically the same car into small scale production, building 13 in all, with G. H. Morill Jr. of Massachusetts having the distinction of being the first American to buy an American automobile.

At a time when Britain was truly 'Great', when the Industrial Revolution had made it 'the workshop of the world', the birthplace of the power loom, the steam engine, the locomotive and railways, the ocean liner and the steam road carriage, it may seem strange that the country should have lagged behind so much in the all-important invention of the horseless carriage. The answer lay primarily in its very prosperity at the time. Proud Victorian Britain, sated with the largest empire ever ruled by one nation, had in effect become fat and lazy. Many decades of technical preeminence were sapping initiative, and the rich were more absorbed in living their lives as gentlemen and ladies, leaving vulgar but at the same time vital commerce, to those paid to understand it.

The red flag

Britain's own bigoted legislation had killed the steam road carriage, an entirely British invention of tremendous promise. Brilliant engineers such as Richard Trevithick, Goldsworthy Gurney, Thomas Hancock, and others had produced these vehicles between 1800 and 1860, and their use steadily spread all over the country. In so doing, they threatened strong vested interests such as the railways, stage coaches, grain merchants, stabling and other dependent ancillaries; direct confrontation ensued, and the railways and horses won. Turnpike trusts savagely raised steam carriage tolls, and an 1861 Act restricting speeds to 10mph on open roads and 5mph in towns was followed by another in 1865 imposing ridiculous limits of 4 and 2mph respectively.

Road locomotives were also required to have a minimum crew of three men, one walking 60 yards ahead carrying a red warning flag, and this virtually confined road traffic to horse-drawn vehicles and steam traction engines. In 1878 an Amendment waived the red flag requirement but kept the man on foot, now 20 yards ahead, while all road carriages had to stop on sight of a horse and were forbidden to emit steam

The early development of mechanical road travel in Britain was stifled by archaic legislation such as an 1865 Act imposing a 4mph limit and requiring vehicles to be preceded by a man on foot with a red flag. An Amendment in 1878 made the flag unnecessary but many councils still enforced it. Pioneer British motorists campaigned against the restrictions, and in this artist's impression (below) a driver mocks the Act by employing a small boy with a very small flag. Right: The first British car which worked reasonably well was this Knight, built as a 3-wheeler in 1895 and converted to 4 wheels in 1896.

or smoke — in case they frighten the animal. Crews trying to meet this idotic law would tie their safety valves down and risk the danger of the boiler exploding.

When the internal combustion engine came on the scene in the late 1880s, these archaic restrictions were still enforced, naturally discouraging British incentive to build cars. Moreover, there was fierce opposition from ignorant people to these 'outlandish devices that barked like a dog and stank like a cat'. The blinkers of prejudice were donned, and few in Britain realized that the petrol (gasoline) car offered not just a wonderful new personal mobility, but also emancipation for that much overworked but limited servant, the horse.

A few enlightened members of the 'gentry' and engineers intrigued by the new mechanical challenge had more foresight, and either imported foreign cars when the crippling Act was still in force, or else tried building their own. Among these adventurers were the Hon. Charles Rolls, the Hon. Evelyn Ellis, Sir David Salamons, Henry Hewetson, F. R. Simms, John Henry Knight, Bremer, Petter and Roots. The last four all developed experimental vehicles, mostly Benz-inspired but immature.

Early British efforts

Bremer's four-wheeler, claimed to have been built in 1892–94, was an unconvincing, pram-like affair with no record of having run effectively on the road. The Knight, probably the worthiest candidate as Britain's first working internal combustion-engined vehicle, began as a three-wheeler in 1895 with a gas engine which had been adapted to run on liquid fuel.

The designer converted it to a four-wheeler in 1896, and it ran reliably if slowly at under 10mph. Knight's closest rival as Britain's 'first' was the Petter four-wheeler which appeared around Yeovil in Somerset later in 1895. Again broadly Benz-based, it had chain final drive and is said subsequently to have covered several thousand miles before being broken up.

The Roots began as a paraffin-burning tricar in 1896, becoming a four-wheeler the following year, while Herbert Austin, later founder of the famous Longbridge marque, experimented at about this time on behalf of his employers, the Wolseley Company. His first effort, a tricar similar to the Léon-Bollée, had a flat-twin engine set to the left of the rear wheel; an advanced feature was mechanically operated inlet valves, but the machine did not work well and Austin abandoned it in favour of another unsuccessful tricar.

These British attempts were woefully inferior to the seasoned German and French products, but in common with British buyers of Continental cars a major objective of their builders was to draw attention to the absurdity of the traffic laws. Headed by Sir David Salamons, several of them, including Rolls, Ellis, Simms, Hewetson, Knight and W. C. Bersey, who built early electric cars, formed the Self-Propelled Traffic Association, gaining encouraging support from MPs and the press in their fight against legal archaism.

Most of them had brushes with the police when out driving, for with a 4mph limit and the need for a man walking ahead, the pioneer British motorist was a 'sitting duck' to any zealous 'bobby'. Furthermore, most magistrates, let alone the 'horsy' county element and an ignorant public pleased to see 'the toffs' discomforted, were blindly anti-motorcar, and this prejudice was to prevail for several years yet.

Daimler in Britain

As in France, the real British automobile industry sprang directly from the engine patents of Gottlieb Daimler. F. R. Simms, engineer, inventor and businessman, first encountered Daimler's invention at a Bremen exhibition in 1890 and was so taken by its potential that he asked Daimler for the British patent rights. An agreement was drawn up and the following year a single-cylinder Daimler engine and a Daimler-powered motor launch were sent to Britain.

In May 1893 Simms formed the Daimler Motor Syndicate Ltd., concentrating at first on boats; but by mid-1895 hopes that the severe road traffic laws might be relaxed, encouraged him to import a Daimler-engined Panhard-Levassor for the Hon. Evelyn Ellis. October that same year brought the first motor exhibition ever held in Britain, a one-day open-air affair organized by Sir David Salamons at Tunbridge Wells. The object was to display publicly the new horseless carriages and to strike a blow against the Acts of 1865 and 1878.

Four vehicles were on show: the Hon. Evelyn Ellis's new Panhard, again with F. R. Simms accompanying him; Sir David Salamons' Peugeot; a De Dion tricycle; and a Daimler fire engine. Demonstrations lasted two hours only, but the event was a great success, drawing fully 5000 spectators. The Daimler Syndicate were by now contemplating the formation of the Daimler Motor Company with additional capital when out of the blue came a surprise offer from a financial group to buy the Daimler patents outright. The then staggering sum of £35 000 was agreed, and Simms handed over all rights to H. J. Lawson, M. D. Rucker and E. T. Hooley, an enterprising trio who promptly formed the British Motor Syndicate to exploit the inventions further. They then

Herbert Austin (above left) with his first experimental Wolseley tricar of 1896.

Another early Italian car, the 1897 Menon built at Roncade di Treviso, had a front-mounted De Dion-Bouton aircooled engine.

Among prominent pioneer British motorists was the Hon. Evelyn Ellis (left) seen with his 1895 Panhard-Levassor at the Tunbridge Wells one-day open air motor exhibition staged in October that year.

floated the Daimler Motor Company, with Lawson as chairman and Simms acting as consulting engineer.

Henry John Lawson, son of a Methodist minister, was a company promoter of considerable ingenuity, offset by questionable scruples. He had been deeply embroiled in the Coventry cycle boom, pioneering the 'safety' bicycle with equal-size wheels and pedal-and-chain drive in 1873–74. Later he founded the Rudge Cycle Co., then fell in with two other financial adventurers, E. T. Hooley, who had himself launched the Raleigh, Singer, Humber and Swift cycle companies, and Martin Rucker. The trio brought off their first joint coup in the flotation of the Dunlop Company, reportedly netting £2 million between them.

Fiddlers three

When the motor car appeared, Lawson immediately saw its vast potential and set out to corner the British market by buying up every possible patent. Hooley and Rucker, having made their profit, withdrew from the venture, and in order to secure further finance Lawson floated yet another company, the Great Horseless Carriage Co. Ltd., in 1896, with a capital of £750 000. He then acquired a large empty cotton factory in Coventry which he renamed the Coventry Motor Mills, and issued an ambitious prospectus. With the licences purchased, he proposed to make, not only Daimler cars and engines, but also Léon-

Bollée and De Dion-Bouton three-wheelers, and cars and motorcycles to the design of a flamboyant American named Pennington.

Like Lawson, Edward Joel Pennington of Chicago was a company promoter and inventor whose brain fermented a flood of improbable vehicle designs and schemes, fortified by wild claims for their performance. His motorcycle of 1895 was depicted in a fanciful sketch flying 65 feet through the air over a river; his quadricycle with its fat 'puncture-proof' pneumatic tires was photographed with nine people aboard; his Kane-Pennington engine, appropriately termed the 'hot air' motor, had no carburettor, no cooling, was readily available with one, two or four cylinders, would start 'with one turn' of the flywheel, and employed a 'light untempered steel' coil spring giving a 'long mingling spark' in the cylinder.

So persuasive was Pennington that even Lawson fell for his eloquence, his Great Horseless Carriage Co. paying £100 000 for the Pennington patents, besides setting aside a floor of the 'Mills' for production of his vehicles. Little came of the American's wildcat notions, but in the meantime Lawson had sold the Daimler rights which he and his partners had so recently acquired from Simms to his own Great Horseless Carriage Co. The negotiations earned him another handsome profit, and at the same time he proposed to demand a 10 per cent royalty from any other British concerns seeking to use the patents!

In 1896 the Locomotives on Highways Bill, seeking relief from the idiotic 4mph limit and the man walking in front, went before parliament. To raise public interest, Lawson formed the Motor Car Club, with the avowed noble aim of liberating British motorists whereas he simply sought a surer market for his wares. He then promoted London's first Motor Show, held at the Imperial Institute, South Kensington, and running from May to August, 1896 during which influential people were lavishly entertained.

Naturally Lawson's companies were fea-tured prominently, but so unproductive were the Coventry Motor Mills that all their exhibits came from abroad. They included Daimler, Panhard and Peugeot cars, a Panhard chassis and some Daimler engines. Backed up by Pennington, Léon-Bollée, De Dion and Lutzmann exhibits, and diverse electric vehicles, this first Show was pronounced a roaring success, climaxing with the passing of the Locomotives on Highways Act itself. Concessions were small enough, with the speed limit for 'light locomotives' raised from 4 to a grudging 12mph, but motorists were freed at last from 'that man in front'.

The Emancipation Run

With typical showmanship, Lawson and his Motor Car Club laid on a special 'Emancipation Run' to celebrate such an important occasion. A cavalcade of cars was to travel from the Hotel Metropole in Whitehall, London, to the Hotel Metropole, Brighton, on the very day the Act became law, Saturday, November 14, 1896. Every available motor car was rounded up: four Panhards, four Roger-Benz, four Léon-Bollées, two Duryeas from the United States, a Beeston tricycle, a Pennington, two Arnold-Benzes, a Lutzmann and an indeterminate number of electric cars.

Gottlieb Daimler himself was there, accompanying F. R. Simms in a Cannstatt-Daimler phaeton; Mayade, winner of France's second big motor race from Paris to Marseilles and back that year, drove the same Panhard, notable in having a four-cylinder engine; while a passenger in another Panhard was Jerome K. Jerome, author of *Three Men in a Boat*. And in the pilot car, the very Panhard in which Emile Levassor had made his epic Paris-Bordeaux-Paris drive a year earlier, rode the Motor Car Club chairman H. J. Lawson himself, who had bought it for £1200.

The weather was wet and cold, and the whole affair badly organized: there were no marshals or officials en route; timekeeping was very casual; and large crowds added to the confusion. With the new speed limit of

Left: The persuasive Mr Pennington (in top hat) and family on one of his creations, the 1896 tricar with 'puncture-proof' tires. Right: Emancipation for British motorists from a 4mph speed limit and other restrictions was celebrated by the famous London-to-Brighton Run in November 1896. Here is Charles McRobie Turrell setting off in one of the Panhards entered by H. J. Lawson's British Motor Syndicate.

14
OWNER   Harry J Lawson
SYSTEM
BUILDER of MOTOR
BUILDER of CARRIAGE

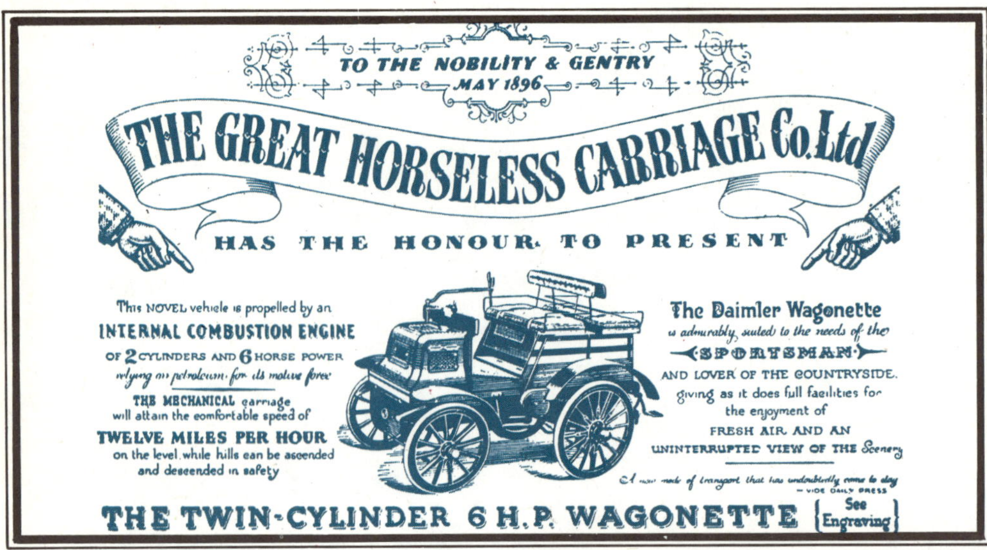

Left: Flamboyance and financial intrigue clouded Britain's entry into the motor industry – an 1896 advertisement for the Daimler. Right: A fanciful interpretation by H. J. Lawson's company of a 'chic horseless brougham'. Below: George B. Selden, an American attorney, cornered US car patents by far-sighted manipulation. His '1877' car was actually built by court order in 1906 to prove that it worked. Below right: The British-built Lanchester of 1897 was a very advanced design with epicyclic transmission and a fully counter-balanced flat-twin engine.

12mph, no race was possible, although the French Bollée drivers decided to make it one, and by missing the scheduled lunch stop at Reigate were first and second into Brighton. The Arnold-Benzes could not reach the start for the crowds, so joined the run farther along the route, and Pennington's vehicle burst one of its 'unpuncturable' tires near Norbury. At least one Bersey electric was quietly put on a train to Preston Park station, near Brighton, to 'finish' the course impressively 'mud-smeared'!

Press information was sketchy, ill-informed and biased, tending to ignore all vehicles in which Lawson had no financial interest. In his 'official report', the Chairman extracted the last drop of publicity by inferring that of the 20 cars claimed to have reached Brighton, 18 had been 'lent' to Motor Car Club members by the British Motor Car Syndicate! In fact, it seems that only ten vehicles actually completed the course in an event which is now celebrated each year on the first Sunday of November by the highly popular London-Brighton Veteran Run.

Lawson's downfall

With British motoring now comparatively unfettered, even though the police began a tyrannical enforcement of the 12mph limit that was to prevail for several years, a spate of orders and activity might have been expected. Certainly some independent engineers such as Frederick Lanchester were encouraged to develop sound car designs, several more foreign cars were imported, and the Peckham firm of William Arnold and Sons began to build Benz cars under licence. But the much-lauded products of Lawson's mighty Coventry Motor Mills were uncommonly slow in materializing. Pennington had departed, but customers for Daimlers, Humber tricycles, etc. began to grow indignant at delivery delays, shareholders became restive, and attacks by the *Financial Times* and other influential papers ensued. Not until mid-1897 did the Mills deliver their first British-made car.

Fortune deserted Lawson in other ways. His blatantly commercial Motor Car Club lost popularity to the newly founded Automobile Club of Great Britain and Ireland –

16e ANNÉE. N° 7. — 18 Février 1911.

63, Champs-Elysées, Paris (8e). Tél.: 645-93.

ABONNEMENTS :
Paris et Départements. Un an . . . . 16 fr.
Étranger . . . . — . . . . 20 fr.

LA FRANCE AUTOMOBILE & AÉRIENNE

Fondée en 1896

Les abonnements partent du 1er de chaque mois.
On s'abonne dans tous les bureaux de poste.

Organe officiel de l'Automobilisme, de l'Aviation et des Industries qui s'y rattachent

Rédacteur en Chef : Maurice CHÉRIÉ

La voiture SELDEN reconstruite sur les plans de l'inventeur et présentée en état de marche à New-York, au moment du fameux procès (Fig. 137).

detailing how it might work. Under American patent law at the time, an invention remained protected for two years after application, and this application could be further renewed by detail amendment every two years.

The cunning Selden thereby prolonged his application by periodically drafting minor changes in its specification until, in 1895, he judged the time ripe to pounce. He finalized his application and was duly granted U.S. master patents for road vehicles propelled by petrol (gasoline) engines — patents which, under U.S. law, he would hold for 17 years! His 'phantom' car virtually gave him prior design claims and hence entitlement to royalty payments on every American petrol car built, also on the use of specified components such as clutches, differentials, universal joints, etc.

Stranglehold attempts

Selden did not even fight the would-be American car makers himself. Instead, in 1899 he sold the controlling interest in the patents to the Columbia cycle and electric car manufacturing concern run by the Pope brothers of Hartford, Connecticut, with an agreed royalty percentage for himself. The Popes were also old hands at patent litigation, having profited handsomely by cornering practically all the worthwhile cycle design principles in the United States. They forthwith demanded royalties of $1\frac{1}{4}$ per cent of the retail price on all American-built and imported cars, and after scoring their first victories over difficult manufacturers they formed a protective Association of Licensed Automobile Manufacturers (ALAM) in 1903, all royalty-paying firms automatically becoming members.

ALAM then tried to restrict membership to about 16 principal manufacturers, thus ensuring a cosy 'closed shop' on the U.S. market and discouraging new enterprises in the ever-growing industry. Resistance hardened, led by Henry Ford who had built his first experimental car at Dearborn, Michigan, in 1896 and began production as the Ford Motor Company in 1903. French makers whose American imports had been seized pending payment of ALAM licence fees joined the fight, and provided invaluable evidence of vital design principles, including the use of liquid fuels, differentials, clutches, electric ignition and gears, all patented before those specified by Selden.

Ford weighed in with a series of advertisements undertaking to support all car makers who resisted licence fee payments, and Ford owners if threatened by litigation. In 1905–06 the U.S. courts demanded that an example of Selden's car, as laid down in his patent specification, should be built to see if his claims were justified. With much difficulty this was achieved by his son, the date '1877' even being painted on the vehicle. Despite aid from a cylinder of compressed air, the 'Selden' car barely covered 1500 feet before expiring. Even so, American law moved as slowly as British, and the Selden dispute hung on until 1911, when the patents were finally ruled invalid — less than two years before they were due to expire.

the future RAC. Then Lawson reorganized the Great Horseless Carriage Co. as the Motor Manufacturing Co. (MMC) and resigned from Daimler owing to 'pressure of work in his other interests'. These included the flotation, with his old crony Hooley, of a tramways construction and maintenance firm, investigation into which revealed fraudulent activities for which Lawson was sentenced to 12-months hard labour. Hooley somehow emerged scot-free, but subsequent murky financial gambles cost hapless investors some £10 million and earned Hooley three years' penal servitude.

The Selden patents

This was the sombre finale in a spectacular bid to establish a stranglehold on the British automobile market by mass purchase of patent rights. But if Lawson's monopolistic machinations hindered the growth of the industry by frightening off investors, they also brought the car wide publicity, irrespective of the motives behind the drum-beating.

Similar unscrupulous dealings were also experienced in the United States. While Pennington was in England selling his fanciful ideas to Lawson, a third fiddler, an incredibly farsighted solicitor from Rochester, New York, named George B. Selden, was setting the seal on a long-planned scheme to set himself up in easy street for life. As early as 1877, one year after Otto had patented the four-stroke principle, Selden drew up plans for a horseless carriage, and in 1879 he filed a U.S. patent application for use of an engine 'of the compression type' in a road carriage! This engine was a hypothetical three-cylinder version of the Brayton 'Ready' two-stroke stationary unit of 1872 origins, running on liquid hydrocarbon, mounted sideways between the front wheels of the vehicle above the axle, and driving the wheels through pinions as a self-contained unit with cart-type, centre-pivot, geared-down steering.

Here was an automobile of sorts, designed 16 years after Lenoir's, but predating those of Benz and Daimler by almost a decade! The only difference was that Selden never built his car, nor had any intention of doing so. As a patent attorney he was well versed in the art of defining a principle without

THE MOTORING

BOOM

Daimler Benz

National Motor Museum

Left: A view of the Canstatt-Daimler assembly shop before the production line system had come in. Above: A poster for France's premier motor show.

By the dawn of the twentieth century, the motor car was a *fait accompli*. Struggling backyard engineering firms saw salvation in the new industry; well-established manufacturers with comfortable rail or service contracts saw an important new outlet for their experience and plant; and major banks and financial groups saw the vast investment potential. In 1890 there were but four makes of car; by 1900 there were over 110, some due for a short life, others for world fame.

Benz and Daimler, the cause of these activities, progressed slowly and methodically. In 1896 Benz at last supplemented his slow-turning single-cylinder engine by a horizontally-opposed 5hp twin-cylinder (i.e. flat twin), logically called the *Kontra*. The crank and con. rods were still out in the air, but the extra power and flexibility were welcome. But apart from this, a steady flow of orders enabled the ultra-conservative Karl Benz to stick to his belt drive and solid tires long after others had abandoned them.

Reconciliation between Gottlieb Daimler and the Daimler Motoren Gesellschaft (DMG) of Cannstatt was followed in 1896 by major reorganization and a serious attempt to produce cars known as Cannstatt-Daimlers. As ever, Daimler was better at engines than cars; after developing the in-line two-cylinder Phénix engine for Panhard, he switched to front engines himself in 1897, and he next produced a four-cylinder model. The Cannstatt-Daimler was high-built and clumsy, though well constructed and able to carry luxury bodywork seating up to six people.

In the meantime France forged ahead, now unquestionably leaders in design and production. Dozens of 'upstart' assembly firms trod in the Panhard and Peugeot footsteps, using De Dion's excellent engines and other proprietary components which enterprising engineers were churning out. Naturally De Dion products were copied, and new 'over the counter' engines included Aster, Buchet, Bruhot, Kelecom and Fafnir, while the firm Lacoste et Battmann became famous as suppliers of chassis and running gear.

Foremost in this new generation was the Renault, founded at Billancourt, a Paris suburb by the Seine. Twenty-year-old

Louis Renault, dismissed as a ne'er do well by his draper father, used an old hunting lodge in their garden for his experiments. He owned a De Dion tricycle with 273cc 1¾hp single-cylinder engine, but was dissatisfied with its bumpy ride, excessive vibration and exposure of self and machinery to the elements. He designed a four-wheeler, brazing up a neat little tubular steel frame and fitted the De Dion unit at the front, its crankshaft in line with the chassis and driving the rear wheels through a three-speed gearbox and propeller shaft instead of chains. Cleaner and quieter, this shaft embodied universal joints for the first time, and Renault's gearbox was novel, not only for its direct drive top gear but in utilising the lathe 'tumbler' gear principle for the intermediate speeds instead of sliding pinions.

It worked well, and so did the car, which was deliberately small and light, though rather top heavy. But it romped up hills and could exceed 25mph, and Renault found himself precipitated into motor manufacture by the rush of orders from acquaintances to whom he had demonstrated his prototype. Louis and his brothers Marcel and Fernand founded Renault Frères in 1899, and the first tiny cell of today's vast Boulogne-Billancourt plant turned out 60 cars in its first six months of production.

Motor racing helped, as usual. Driven by Louis and Marcel, the neat little cars were already winning by 1899, and with larger 3½hp De Dion engines fitted, their victory in just one event of 1900, the 705-mile Paris-Toulouse-Paris, brought in 350 orders. As the twentieth century advanced, so too did Renault, making their own engines instead of buying De Dions, pioneering their famous 'coal scuttle' sloping engine cover with dash-mounted radiator behind, and widening their range to encompass full size twin- and four-cylinder models, taxicabs, vans, buses and trucks.

Developments under the new boom conditions were so rapid and diverse as to confuse, and originality and ethics often took a back seat in the scramble. While other French, German and British firms were glad to follow Renault's example and buy De Dion, or similar engines, others such as Argyll of Scotland, Corre of France, Adler of Germany, and Bianchi and Isotta-Fraschini of Italy swiftly copied the Renault itself.

Over 20 new marques in France, Britain, Germany, Holland and Switzerland were based on Benz designs, another half-dozen on Daimler's, yet others copied the *système Panhard*, while the Amédée-Bollée four-wheeler drew its admirers too. Many copies were legal, having acquired the necessary licences, but others merely 'borrowed' from other manufacturers. Confusion was added when cars like the French Hurtu, a Benz copy, was itself copied by the British Marshall; de Dietrich built a Bollée-type car, then switched to a Belgian Vivinus pattern, this same design appearing in Britain as a New Orleans and in France as a Georges Richard!

Contemporary with the Renault was another important French newcomer, the Decauville, product of a firm of locomotive makers. Léon-Bollée having cornered the attractive title 'voiturette' in 1896, Decauville called their 1898 small car the 'voiturelle'. They ingeniously secured more power by coupling two De Dion motors together, and also boasted independent front suspension by a transverse leaf spring and sliding pillars. Like Renault they boosted their name through racing, and swiftly sold licences to Wartburg and Falke in Germany and Marchand in Italy.

More cars from Europe

Holland's first contributions to the world motor car production consisted of the Eysink and the Simplex in 1897, both relying on Benz engines and inspiration at first. Eysink soon developed their own power units, however, and became well established as motor manufacturers, finding a useful market in the Dutch East Indies.

Although Denmark has never undertaken serious car production, it can claim two unusual pioneers. One, still to be seen in the Copenhagen technical museum, is the Hammel, built by Hans Urban Johansen for the Hammel works in that city. It had a large 2.7-litre twin-cylinder engine giving perhaps 3hp and 6mph, and is said to have been driven 12 miles daily for two years despite the considerable handicap of steering gear which had to be turned left to make a right turn and vice versa!

The Hammel is dubiously dated as of 1886 origin, but 1896 is probably more accurate. Another Danish pioneer, the Brems, was in fact a copy of the Wartburg, first made in 1900 by two brothers, Aage and Jakob Brems of Viborg, who had worked in the Wartburg plant at Eisenach, Germany. A hefty 3.8-litre engine, two speeds and friction drive were featured, and a Brems could be ordered up to 1907.

Austria-Hungary weighed in with an experimental French-engined petrol car from the Vienna coachbuilders, Jacob Lohner in 1896, who then unexpectedly dropped it for electric power. In 1898 a youthful Ferdinand Porsche joined them, designing a battery-powered Lohner-Porsche in which each front hub contained an electric motor. The intrepid inventor even raced this unique front-drive machine in Austrian mountain events, but then decided that the weight of batteries might better be replaced by that of an engine for generating the current through a dynamo. Thus evolved the first of the 'petrol-electrics' which enjoyed quite a vogue early in this century.

Other Austrian pioneers were the front-drive De Dion-engined Graf from Vienna, and the Nesselsdorf of 1897, built by a rolling stock factory in that city later renamed Koprivnice. Using a Benz engine and chain drive, it was called the 'Praesident' and survives today in a Czech museum as the ancestor of the modern Tatra. Coincidentally, Sweden's first car, the Vabis of 1897, was also the product of a railway rolling stock maker at Södertälje. Somewhat Germanic in pattern, Vabis cars had to be tough to survive Scandinavian conditions; they combined with the Scania truck concern in 1911, and today the Scania-Vabis group also controls the Saab car enterprise.

Even Czarist Russia dabbled in the new locomotion, unlike Soviet Russia that followed which denounced motoring as an 'affectation of the rich'. The first Russian car came as early as 1896, and was called a Yakovlev-Freze. It was built in St Petersburg (now Leningrad) vaguely based on Benz specifications, with a 2hp single-cylinder engine and twin rubber-cum-canvas belt drives on different sized pulleys; skis for the front wheels and toothed chains

Louis Renault, discontented son of a linen draper, preferred to experiment with cars. His first (far left), built around a front-mounted De Dion engine, appeared late in 1898. By 1905 Renault Frères was one of France's biggest car makers, taking a prominent stand at the Paris Salon (left). A rival contender for the ever-widening small car market from 1898 was the Decauville 'Voiturelle' (right), well ahead of its time in having independent front suspension by a transverse leaf spring.
Below: Renault's little 402cc single-cylinder watercooled car proved immensely popular all over Europe, besides being widely copied. It was first in the world to use universally-jointed shaft final drive.

THE DECAUVILLE'S VOITURELLE.

At the last steeplechase of Auteuil a very pretty little motor-car made its first appearance and was greatly admired. Light, very elegant, painted in bright golden yellow, with two comfortable seats.

This motor-car merits considerable attention, as it is very easy to manipulate, and can be turned in a small space.

Later on, at the Paris Agricultural Show, it was one of the greatest attractions of the Exhibit of the Société Decauville.

Full particulars of the car may be obtained at the offices of THE SOCIÉTÉ DECAUVILLE :— **13, Boulevard Malesherbes, PARIS.**

Subjoined is a description of a few of the principal features of the car :—

The "Voiturelle," as it is called, is suspended at the front on springs, and rests on a spring cushion at the back. By these means all disagreeable motion

The "Voiturelle" is 2m. 30 long and 1m. 25 wide ; a convenient size for the coach-house.

Its weight is of about 200 kilos, and with 10 litres of oil of petroleum it will travel 150 kilomètres.

Its two cylinders are able to develop force equal to three horses, and, supposing that the car and its occupants together do not exceed 400 kilos, this power is sufficient to enable the "Voiturelle" to ascend hills at a good speed.

The cars are constructed in the workshops at Petit-Bourg.

The Price is

£140

One-third to be paid when ordering, and the balance on delivery.

The Société Decauville considers that it has reason to congratulate itself on this new creation, as this motor-car is the cheapest and most comfortable yet placed before the

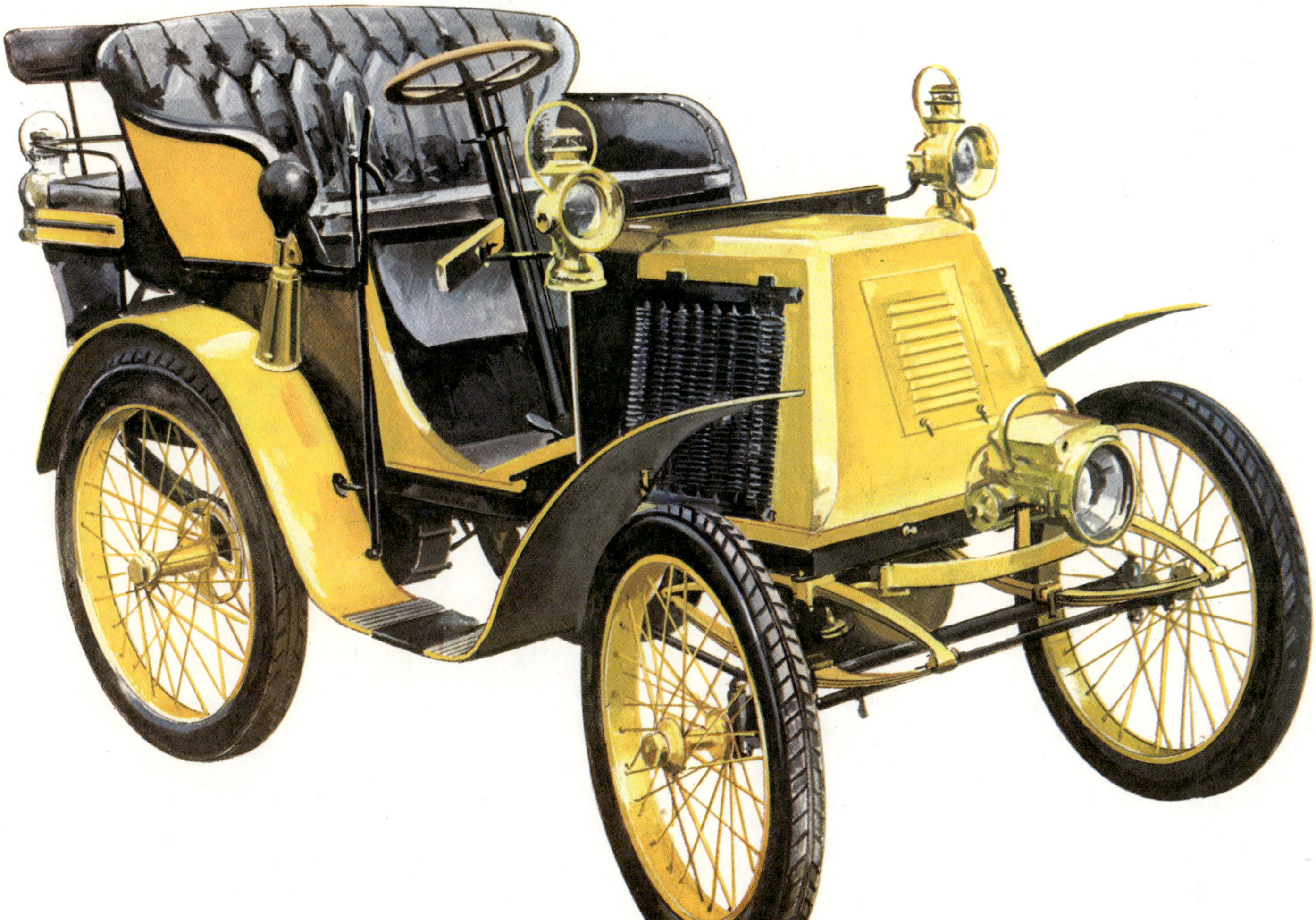

The "VOITURELLE" is already so great a success that intending Purchasers desiring EARLY DELIVERY

for the rear were optional winter fitments. Another early Russian car was the two-cylinder Puzyrev of 1899, also built at St Petersburg, but superior imported cars soon killed off these domestic enterprises in a strictly limited market.

As the automobile spread its influence the world over, its design was continually improved and refined, and better methods of production were devised. The last vestiges of its horse-drawn carriage ancestry were rapidly departing; it was no longer a freak but a vehicle in its own right, accepted if not loved by all. It remained largely a rich man's indulgence, but was becoming of growing importance to professional and business people requiring speedy mobility.

De Dion democracy

But 'democratization' was on the way; it was already evident, in fact, in the relatively inexpensive Renault, the Léon-Bollée *voiturette* and the Decauville *voiturelle. La petite voiture* was about the only appropriate name left for a French rival car which did more than any other to popularize motoring in the next eight years. This was the De Dion-Bouton four-wheeler, which first emerged in 1898 with rear-mounted $2\frac{3}{4}$hp single-cylinder engine and unsprung rear axle, and a year later was given a $3\frac{1}{2}$hp watercooled engine and the famous De Dion rear suspension. This permitted rigid mounting on the tubular frame of the gearbox/final drive unit, with universally jointed halfshafts linked by a transverse tubular beam and suspended by $\frac{3}{4}$-elliptic leaf springs.

A further mechanical novelty was the two-speed gearbox in which each gear had its own automatic clutch running in oil, selection being by a lever (a hand wheel was originally used) pulled back for first gear and pushed forward for second, with neutral in between. By pushing down, the same lever also operated the rear brakes, so that with the hand throttle customary at the time, one-pedal motoring was quite practical at the turn of the century! As the De Dion *petite voiture* also handled well and was commendably reliable, it proved especially popular with women drivers daunted by the early straight-tooth 'crash' gearbox and the need to double-declutch for all changes.

Engine size rose to $4\frac{1}{2}$hp in 1901, and 6hp by 1902. Over 12 500 of these cars were built up to 1904, being sold, not only in France and all over Europe, but also in the U.S.A., South America, Australia, India and China. As fashion tended to favour front-engined cars by 1902, De Dion added a front-engined model with an optional 6 or 8hp watercooled single-cylinder engine, still with the famous expanding clutches and De Dion rear axle. A Renault-like bonnet was hinged at the scuttle end, a normal handbrake was fitted, and a three-speed gearbox became optional. Twin- and four-cylinder models of greater power followed, and by 1904 the firm claimed to be the world's largest car manufacturers, employing many clever multiple engineering methods in their vast Puteaux factory near Paris.

A third French marque to plunge into quantity production alongside Renault and De Dion was Darracq. Whereas prosperity came to the first pair largely through enterprise and enthusiasm, Alexandre Darracq was more openly spurred on by the profit motive. He had begun in 1891 by turning out Gladiator bicycles en masse so cheaply that British interests had to buy him out to preserve their markets. He then set out to build a Bollée four-wheeler under licence, but quickly changed his mind on seeing the little Renault. By 1900 he had a fair imitation in production at his works in the Paris suburb of Suresnes. It was slightly larger, with a 785cc, $6\frac{1}{2}$hp single-cylinder front-mounted engine and shaft drive, also differing in its three-speed sliding pinion gearbox and steering column gearchange — fondly imagined by many to be an innovation of the 1950s.

Few firms spread the motoring movement more widely than De Dion-Bouton, their engines and cars reaching all corners of the world. The front-engined 6hp 'Populaire', (below) introduced in 1901, thoroughly lived up to its name. Bottom: This 1901 $4\frac{1}{2}$hp rear-engined 'vis-à-vis' was the first to be imported into Australia for proud owner A. J. Penier. Bottom right: The first FIAT, the $3\frac{1}{2}$hp model with 697cc rear-mounted flat-twin engine and chain drive, appeared in 1899. It was a much improved version of the Welleyes, designed by Faccioli and built by the Ceirano concern which was absorbed by the new FIAT organisation headed by the dynamic Giovanni Agnelli (right).

Roger-Viollet

National Motor Museum

Although rather crudely engineered, the Darracq was light, reliable and cheap, finding a ready market all over Europe. Opel secured a licence and built the Opel-Darracq in Germany, and from 1902 on Darracq aped his Parisian rivals and widened his range to include twin- and four-cylinder models. So great was the volume of car exports from French factories that Italy, Britain and Germany were all spurred into making greater efforts.

The birth of FIAT

A group of Turin businessmen, worried by the steady flow of Panhards, Peugeots, Mors, De Dions and other vehicles into Italy, resolved to create a new car factory in their city. Having secured adequate capital, they began by acquiring a small established concern, Ceirano e Cia, cycle makers who had ventured into the motor industry with a prototype called the Welleyes. Designed by Aristide Faccioli, this was built for Ceirano in 1898 by the Martina works, which had earlier produced the first Lanza. The new group, led by Giovanni Agnelli, bought out Ceirano's patents in July 1899 and took over the staff, including Faccioli and his car, for 30 000 lire.

They named their new enterprise Fabbrica Italiana Automobili Torino, which at Faccioli's suggestion was abbreviated to FIAT (becoming Fiat in 1906), and promptly set about erecting a new factory. The Welleyes design was improved, notably with chain instead of belt drive. Its $3\frac{1}{2}$hp, 697cc flat-twin watercooled engine was at the rear, driving through three speeds, the frame was of armoured wood, and steering was by tiller. This was the new FIAT, all the components for which, apart from the body-work, were made in their own factory, and considering they began from scratch in a country lacking in natural resources such as coal, iron or oil, their 1900 output of 24 cars was creditable.

Inevitably, larger engines were soon fitted, and in 1901 Faccioli was succeeded as designer by Enrico, who swiftly produced a front-engined FIAT to the *système Panhard*. Output rose to 73 cars in 1901, to 107 by 1902, and to 134 by 1903, when a significant proportion was exported. A new contender for world car markets had arrived . . .

In the meantime there was trouble in the two German camps. Gottlieb Daimler's health was failing through overwork, and much of the pressure was taken over by his son Paul and his old partner Wilhelm Maybach, with a new spur from a remarkable personality named Emile Jellinek. A wealthy Czech who was not only the consul-general for Austria-Hungary in Nice, but also a fanatic for cars, Jellinek knew all the 'right' people and his influence had gained Cannstatt many valuable orders. In 1899 Paul Daimler evolved a prototype called the PD, chiefly notable for its compactness, foot-controlled accelerator, and a honeycomb radiator instead of the accepted coiled tube type.

The Mercedes era

Jellinek ran one of the 1899 Cannstatt-Daimler racing cars, a cumbersome, high-built, short wheelbase machine, though important in having a pressed steel frame instead of the usual armoured wood type, a big, low-hung honeycomb radiator, and a gate-type gearchange anticipating the modern 'H' layout. Unfortunately one of these cars crashed in the yearly hillclimb contest held at La Turbie in France, killing the driver; as a result Jellinek vehemently urged DMG to scrap the heavy, ill-balanced machine and design a new car.

Then Gottlieb Daimler, the genius whom the Marquis de Dion had toasted as 'the father of the internal combustion engine and all the benefits it brought to mankind', died in March 1900, and the destiny of his famous firm was left in the hands of a non-technical board of directors, Wilhelm Maybach and the dynamic Jellinek. With the promise of an initial order for 36 cars if the first could be delivered by October 15, 1900, Jellinek asked Maybach to construct a new car with 35hp engine, a low, light chassis, and a honeycomb radiator; he further stipulated that the car be given the inter-national-sounding name of Mercedes (after his daughter) rather than the Teutonic one of Daimler.

DMG could not meet the deadline, but the first 35hp Mercedes was completed early in 1901, when it virtually revolutionized car design. It had a 5.9-litre 116× 140mm four-cylinder engine, novel for its use of mechanically-operated inlet as well as exhaust valves at a time when 'automatic' suction operation was accepted practice. Inlet and exhaust valves were on opposite sides, i.e. forming a T-head, operated by two camshafts in the block. Light alloys kept engine weight down, and ignition was by

Miss Mercedes Jellinek (left), 11-year old daughter of Emil Jellinek, international diplomat and 'merchant prince' from Nice (far left), gave her name to one of the world's most famous cars. Built by the German Daimler company to Jellinek's commission, the 35hp Mercedes of 1901 set new design trends which other makers quickly followed.
Below: A 1902 example of the famous Mercedes, with engine enlarged to 40hp. Light alloys were used in the big four-cylinder engine, which had mechanically operated valves, magneto ignition and cooling by honeycomb radiator. A pressed steel chassis and 4-speed gearbox made this an advanced but expensive pioneer of the grand touring car.

low-tension magneto. Cooling was by a neat honeycomb radiator and a flywheel fan drawing air through an engine under-shield, and there was a foot-operated accelerator combined with a hand throttle, giving truly responsive engine speed control. A spiral spring clutch transmitted to a four-speed gearbox with gate-change as on the 1899 Cannstatt, and final drive was by side chains.

The internal expanding rear brakes were watercooled, while the chain sprockets and wheels ran in large ball races. The engine was bolted straight to the pressed steel chassis instead of in the usual subframe, all helping to improve the power-to-weight ratio. As ever, racing was the acid test. The new Mercedes failed through clutch trouble in its first event at Pau in Southern France, then atoned dramatically by winning the 262-mile Nice-Salon-Nice race, the Nice speed trials and the La Turbie hillclimb in quick succession.

Galling though it must have been to patriotic Frenchmen, it was a French journalist, Paul Meyan, who wrote that year "We have entered the Mercedes era." Jellinek sold his 36 cars and more, supplying an eager clientele including royalty, nobility and at least four American millionaires (Vanderbilt, Gould, Dinsmore and Astor). The 35hp Mercedes is generally proclaimed the world's first sports car, designed for road use rather than racing. By 1902 it became a 40hp, and was firmly established as *the* car to copy.

While DMG was reinstating the pre-eminence of Germany, its Benz compatriots were undergoing a bad spell. Since 1897 Karl Benz had reluctantly fitted pneumatic tires, raised the power of the *Kontra* to 9hp, and adopted a sliding pinion three-speed gearbox, though the belt final drive, horizontal rear engine, surface carburettor, tiller steering and complex controls all remained. Slow, plodding reliability still achieved sales of 572 in 1899 and a peak of 603 in 1900; they then took a downward slide in 1901, reaching 226 by 1902.

The management became alarmed, over-rode Karl Benz and hired a new designer, the Frenchman Marius Barbarou. He promptly switched to a combination of Panhard and Mercedes systems in a new, conventional front-engined car in two- and four-cylinder forms called the Benz Parsifal. Popularity once lost is hard to regain, however, and when Benz reemerged as an influential name it was with much more powerful cars in 1907–08.

British success at last

It was now Britain's turn to come to the fore, and the first sign that she was no longer an 'also-ran' came in the Thousand Miles Trial of 1900, organized by the ACGBI, the forerunner of the RAC. This was Britain's first long distance motor event, the route being London to Edinburgh via Bristol and Manchester, and then back via Leeds and Nottingham. Of the 65 starters, 35 finished, and among the twelve class winners were four British vehicles: an Ariel quadricycle, an MMC, a Wolseley voiturette and an 8hp Napier.

The Wolseley and the Napier were both important representatives of the growing British industry. Forgetting his early tricars, Herbert Austin had now designed a small $3\frac{1}{2}$hp four-wheeler Wolseley with front-mounted single-cylinder horizontal engine. In its successful Thousand Miles Trial form, when Austin himself drove, it had a wrap-around tubular radiator, three speeds, belt-cum-chain drive and tiller steering. Improved chain-drive versions of this pleasant little car were built in hundreds in the following few years, setting Wolseley firmly on the road to prosperity.

The Napier was a newcomer of distinguished pedigree. D. Napier & Sons of London had made coin-minting machinery, hydraulic equipment, balances, printing presses, etc. since 1808. In 1899 proprietor Montague Napier was asked by a famous pioneer British cyclist, tricyclist and motorist.

Selwyn F. Edge, to fit wheel steering, a tubular radiator and pneumatic tires to his 1896 6hp Panhard. Napier did so, then offered to build a new vertical twin coil ignition engine for the car. The resultant Napier engine was light, powerful and reliable, and the next stage was a complete car, following general Panhard pattern but with many practical improvements.

It was completed just five days before the Thousand Miles Trial, in which Edge drove it to win his class, finishing second overall. Encouraged, Edge now arranged to market Napier cars, and a four-cylinder soon augmented the range. The year 1902 brought resounding success to Napiers, when S. F. Edge's 40hp car won the Gordon Bennett Cup race from Paris to Innsbruck, rudely shattering the complacent French, whose cars had led easily until they broke down. This racing Napier had shaft drive and 'square' engine dimensions, i.e. equal bore and stroke of 5in×5in, and also utilised an aluminium cylinder block with dry steel liners.

Edge now aspired to market an ultra-smooth luxury car, and urged Napier to design a six-cylinder unit. Isolated 'sixes' had already been built, but Napiers were the first to commercialize the type's virtues of silence, smoothness and flexibility. Their first 'six' would proceed at walking pace in top gear without snatch, yet romped up hills without need for continual gear-changing. By 1904 the six-cylinder Napier was in production; by 1905 one example, built to carry limousine bodywork, had broken the world speed record at 104.65mph, and by 1906 there were over 30 imitators, including Mercedes, Panhard and Fiat.

Rolls meets Royce

By then, other noteworthy British cars such as Humber, Sunbeam, Rover, Singer, Vauxhall and the Scottish Arrol-Johnston and Argyll, had come forward to ruffle Continental confidence and reduce their exports into Britain. A master designer whose work was never fully appreciated was F. W. Lanchester, whose first car, begun in 1896 and in production by 1900, had a centrally-located 10hp flat-twin engine with two contra-rotating crankshafts and flywheels to achieve perfect balance, an epicyclic three-speed gearbox, propeller shaft final drive, and a combined chassis/body.

In 1904 an aristocratic young sportsman, the Hon. Charles Rolls went to Manchester to meet an electrical engineer, Henry Royce. The result of the meeting was historic. Royce had acquired a secondhand Decauville in 1903, had maintained and tinkered with it, and felt he could build a better car himself — and did so. His prototype with 1.8-litre in-line twin-cylinder engine and shaft drive performed so well in 1904 that news of it reached Rolls in his London car showrooms in Brook Street. The smoothness, silence and refinement of the Royce twin so impressed him that a business agreement was soon drawn up, and the Rolls-Royce marque was founded early in 1905, distinguished by the noble Grecian radiator lines still retained today.

The engine was enlarged to 2 litres, and clever multiplication of components produced Rolls-Royce 3-litre 'threes', 4-litre 'fours' and a 6-litre 'six' by 1906, when Rolls himself drove a 4-litre 'Light Twenty' to victory in the Isle of Man TT race for catalogue touring cars. A 20hp V8-engined town car called the 'Legalimit', deliberately governed not to exceed the official 20mph speed limit, proved a rare R-R flop, and in 1907 the firm adopted a one-model policy, building a 7-litre 40/50 six-cylinder only for the prestigious luxury market. There was nothing sensationally advanced about this big side-valve twin ignition car; it was merely built to the most exacting engineering standards irrespective of cost. Called the Silver Ghost, which sold at £985 for the chassis only (complete examples today fetch over £30 000), this glorious car was made, with periodic improvements, right up to 1925.

The American way of transport

Meanwhile the automobile was revolutionizing the American way of life. The United States had a poor road system in the early 1900s, with long stretches of dirt roads that became thick mud in winter or choking dust in summer. This precipitated a rash of nimble, high-wheeled, motorized buggies, most of them fitted with rear-mounted Benz-like engines and primitive transmission. Steam cars thrived particularly well there water being more easily available than gasoline, while light battery electric cars with a range of about 20 miles were popular for city use. Before 1900 there were scarcely 50 American-built cars existing, yet a year later the figure was 4192 and by 1905 had rocketed to 24 250. In addition there were substantial imports from Europe.

Some epic endurance runs helped to convince 'John Public' of the value of the automobile. Remarkable for 1903 was the 6000-mile coast-to-coast drive by Colonel Nelson Jackson in a 20hp Winton in 63 days, when there were no proper highways, garages or gas stations. Tom Fetch in a 12hp Packard made the same trip in two days less, while in 1904 L. Whitman in a 10hp aircooled Franklin lowered the time to 33 days. That same year F. de la Roche in a Darracq drove 3650 miles from New York City to St Louis and back in 16 days, the engine never stopping save on the Staten Island ferry at the finish.

Such feats fostered confidence in the automobile right across the Americas, and despite the inevitable short-sighted reactionaries the result, as in Europe, was an unprecedented boom which spawned hundreds of new makes. Some hired European designers; some copied European models; others bought up the main parts and assembled them, while yet others learned as they built. Cars were built in over a dozen states: runabouts, buggies, buckboards, high-wheelers, tonneaus, stanhopes, pullmans, roadsters, even 'bugs' and 'buggyabouts'. There were 'gearless' cars and 'waterless' cars, and the inevitable 'noiseless', 'vibrationless' and 'dustless' ones.

The Packard ('Ask the man who owns one') was a quality car right from 1899, when James Packard, complaining of

Alliterative, co-operative, superlative: no two names formed a finer or more famous alliance in motoring than Rolls and Royce. Inset left: The Hon. Charles S. Rolls, third son of Baron Llangattock, and a pioneer motorist and sportsman, who visited Frederick Henry Royce (inset right) in Manchester in 1904 to see his 2-cylinder Royce car and was immediately captivated. The Rolls-Royce marque was formed the next year. Above: The Hon. C. S. Rolls taking the Duke of Connaught for a 75-mile demonstration run along the South coast in one of the prototype Royce cars in December 1904.

Left: The 1902 10hp Wolseley with transverse horizontal twin-cylinder engine, a successful British model designed by Herbert Austin before he formed his own company. The cylinders were parallel, with the heads at the forward end, and the flywheel on the offside. The body has an 'occasional' third seat at the rear, one of several options in coachwork.

faults in his Winton, was told: "Young man, if you think you can do better, go and try it," and did so, aided by an ex-Mors engineer named Schmidt. David Buick had earned a fortune making bathtubs when he began on cars in 1903. He used an underseat 2.6-litre overhead valve twin-cylinder engine and two-speed planetary gearbox, and couldn't build enough to meet the demand. Bigger models followed, and in 1908 Buick became a pioneer member of the powerful General Motors Corporation.

The Cadillac, also a product of the GM stable today and named after the French founder of the city of Detroit, appeared in 1903 as a well-made small car with under-seat 6½hp single-cylinder engine and the popular planetary two-speed transmission. It was one of the first American cars to be exported in appreciable quantities to Britain, and improved versions were made right up to 1908. By then the makers were 'quality conscious', and to publicize their high-precision manufacturing methods under-went a 'standardization' test at Brooklands, Surrey. Under RAC observation three cars from stock were completely dismantled, their parts intermixed, and three new cars assembled, all working faultlessly — a feat that won Cadillac the coveted Dewar Trophy.

Yet another important recruit to General Motors in 1909 was Oldsmobile, a make of particular import as pioneers in mass pro-duction. Ransom Olds, who said he couldn't bear the smell of horses, made the usual experiments with steam and electric cars before getting his first serious gasoline car into production by 1901. This was the famous runabout with 'scroll' front called the Curved Dash, a tough, simple design with its front and rear springs in one piece forming chassis side members as well as axle supports. A slow-turning 1.6-litre watercooled single-cylinder engine lay flat amidships under the body, and the whole car weighed only 800lb and did 20mph.

Drama attended its first appearance, when a factory fire destroyed all working drawings, parts, dies and patterns. Fortunately the prototype car was saved, fresh drawings and patterns were prepared, and production began in a month. Olds developed line pro-duction where cars were rolled along to assembly stages, with groups of workmen concentrating on fitting one item only. The 1901 output was 425 cars, and this figure rose to 2100 in 1902, 3750 in 1903 and 5000 in 1904. An output of 36 cars per day by 1905 was impressive by any standard.

Another make to employ mass production methods to a degree was Rambler, ancestors of today's cars of the same name built by the American Motors Corporation. With long experience of churning out bicycles in quantity, the Jefferys, father and son, of Kenosha, Wisconsin, easily adapted their assembly line system in 1902 to the spidery wire-wheeled, front-engined Rambler run-about. Some 1500 cars was an impressive first year's output, and this achievement, coupled with that by Oldsmobile, hardened the resolve of the stubborn, farseeing son of a farmer from Dearborn, Detroit, to build cars for the masses. This was Henry Ford.

'Curved Dash': So called because of its scroll front, this famous Oldsmobile was one of America's first quantity production motor cars. Designed for extreme simplicity, lightness and dependability, it had a horizontal single-cylinder engine amidships, single chain drive, combined front and rear springs also forming frame side members, an epicyclic 2-speed gear and tiller steering. It weighed 800lbs, could achieve 20mph, and cost under $700. Over 12 000 were built between 1901 and 1905.

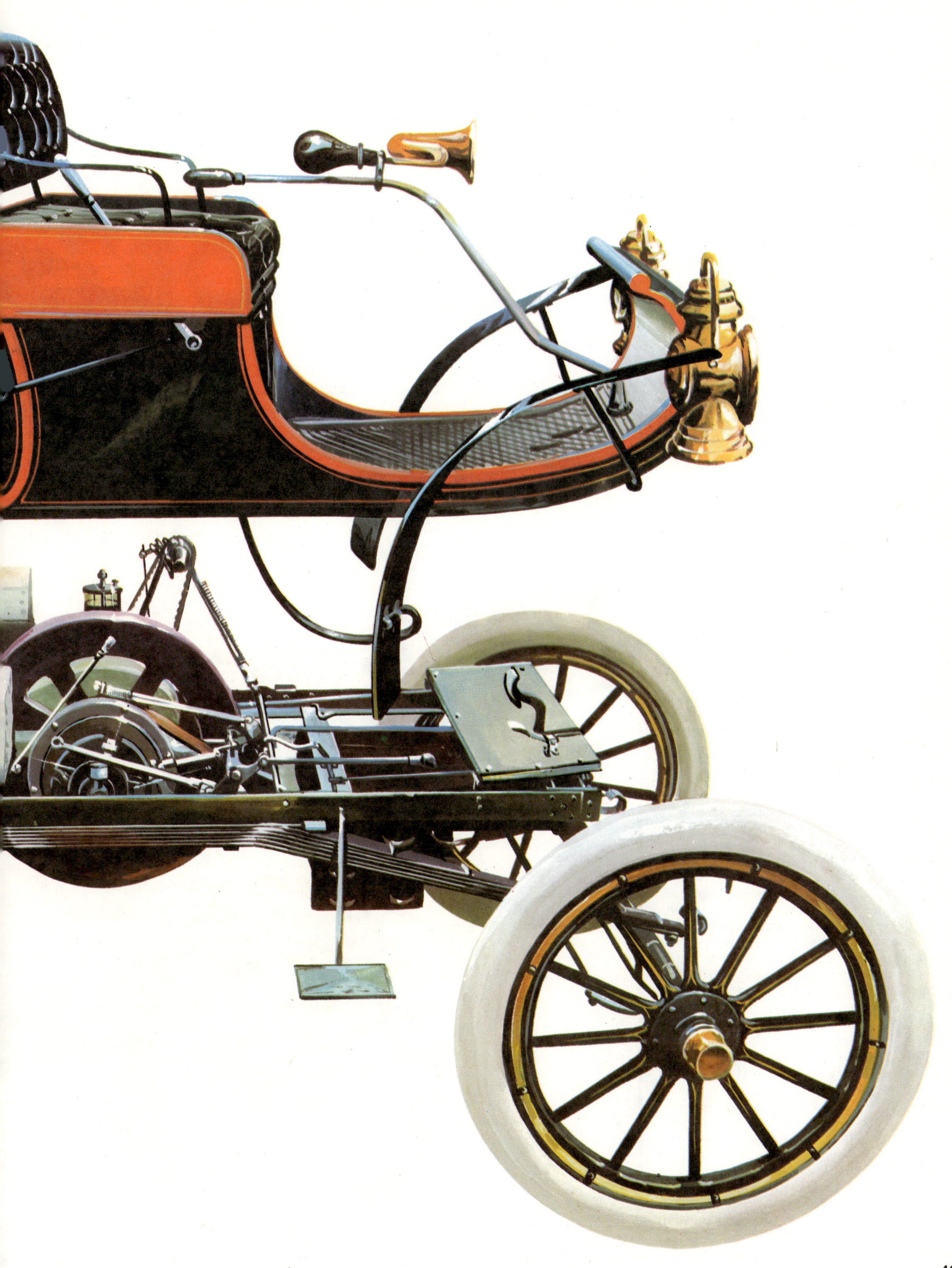

ALL SORTS

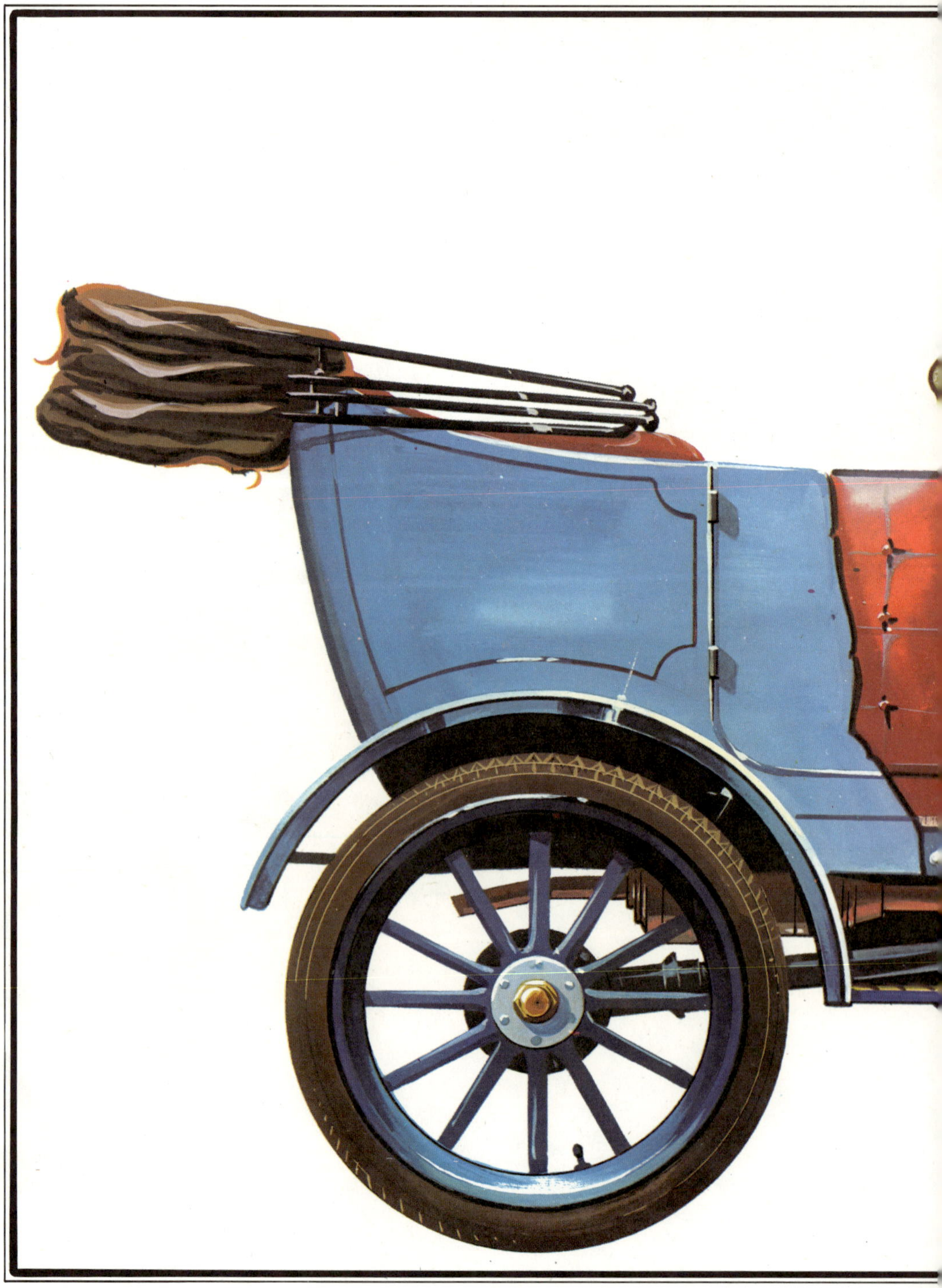

I t is often thought by many people that Henry Ford 'invented' mass production of cars. This is not so; De Dion-Bouton Renault, Oldsmobile and Rambler all anticipated him to a degree, but he certainly perfected the system in the production of his unforgettable Model T. Mass production really began back in the bicycle days of the 1880s, when it was logical to make identical parts in quantity and build the embryonic machines in rows, with workers fitting certain parts in a certain order, and completed bicycles coming off the end of the line.

Birth of the 'Tin Lizzie'

Henry Ford, however, made a science of it, timing every operation with a stopwatch, saving wasted movements by bringing parts close to hand at the right moment on moving platforms, and guiding components to join the main flow at precisely the correct second. Thousands of different operations had to be correlated, and every action streamlined to secure the greatest output in the least time, thereby cutting costs. One man did one job, maybe putting a bolt through a hole, or screwing on a nut, all day long. Many jokes on the subject abounded, such as the operative on line E who dropped his wrench and was fired because 15 cars passed him while he was picking it up.

Ford employees certainly worked hard, but if the system sounds inhuman today, it should be stressed that they were paid well — the ten-hour working day was cut to eight hours — and Henry Ford never went short of labour at any time. It took several years for him to develop the system. His first production car, the Model A of 1903, was virtually an assembly job of parts made outside the Ford plant; 1708 units were built in the first 12 months, but Ford was only just feeling his way. He had very set, practical ideas about cars, and hated excess weight: ''The old ox cart weighed a ton — and had so much weight that it was weak'' he would snort.

Experience in building subsequent models such as the B, C, K and N then converted him to a one-model policy — ironically like Rolls-Royce at the opposite end of the scale — and the Model T was born. This, the famous 'flivver' or 'Tin Lizzie', was the most

AND SIZES

The immortal 'T': The world's first 'people's car', without doubt, was the Model T Ford, introduced in 1908 by Henry Ford (top left). Over 15 million of these cars, progressively modernised in style, were sold in the next 19 years, but the basic design remained unchanged. It included a sturdy 2.9-litre 4-cylinder side-valve engine, an epicyclic 2-speed gearbox, shaft final drive and transverse leaf springing at front and rear.

important car of the first decade of the twentieth century. It was a 'people's car' 30 years before Nazi Germany announced the Volkswagen in 1938, and it gave clear notice that the United States had no more to learn about manufacturing cars from Europe.

Everything about the T was utilitarian. It had a 2.9-litre four-cylinder monobloc side-valve engine with detachable head, a two-speed planetary gearbox, flywheel magneto, shaft final drive, suspension by transverse leaf springs front and rear, and left-hand drive. With its square brass radiator and erect lines it was no worse and no better looking than dozens of contemporaries, but 'the universal car', as Henry Ford called it, offered greater reliability, even when grossly abused, ample power for its weight, a 40mph maximum, remarkable agility over the deplorable roads of the time, and unparalleled value for money.

Sales figures speak for the T. In its first full production year, 1909, 10 607 cars were built – and snapped up. The figure was 18 664 in 1910, 34 528 in 1911, 78 440 in 1912, 168 220 in 1913, 248 307 in 1914, and 533 921 in 1916! In 1911 the firm had moved to a new factory at Highland Park, Michigan, planned from the start for assembly line production, and with ever-mounting output the purchase price was progressively reduced. The harshest lesson to other makers was that production had increased more than sixfold in four years yet the workforce had scarcely doubled, while skilled men were far less at a premium. Model Ts were also built in Britain from 1911, and with periodic improvements the car was in production right up to 1927, the total production being a staggering 15 007 003.

Unbeatable bargain though it was, the Model T was not all virtue: it had its moods and idiosyncrasies and could be both a difficult starter and stopper. It inspired countless jokes, Henry Ford's own favourite, pleasing his own vanity, going something like this: ''Part of a famous magician's act is to make a horse vanish. That's nothing though – Henry Ford did it!'' His car brought both an industrial and social revolution to the United States and other nations, and finally established the automobile as a necessity to mankind and not merely a luxury.

Britain fights through

Back in 1895, before Britain's Emancipation Act came into force, a Scotsman named Joseph Wright applied to the Glasgow city chambers for permission to drive his horseless carriage on local roads. He was advised that it would be imprudent, and in his reply he wrote: ''Allow me to say that those in authority . . . might as well try to beat back the waves of the sea with a broom as try to stem the tide of horseless carriages which are looming in the distance.''

Time was to prove the wisdom of these words, but the way was made needlessly hard in Britain by legal and personal prejudice. Although the 12mph speed limit was reluctantly raised to 20mph in 1903, the police continued their vendetta against motorists and lawful vigilance often degenerated into persecution. Fines were

Motoring for the millions: The main street in any American town from 1909 looked like this, with Model Ts in abundance.

heavy and eventually the victims got together and organized private warning systems. From these sprang the Automobile Association, an infinitely more militant body in its youth than it is today. It set up scout patrols to warn of police traps, arranged free legal services and a phone box rescue system for breakdowns, and with both the AA and the RAC to back him up, the British motorist felt less of a pariah.

Even so, guerilla warfare between motorists and the police continued throughout this early period, while there was the added irritant of 'car haters' who threw stones at passing cars, dug damaging holes in the road, or strewed it with nails or broken glass. This was not exclusive to Britain, for there were anti-motoring elements in every country. German and Swiss police were just as vigilant as the British force. The Austrians would scatter horseshoe nails around, Italian peasants rolled rocks onto the road, and U.S. farmers would plant broken bottles, the sharp end upwards, where the detested autos passed. But the motor car came through it all.

By 1910 the top luxury car offered a suave combination of mechanical efficiency and every passenger comfort: good suspension, large diameter pneumatic tires, and enclosed, well-upholstered coachwork. Shaft drive had largely displaced whirring side chains, four-speed gearboxes were smoother, and with a ready source of professional chauffeurs long-distance road travel was quite 'the thing' among those who could afford it.

Of the great makes, Napier's once avant-garde six-cylinder models had lagged sadly behind the rival Rolls-Royce 40/50. The Hon. C. S. Rolls had been killed in an air crash in 1910, but the company, by then transferred from Manchester to Derby, had gone from strength to strength. In 1911 a

Motoring for the few: For sheer magnificence and grace the Rolls-Royce 40/50 six-cylinder 'London-Edinburgh' open tourer was hard to match.

Silver Ghost with superb open 'torpedo' bodywork was driven from London to Edinburgh in top gear only, averaging 24.32mpg, and in 1912 a 'Continental' variant took part in the gruelling Austrian Alpine Trial. To the firm's intense shame the car failed on one pass due to a too high bottom gear, so they tried again in 1913 with a new four-speed gearbox. This time they emerged with full honours, and in 1914 they managed to repeat their 1913 Alpine success. Certainly the pre-war Rolls-Royce tourer was of timeless beauty with its clean, sweeping lines and perfect balance.

In Germany, Mercedes and Benz had become great rivals (the merger did not take place until 1926), both in the high-powered luxury car class and in tough, long-distance events such as the Herkomer and Prince Henry Cup Trials, fielding massive four-cylinder overhead valve machines, each valve the diameter of a modern piston.

In France, Panhard-Levassor, long since free of Daimler-licensed engines, had joined the 'sleeve valve school' initiated when the American, Charles Knight, licensed his engine patents, first to the British Daimler company in 1908, and then to several other marques including Mercedes, Minerva and Panhard. The larger Panhard chassis, like those of the conservative Lorraine-Dietrich and Delaunay-Belleville cars, habitually wore superb coachwork from the fashionable Paris *carrossiers*.

Métallurgique of Belgium had joined the ranks of the elite with some finely built fours and sixes distinguished by their sharp vee radiators, a style then becoming distinctly popular. Daimler of Coventry, their Lawson days happily forgotten, increased in size and elegance, their 7.4-litre six-cylinder sleeve-valve model of 1913–14 carrying lofty, luxurious coachwork and the cachet of royal patronage, its silent but modest performance ensuring remarkable longevity. Sunbeam of Wolverhampton marketed a well-proportioned 6.1-litre six-cylinder which attracted the coachbuilders of the day, while Lanchester, who had stuck firmly to engine location between the passengers since 1904, yielded at last to convention and produced a much better looking front-engined 40hp six.

Italy's Isotta-Fraschini, which began as an Italianized baby Renault, had grown into an aggressive four-cylinder vee-radiatored 100hp machine with four overhead valves to each cylinder, operated by an overhead camshaft. One of the last makes to

Radio Times Hulton

National Motor Museum

Glorifying the benefits of petrol to mankind, this 1911 magazine cover (left) stresses its uses on land, sea and air, with HM King George V's Daimler in royal purple as the centrepiece.

Top French quality in pre-Great War automobiles was epitomised by this 1911 27hp Delaunay-Belleville (below left). The characteristic circular radiator symbolised the marque's long-established profession as marine boiler makers. At the other end of the scale, the cyclecar (right) appeared in around 1910, offering the cheapest form of basic motoring. Despite its unusual layout with the driver behind the passenger and the long drive belts, this French-built Bedélia was one of the better examples. The British Humberette (bottom) came midway between the frugal, spidery cyclecar and a normal small car. With an aircooled vee-twin engine in a tubular frame, three speeds and shaft drive, it cost £120 in 1913–14.

retain chain drive to 1914, albeit enclosed in elegant casings, I-F were paradoxically the first to standardize four-wheel brakes in 1909, whereas more timid makes tried them out but found them wanting and hurriedly dropped them. The Isotta-Fraschini enjoyed considerable popularity among wealthy Americans with a sporting bent, at a time when the United States had several prestige cars of her own. These included the Locomobile, Simplex, Pierce-Arrow, Cadillac and Packard, some of which reversed the former order of things and were exported to Europe.

There was such a large variety of cars available on the market by 1910 that even 'the man of modest means' as the advertisements tactfully put it, could contemplate motoring, aided by new down-payment schemes, while 'the professions' used cars

more and more for business. An uncertain new species of vehicle, half motorcycle, half car and very cheap, was invented; it was called the 'cyclecar', and it offered basic, unsophisticated transport, no more. France, Britain, Germany and Italy all built them, in frightening variety. Some had three wheels, one at the front and two at the rear, others vice versa, while some sported the full four. Some were desperately crude, with nineteenth-century style belt drive over sliding pulleys or movable rear axles and centre-pivot steering, while others were simplified, scaled-down large cars.

Most of them had twin-cylinder proprietary motorcycle engines, located at the front, the side or the rear; wheels were spidery and tires thin, and gossamer-light bodies had side-by-side or tandem seating. At prices well below £100 self-maintenance

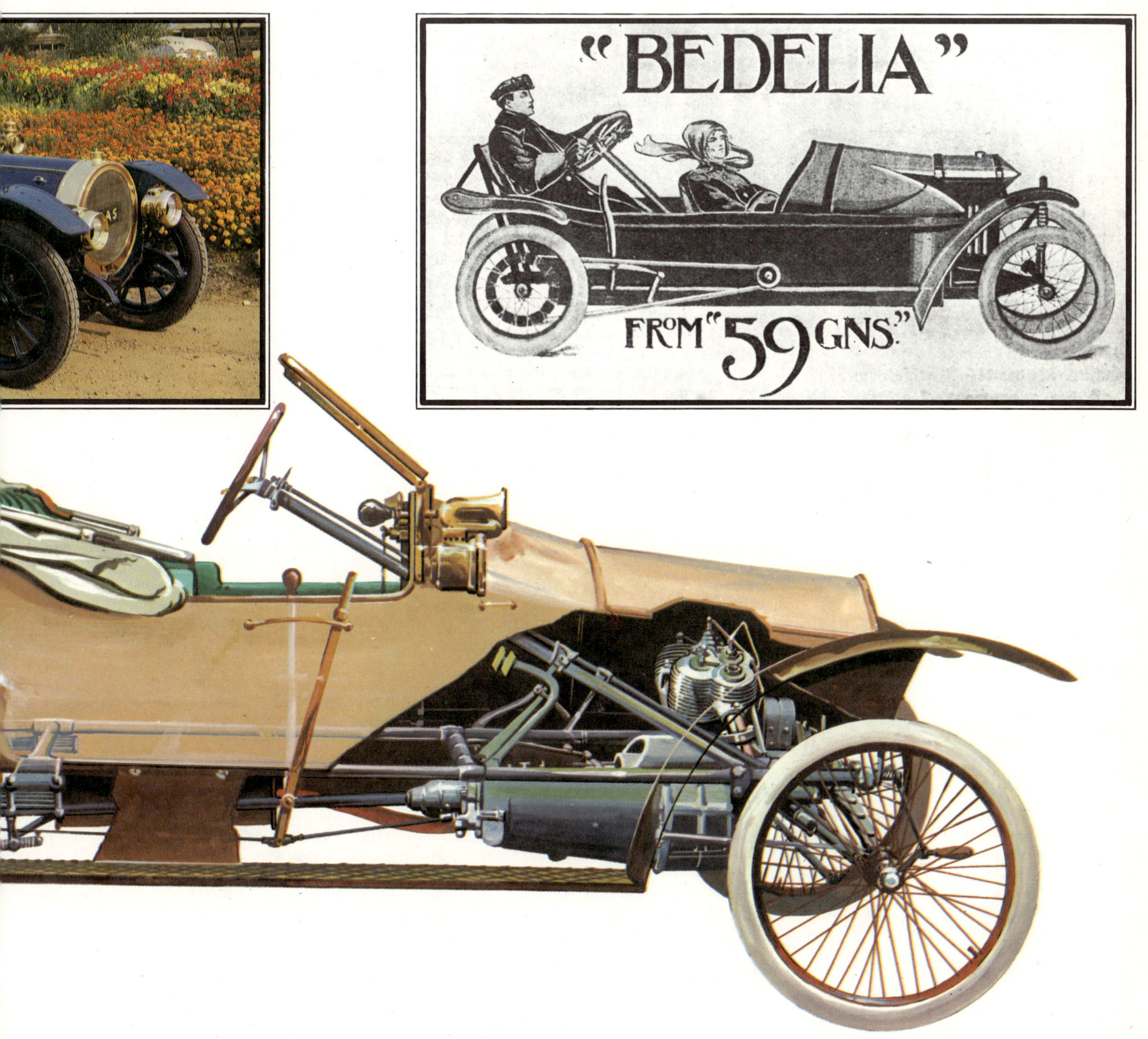

D. Burgess Wise

Brian Hatton

was almost essential, and with agility and physical endurance also desirable requisites, the cyclecar was essentially a young man's vehicle. Yet they gave many thousands of people their first taste of motoring, and helped breed an invaluable self-reliance on the road.

Excessive fragility was the undoing of most cyclecars, but a thriving market remained for the miniature car proper, with small four-cylinder engine, shaft drive and other civilized features. Epitomizing this class was the Bébé-Peugeot of 1912, an exquisite little vehicle of deceptively delicate appearance, with diminutive 856cc mono-bloc four-cylinder side-valve engine and two speeds. A practical pioneer 'mini-car', it was designed by Ettore Bugatti, the Milan-born, French-naturalized genius whose name also shone in higher performance spheres.

Other makes exploiting the same theme used slightly larger engines. Mathis, neighbours of Bugatti at Strasbourg, introduced an 1100cc 'Babylette' that same year, while FN of Belgium marketed a 1250cc 'baby'. Wanderer of Germany wrought a variation in their 'Püppchen' (or 'doll') which resembled the Peugeot but had a 1145cc engine, a body with two seats in tandem, and a central steering wheel. This reduced width but proved so unpopular that the makers switched to conventional side-by-side seating.

British contenders in this new 'little big car' sphere included an 1100cc Singer with gearbox on the back axle, an 1100cc Swift Ten, both with four cylinders, and a new 'economy' model by Wolseley called the Stellite, with 1076cc four-cylinder motor, two speeds and quarter-elliptic springing all round.

Between the extremes of ultra-luxury and economy small cars, the motor car made further divergences catering for all depths of pocket. Renault, Opel and Fiat all borrowed American mass production methods. Agnelli of Fiat announced the 'Zero', a utilitarian car with only one style body — an open four-seater — to be produced in large quantities with minimum complication. It had a sturdy 1.8-litre four-cylinder mono-bloc side-valve engine, and many parts, including the body panels, were formed on large presses. From 1912 over 2000 of

these cars were built until the intervention of war.

Louis Renault had visited the United States in 1912, returning deeply impressed, particularly by the manufacturing methods pioneered by the American efficiency engineer, Frederick W. Taylor, such as time and motion study. He resolved to employ such methods at Billancourt, but his enthusiasm quickly resulted in a strike, the independent Parisians objecting to 'the dictatorship of the chronometer'. The dispute lasted many days before the workers yielded to the lure of higher earnings. Opel in Germany managed to speed up their production with fewer complications. A serious factory fire proved fortuitous for it obliged them to refit their plant, and they naturally installed the latest line assembly equipment.

Morris on the road to fame

Yet another who learned from the United States was Britain's William Morris, who had graduated from bicycles and motor-cycles to motor manufacture by 1912. Morris approached car production both as an experienced mechanic and a business-man, fully conscious of the need for high output and low price at a time when 'the pound in your pocket' often rated a full week's wages. Ford were selling their Model T from the Trafford Park works in Manchester at about £160 in right-hand drive, four-seater form, but its 2.9-litre engine was large for British conditions and Morris planned a smaller car.

Rather than attempt to make major components himself, Morris bought them from other manufacturers. White & Poppe supplied the 1-litre four-cylinder T-head engine and three-speed gearbox for a combined £50 per car; axles and steering came from Wrigleys, Redpath Brown made the chassis, and Sankey pressed steel wheels were used. The car, called the Morris Oxford, was built as a two-seater only, costing £175. But Morris had only just started; he visited Detroit in late 1913, saw Ford's fantastic system at work in the great Highland Park plant, and devised a smaller anglicized version at his 'assembly' works in an Oxford drill hall.

While in America, Morris also visited the Continental engine company and negotiated

bulk purchase at a mere £18 apiece of their $1\frac{1}{2}$-litre 'Red Seal' engine, destined to power his first four-seater car, the Morris Cowley. By combining selective 'buying out' with coordinated assembly methods, Morris was launched on the road to fame, and his tentative introduction of mass production methods, which 30 years later he called 'specialization', was to influence the entire British motor industry after the Great War.

If car production methods had changed radically in the five years preceding war in 1914, technologically the period was more one of refinement. Major design innovations had ceased and the turmoil of ideas around 1900 had settled to a general format in which most cars looked fairly alike. Engines were firmly at the front and had either two, four or six cylinders with side valves, although more adventurous marques employed push-rods and overhead valves or even a single overhead camshaft.

Forced lubrication and magneto ignition were now the general rule, and three- or four-speed 'crash' gearboxes were generally separate, linked by a cardan shaft forward to the engine and clutch, and back by pro-peller shaft to the bevel or, more rarely, worm-drive rear axle. Chain drive was abandoned in all but a few, while the armoured wood frame survived on 'economy' models such as Wolseley's Stellite. Suspension was chiefly by semi-elliptics, although cantilever types, $\frac{3}{4}$-elliptics, $\frac{1}{4}$-elliptics and transverse leaf added variety, while shock absorbers, from being racing novelties in 1903, were now taken for granted on quality cars.

The open body had yielded to the saloon, be it a box-like structure on a small chassis or a spacious limousine, landaulet or berline, with only 'James', 'Jacques' or 'Johann' the chauffeur out in the open to distinguish master from servant. The gear lever and handbrake were still outside the body so why give the chauffeur a side screen any-way? Upholstery was made of real, often buttoned leather or Bedford cord (syn-thetics hadn't been thought of), and wood abounded both structurally and decoratively, although all-steel bodies were on the way, inevitably from the United States.

The mechanical screen wiper had yet to

56

The pre-war cult of miniature cars, as exemplified (far left) by the exquisite little Bébé Peugeot and the Wanderer 'Püppchen' with tandem seating (middle left).
Designers of contrast: Ettore Bugatti (near left), who created the 'Bébé' for Peugeot, and whose artistry in the world of high-performance cars became legendary; and William R. Morris (right), later Lord Nuffield, whose shrewd commercial mind brought quantity assembly methods to Britain by 1912, when he introduced the 1-litre Morris Oxford two-seater.
Below: Completed Morris Oxfords ready for delivery from the works.

The 'Zero', Fiat's first effort at quantity production, was a utilitarian 1.8-litre car introduced in 1912 with a single open four-seater body style.

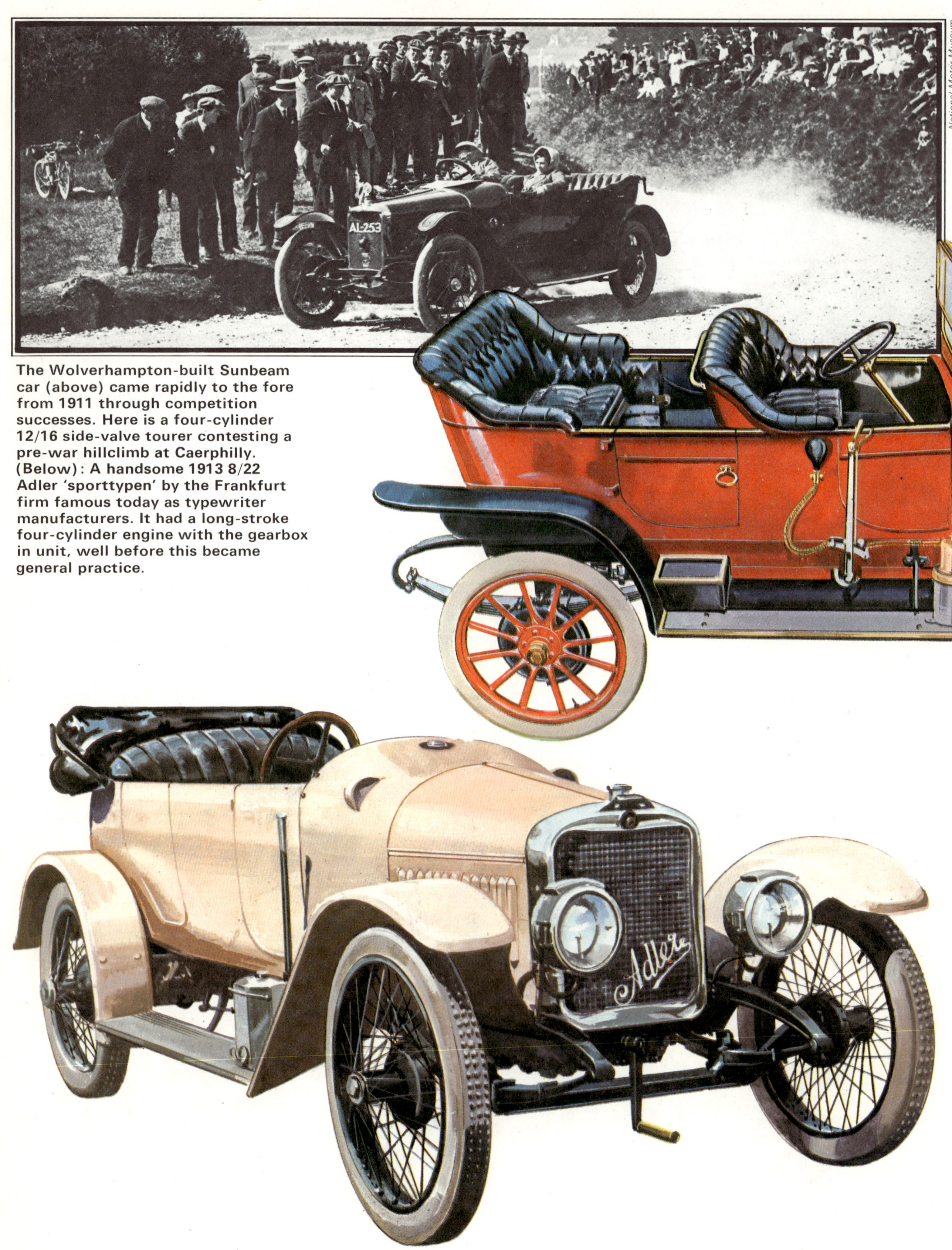

The Wolverhampton-built Sunbeam
car (above) came rapidly to the fore
from 1911 through competition
successes. Here is a four-cylinder
12/16 side-valve tourer contesting a
pre-war hillclimb at Caerphilly.
(Below): A handsome 1913 8/22
Adler 'sporttypen' by the Frankfurt
firm famous today as typewriter
manufacturers. It had a long-stroke
four-cylinder engine with the gearbox
in unit, well before this became
general practice.

be invented, but in bad weather 'James' could work a primitive felted blade by hand now and then, in between steering, gear-changing and 'sounding the horn'. The starting handle at the front was an essential feature, although electric starters, pioneered by Cadillac in 1912, were just coming into general use when war broke out. Electric lighting, too, was about to displace the long-endured acetylene lamps, fed by large brassy cylinders on the running board, containing calcium carbide and a water feed. Car heating had yet to come, although some U.S. cars bypassed the warm exhaust gases to an underfloor heating box. Most prewar motorists equipped themselves with hot water bottles and foot and hand muffs, or special charcoal-heated boxes.

Synchromesh gears were 15 years away yet, and double declutching was the order of the day. After the bewildering variety of 1900, controls had become fairly standardized with foot accelerator, brake and clutch, and a hand ignition control. Obtaining petrol was no longer a fevered rush from pharmacist to pharmacist buying little bottles; two-gallon cans in Britain and the *bidon* on the Continent were now widely stocked at garages mostly descended from cycle repair shops, but the roadside petrol pump had yet to appear, invented, inevitably, by go-ahead America with her staggering car population of around 650 000 before the Great War.

Tires had improved enormously since the bad days of 1000 miles per cover 'if you were lucky', but a Stepney wheel, bolted next to the punctured one, or a spare, were essential equipment. Wheels were now of equal size front and rear and wire spokes were popular on most European quality cars from Rolls-Royce downwards, often with Rudge-Whitworth splined hubs for quick release. Americans preferred wooden spokes, generally of hickory; wood or pressed steel artillery-type wheels largely featured in the middle and 'moderate priced' classes, while spidery motorcycle-type wire wheels often figured on the smaller economy vehicles.

An important development between 1910 and 1914 was the growth of the sports car movement. Vauxhall, Sunbeam and Talbot in Britain all produced fast, easily manoeuvrable models around side valve engines, while the cosmopolitan Hispano-Suiza, launched in Spain in 1904 to the designs of the Swiss Marc Birkigt, and later also built in Paris, fielded a most covetable sporting car in their long-stroke 3.6-litre T-head 'Alfonso X111' from 1912. The great Alfa

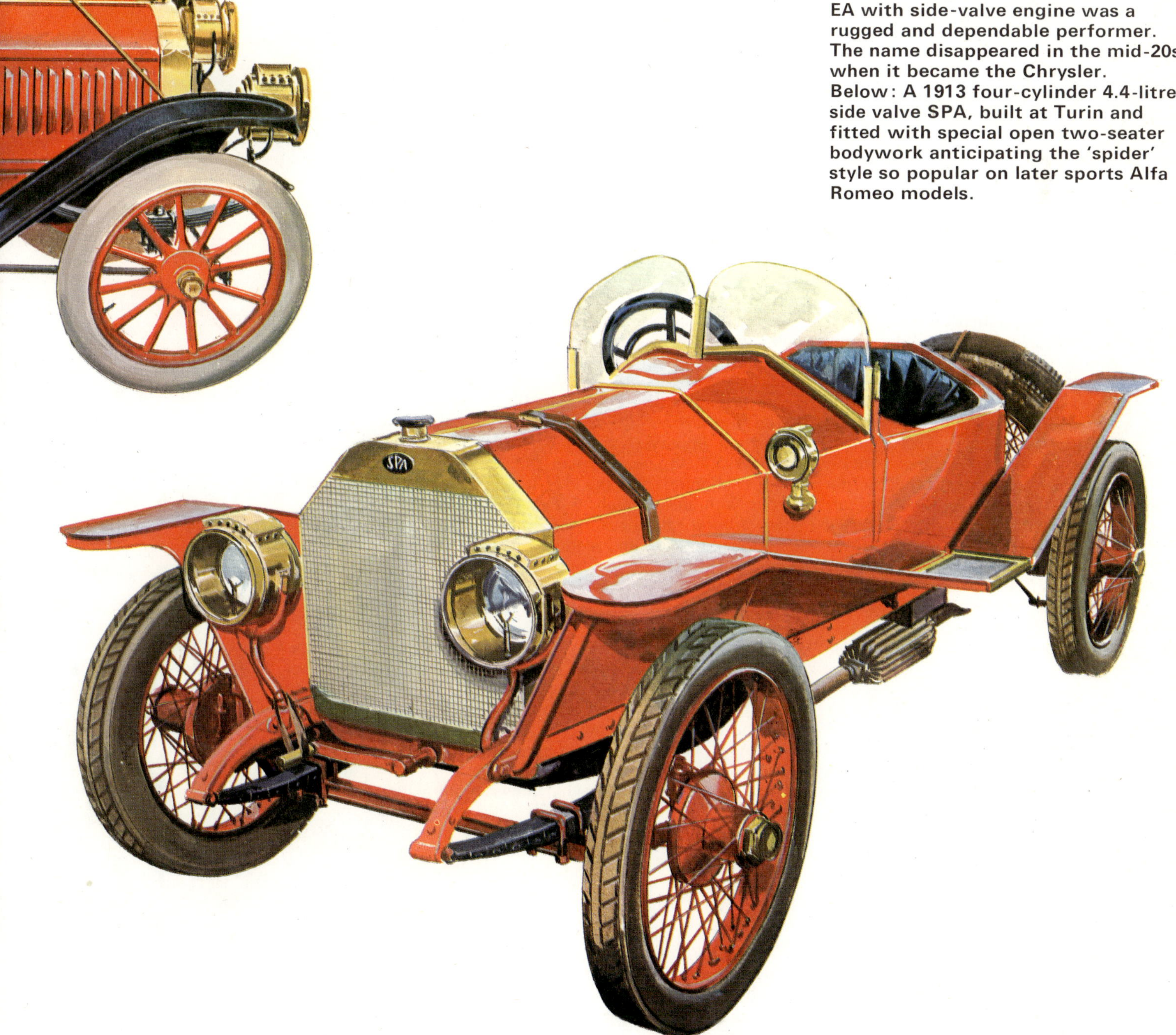

Left: The Detroit-built 1911 Maxwell 'Big Four' model EA with side-valve engine was a rugged and dependable performer. The name disappeared in the mid-20s when it became the Chrysler.
Below: A 1913 four-cylinder 4.4-litre side valve SPA, built at Turin and fitted with special open two-seater bodywork anticipating the 'spider' style so popular on later sports Alfa Romeo models.

Romeo marque was born as the ALFA in 1910, while the Bugatti Type 13 appeared the same year; with its watch-like overhead camshaft four-cylinder 1.3-litre engine and neat chassis, it was all the Edwardian enthusiast could ask for in a small sports car.

An intriguing design from Vienna was the Austro-Daimler of 1910, designed by Dr Ferdinand Porsche. Its 5.7-litre four-cylinder engine had an overhead camshaft operating no fewer than four exhaust valves and one inlet valve to each cylinder, and although such sophistication was slightly offset by chain drive, the car took the first three places in the 1910 Prince Henry Trial very impressively, Porsche himself at the wheel of the winning car. A smaller side-valve with shaft drive won the Austrian Alpine Trial the following year, yet this very sport-minded firm also contrived to manufacture a range of touring cars of great refinement.

The United States also had some fine sporting models, outstanding being the Mercer Type 35 'Raceabout' with big 4.8-litre T-head engine and characteristic bucket seats, 'monocle' windscreen and bolster rear fuel tank. Its famous rival was the Stutz 'Bearcat', with similar bodywork but the advantage of 5.4 litres; tradition has it that whereas Stutz fans declared: "You couldn't do worser than buy a Mercer," Mercer adherents retorted: "You have to be nuts to buy a Stutz." Both were great cars, attracting numerous imitators on the fruitful American market of those carefree times.

What they wore

As motoring fashion changed with the years, personal fashion changed with it. The right gear for riding a horse proved wildly wrong for a car from the very start, when it became immediately apparent that protection from draught, let alone flying hot oil, steam, sooty exhaust gases, dust or mud demanded the sacrifice of elegance for something more practical. Protective clothing of any kind was therefore the first requisite, but as the car became more civilized in the 1900s and the first windscreens appeared, the fashion houses turned their attention to the problem.

Quoting from a 1902 magazine, "The dust nuisance is as trying to ladies as the wind nuisance and, be the cushions in your ton-neau ever so comfortable, no woman will like a 30-mile drive on a dusty road, for the result is always that she arrives a dust-begrimed specimen of humanity — too *poudrée* by half!" In such conditions, 'fly-away' hats were out, and veils, toques, bonnets and capotes with ribbons were in. There was a grisly outbreak of fully-enveloping 'Martian' headgear for ladies, with celluloid eyepieces, while even the motoring dog was equipped with a hood-cum-goggles! As for the man at the wheel, he sported the essential goggles, a goatskin, fur-lined Melton or other heavy coat, or, in fine weather, leather-lined Norfolk suiting that left his arms relatively free for working all the levers.

The Continentals, women as well as men, had a great love for the peaked chauffeur's cap, and although H. J. Lawson and his cronies tried to popularize similar yachting caps in England, the average Briton preferred the anonimity of a cloth cap. As protection improved to the extent of side windows, headgear such as the 'Tammy' (Tam-o-shanter) and the fur 'turban' won favour with the women, with an essential scarf around the neck, not forgetting a 'generosity of skirt' and plenty of rugs lower down.

Later, when fully enclosed bodywork insulated the occupants from the elements, fashion had full sway. 'Madam' could indulge her love for tall, elaborate hats adorned with large feathers, flowers and even stuffed birds, while 'Sir' could safely wear his top hat, all of which helps to account for the lofty build of many pre-Great War landaulets and limousines. Incidentally, an early woman driver and writer, Miss Dorothy Levitt, advised the *motoriste* to carry, not only beauty aids, gloves, pins, mirror, etc., but also 'a small revolver' and a dog, adding that "some chocolates are very soothing sometimes."

The 'might have beens'

Should it seem that, apart from the sporting class, car design by 1914 had advanced little beyond side valves, four or six cylinders in line, crash gearboxes and shaft drive, this does not mean that shrewd technical minds had not explored further. Indeed, it is humbling to realize just how many 'modern'

'Raceabout' was the name adopted for the 4.8-litre four-cylinder side-valve Mercer (left) built at Trenton, New Jersey, USA from 1911 to 1914. This classic American sports car had a 70mph maximum, and the bucket seats and round 'bolster' type fuel tank were popular features at the time. The British Maudslay (right) was a well-engineered car notable in having overhead camshaft operation of the valves from its inception in 1902 until 1914.
Personal protection was very necessary in early motoring days. The intrepid voyageurs off to a shoot (below) are well guarded against flying dust, wind or mud with goggles. The long basket on the side carried the guns – or a picnic.

Stephen Benson

Radio Times Hulton

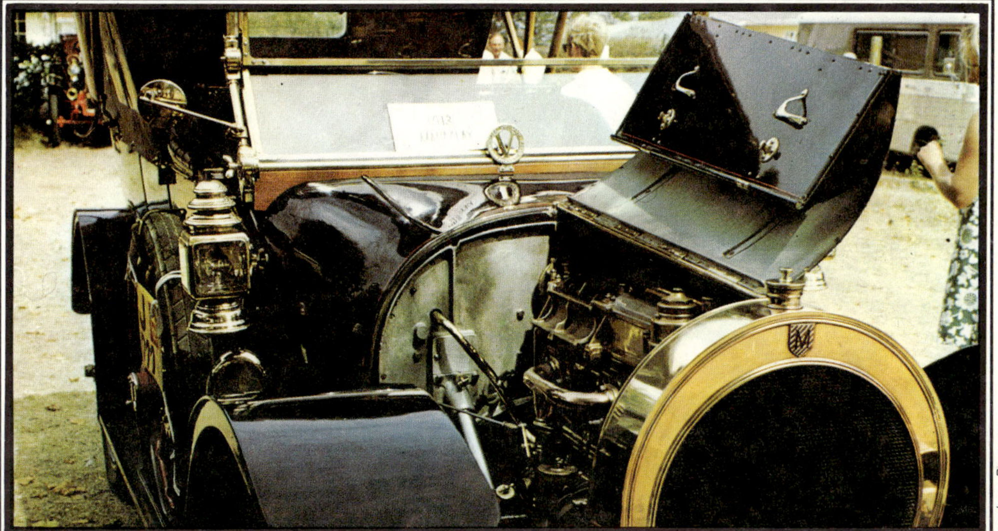

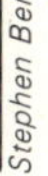

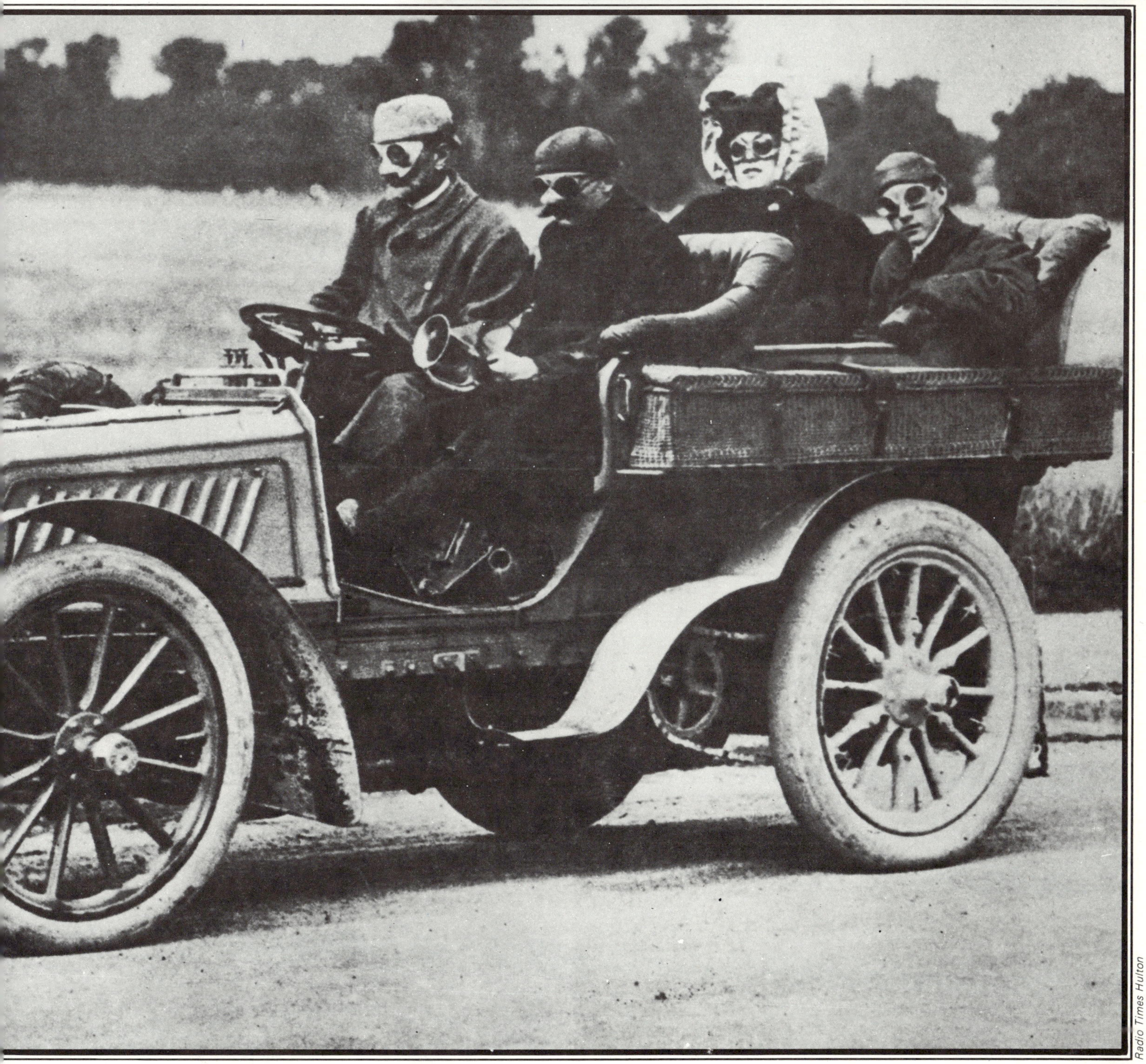

Right: This early aerodynamic effort
added about 15mph to the speed of a
standard 1914 40-60 ALFA. The
streamlined body was built by
Carrozzeria Castagna of Milan to the
order of Count Mario Ricotti, who
achieved over 86mph with his
'teardrop' car. The curved glass
windscreen was a novelty then, but
visibility for the driver, set so far back,
must have been restricted. In spite of
such advanced technical achievements,
everyday motoring remained fairly
primitive. Above: Women and children
wearing some of the necessary
protective clothing.

ideas were conceived in those early days; only limitations in metallurgy, research and manufacturing methods, or lack of funds prevented their further exploitation at the time.

Front wheel drive, so popular today but complex in its need for steering and universal joints, featured on the 1897 Graf from Austria and the 1899 Latil from France. The V4 engine was used by Mors in 1897, the V8 by Ader in 1903, the in-line 8, strictly two fours on a common crankshaft, by CGV in 1902, and the V6 by Delahaye in 1911. Fuel injection for a petrol engine was patented by Amédée Bollée in 1903. Christie of the United States had a transverse-mounted engine, gearbox and front drive *à la* modern Mini in 1909. Spyker of Holland had four-wheel drive *and* six cylinders in 1902; while the British Maudslay featured an overhead camshaft, designed to swing back for easy maintenance, from 1902 to 1914.

Automatic transmission was an optional fitment on the American Sturtevant car in 1905; hydraulically-operated brakes were offered a year earlier on the British Hutton; Lanchester patented disc brakes in 1902; while Louis Renault patented an ancestor to the modern British Leyland 'Hydrolastic' suspension in 1914. Nor were the foregoing necessarily the first of their kind, for in the world's patent offices can be found abounding evidence that, if there's anything in it, 'somebody has thought of it before'.

Even during the First World War when the car was brought into army service, this was nothing new; the ancestor of all mechanized road vehicles, Nicolas Cugnot's steam *fardier* of 1769, had been built to tow guns for the French Army. The wheels had turned full circle, and this time were to give infinitely more effective service.

The progress of the automobile was drastically interrupted by the Great War of 1914–1918. The immediate effects were deceptively minor, apart from some anxiety over petrol supplies and prices, and War Office powers to commandeer any vehicle during the early weeks of the war. Keeping up the front of 'business as usual', many British and French makers announced their 1915 models, which in general seemed to trail some two or three years behind American design. Then, suddenly, the war pattern changed. Comforting beliefs that 'it would all be over by Christmas' were quickly dashed. Car firms increasingly switched to armaments production, many garages closed, and the private car became a rare and valuable commodity.

Incredibly, the British Army possessed not a single unit of mechanical transport when war began, the Boer War-minded generals firmly agreeing that plenty of infantry and horses were the key to victory. In contrast, Germany had used cars for liaison and communication duties in military manoeuvres since around 1900, and by 1914 had numerous specialized vehicles in production. France had seen their potential value as early as 1905, and experimented with Panhards, Peugeots, and the like, equipped with machine guns, while Italy had found motor transport indispensable in her Libyan campaign of 1911. Yet all Britain could show by 1913 was a 'subsidy scheme' whereby owners of potentially useful vehicles were paid a retainer to hand them over to the Services in a time of emergency. When that emergency came, this reserve proved quite inadequate, and Government purchasing agents searched the country for motor cars. The result was a round-up of vehicles ranging from cyclecars to limousines, hastily painted in service colours and despatched to France, where many of them suffered a swift doom in the gruelling conditions.

In Britain this aggravated the already serious shortage of cars on the civilian market, and it was here that the United States stepped in. Uninvolved in the War until 1917, she became a giant store for Allied needs, and among the unceasing flow of goods crossing the Atlantic to Europe were thousands of cars. In appearance and specification most of these

WAR AND PEACE

imports outdated their European contemporaries. They all looked surprisingly similar, for even then American cars were built in such huge quantities that many parts were standardized. Their engines, mostly side-valve fours, were large by European standards, giving good performance with reliability, though less economical on fuel consumption. In those harassing days when Europe was wholly embroiled in war, America undoubtedly set the standard in car design.

V8s and V12s

Electric lighting and self-starters using the new Bendix drive off the flywheel were taken for granted by 1915, as were refinements such as folding or divided windscreens, side windows, efficient folding hoods, dashboards with instruments, proper fuel gauges and even ignition locks. As to styling, this had been vastly improved by merging the bonnet line into the scuttle with a smooth curve instead of a step; mudguards took on graceful curves and became part of the overall design, exteriors were refined with evenly raised sides, the spare wheel moving from the running board to the rear of the body, and control levers, horn, etc., being transferred to the inside of the car. There were also major advances under the bonnet, most important being the adoption of the V8-type engine by Cadillac and King, and the V12 by Packard, all three makes coming from Detroit, already established as 'the motor city'.

The V8 cylinder arrangement was not new, but American engineering made the very best of its virtues of good torque, smooth running, compactness and light weight. The Cadillac unit, unveiled at the New York Show early in 1915, was in fact a fairly close

On active service: Cavalry-minded British generals had to admit the superiority of the motor car over the horse for many duties. Top left: A Vauxhall 25hp staff car, of which nearly 2000 were supplied to the War Office. Left: HM King George V with General Sir Arthur Paget inspecting a Scottish division in 1916 from the comfort of a 25hp Vauxhall, closely followed by a Sunbeam.

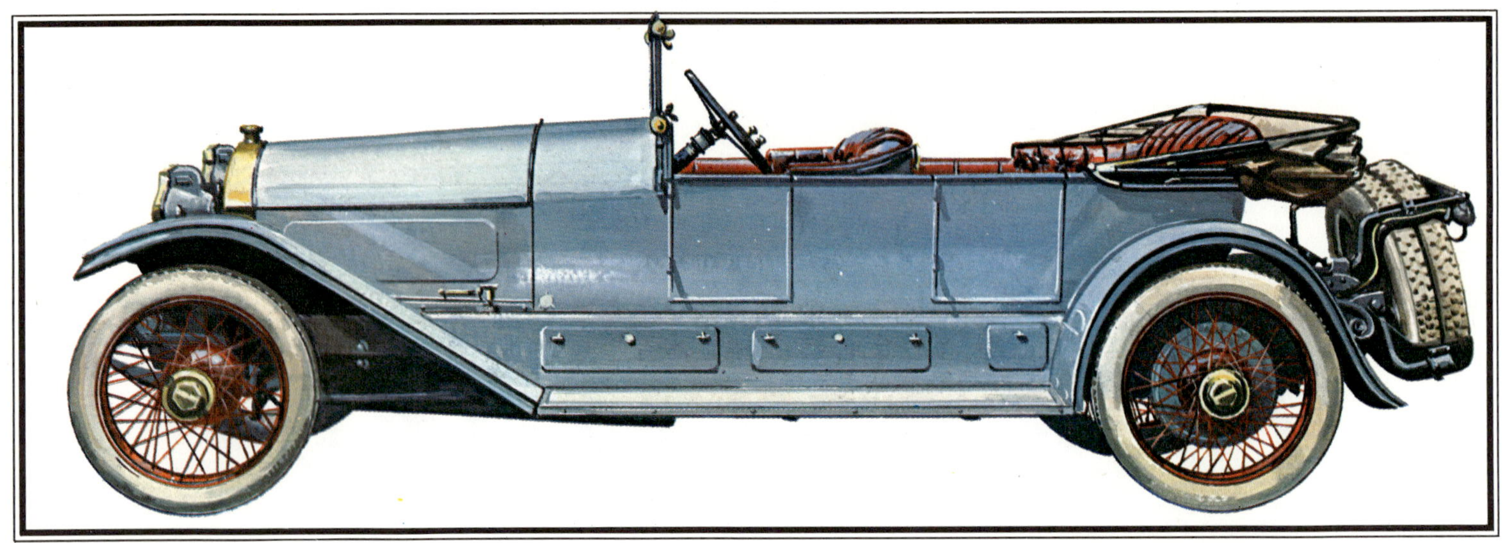

copy of the De Dion-Bouton 90° V8 introduced in late 1909. But the French marque
kept their engine speed (and hence performance) down to a cautious 1500rpm. Cadillac
opted for a sturdy three-bearing crankshaft
and boldly raised revolutions to 2400rpm,
attaining 70bhp, and also replaced magneto
with Delco battery-and-coil ignition. Dimensions were 79×130mm (5100cc) and the
smoothness, silence and flexibility achieved
were a challenge to more expensive cars
such as the six-cylinder Rolls-Royce. Signi-
ficantly, the V8 engine layout still remains
the most popular in American cars today.

An important advance in the Cadillac (of
which 47 000 were built between 1915 and
1917) was its use of a three-speed gearbox
in unit with the engine, and a central gearchange lever working through a ball joint.
Besides being convenient both for the left
and right-hand drive versions which the
Americans built at that time for different
markets, this was a neat and logical location
for the gear-change lever and was later
universally adopted. The King V8 was
broadly similar in concept, and Packard's
12-cylinder eclipsed them both for originality, although more expensive to produce.
It was not the first of its kind, for George
Schebler, a famous Detroit carburettor
manufacturer, had built a V12 in 1908. It was
never marketed commercially, whereas
Packard's chief engineer, Col Jesse Vincent,
firmly planned series production for his new
luxury design.

American boom

The V12 had two banks of six cylinders at
60°, side valves, aluminium pistons, and a
bore and stroke of 76.2×127mm (6950cc),
giving 85bhp at 3000rpm. The unit was so
flexible that the 'Twin Six' Packard, as it
was called, could idle smoothly at 3mph in
3rd (top) gear, and accelerate from 0 to
30mph in under 12 secs. Its maximum speed
was an impressive 80mph, and its introduction aroused nationwide interest, some
20 000 people queueing in San Francisco
alone in the first two days it was displayed
there. 10 645 of this prestige leader were
built and sold in its first full year of production. When the USA joined in the War in
1917, both Cadillac V8s and Packard 'Twin
Six' V12s were used by high-ranking US

While Europe was embroiled in war the USA produced many fine new cars until its own involvement in the war in 1917. Top left: The elegant 1916 Locomobile 'Sportif' had a 90hp, 8½-litre big-four engine. Centre left: Cadillac introduced America to the V8 engine with this 5.1-litre unit in 1915. Below left: The car into which it was fitted. Below: Even more sensational was the Packard 'Twin Six' with 7-litre 12-cylinder engine, bringing new standards in effortless luxury transport.

officers in Europe; it was Enzo Ferrari's experience with these Packards in Italy that began his admiration for the 12-cylinder engine, manifested in the superb Ferraris of modern times.

On mass production levels, American manufacturers found that 1914–1917, so grim in Europe, was a boom time for them even though the so-called McKenna duty of $33\frac{1}{3}$% per car was levied on their exports to Britain from September 1915. Many turned out trucks for the battlefronts as well as private cars. Overall sales of the Model T Ford rose from 240 000 in 1914 to 418 000 in 1915, and 585 000 in 1916, hitting 834 000 in 1917 – with 80 000 orders unmet at that! In 1916 alone, US makers collectively produced over 1½ million cars, yet the world's insatiable demand for them was unsatisfied. It was not only the overseas

car 'famine' that fostered such demand, but also massive American road improvements. These began with the launching in 1913 of ambitious plans for the trans-Continental Lincoln Highway from New York to San Francisco. Fourteen years elapsed before this was completed, but great legs were completed in between, as state tried to outdo state in laying inter-city links and creating a roads network that opened up vast rural areas and connected them with major towns, making the automobile increasingly important to ordinary American citizens.

Meanwhile in Europe, cars of widely different makes and nationalities were proving their worth in all theatres of the war. The humble Renault twin-cylinder AG taxi, built in large quantities at Billancourt before the war, had its finest hour in September 1914, when Marshal von Kluck's army

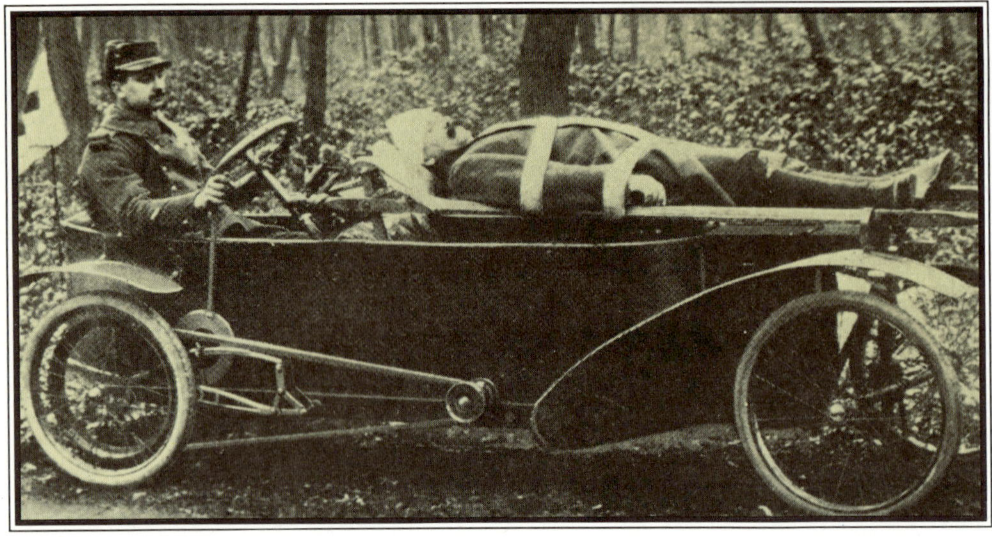

advanced rapidly on Paris. The Germans had reached the Meaux road, a mere three days' march from the capital, when General Gallièni proposed a flank counter-attack with 12 000 French reservists rushed out from Paris. Half of them were transported by rail, but Generals Maunoury and Clergerie literally 'conscripted' 600 Renault taxis from their Paris 'beats' for the rest, each vehicle carrying five soldiers and their arms to Nanteuil during the night, then returning for a repeat load. The French attack at dawn next day took the Germans completely by surprise; they retreated *en masse*, the front was consolidated, and Paris out of danger. The gallant Renault AGs thereafter became known as 'the taxis of the Marne'.

The car in battle

Henry Ford's rugged Model T, exported in thousands, was used for ambulances on every front, while British Crossleys, Napiers, Vulcans, etc., and French de Dions, Renaults, Berliets and other makes also served nobly. Even the spidery, improbable Bedélia cyclecar was hauled in for field first-aid, with a stretcher mounted above its stuttering twin-cylinder engine to carry the wounded. The aristocracy amongst automobiles were also enroled. Writing from a base camp in France, 2nd Lt Henry Segrave, later one of Britain's most famous racing drivers, told his family: "You see beautiful Daimler limousines and Rolls-Royces flying about, all battered up in some way, the bodies dinged, mudguards torn off etc., all with some mark to show what they have been through".

Rolls-Royce's famous six-cylinder 'Silver Ghost' served with distinction as personal transport at the front for Sir John French, Commander-in-Chief of the British forces, General Haig, Maréchal Foch and many other senior Allied officers. Rolls-Royces were also used for ambulance work, and as armoured cars. The 40/50 chassis coped nobly with 3 tons of armour plating, and performed with remarkably reliability in France, Gallipoli, Africa and the Middle East.

Before the war the motor car had been a desirable asset for those who could afford it, but in 1914–1918 it proved itself indispensable. The figures speak for themselves: at the outbreak some 6000 vehicles were 'scratched up' for the French front. By the Armistice in November 1918, 92 000 vehicles were serving there, with no less than 115 000 trained drivers, while throughout Europe thousands more were made familiar with the magic of the once mysterious motor car. The war had, indeed, wrought a social revolution. The pre-1914 revels and splendour of *la belle époque* had gone for ever and the car, once considered a pleasure 'for the gentry and not the likes of us' by much of the population, had by 1919 become familiar, desirable and even attainable. In the first unbelievable, exciting months of peace, many thousands of people determined to become motor car owners.

Unprecedented demand far outran supply. Cars were now extremely rare, apart from American imports still coming in at cost plus $33\frac{1}{3}\%$ duty, and the quest for second-hand cars became frenzied. Prices inevitably soared, while sluggish bureaucracy blocked one potential source when many surplus Army vehicles were 'frozen' at depots pointlessly. When these were finally sold off in small lots they commanded intimidatingly high prices, so that in general most people had to curb their impatience and wait for peacetime production to get under way.

Many of the old-established factories resumed car manufacture as soon as possible, the wise ones adapting basically 1914 designs for which they still retained jigs and patterns rather than developing new models. Cancellation of war contracts left many engineering and allied concerns with factory capacity and a large pool of skilled workers in need of fresh employment. Confronted by the enormous sellers' market of post-Armistice days, several decided to take up car manufacture. Skilled designers and engineers were attracted by the same idea, and with capital readily available from war gratuities and other sources they, too, launched new businesses making cars, or components for them.

Before the war small manufacturers had been able to buy major car parts such as engines, gearboxes, chassis, axles, steering units etc. 'at trade', and prospects of a resumption of these supplies in 1919–1920 induced yet further 'hopefuls' to take the plunge and assemble motor cars. New makes positively mushroomed in Britain and France, and when the first post-war

Renault

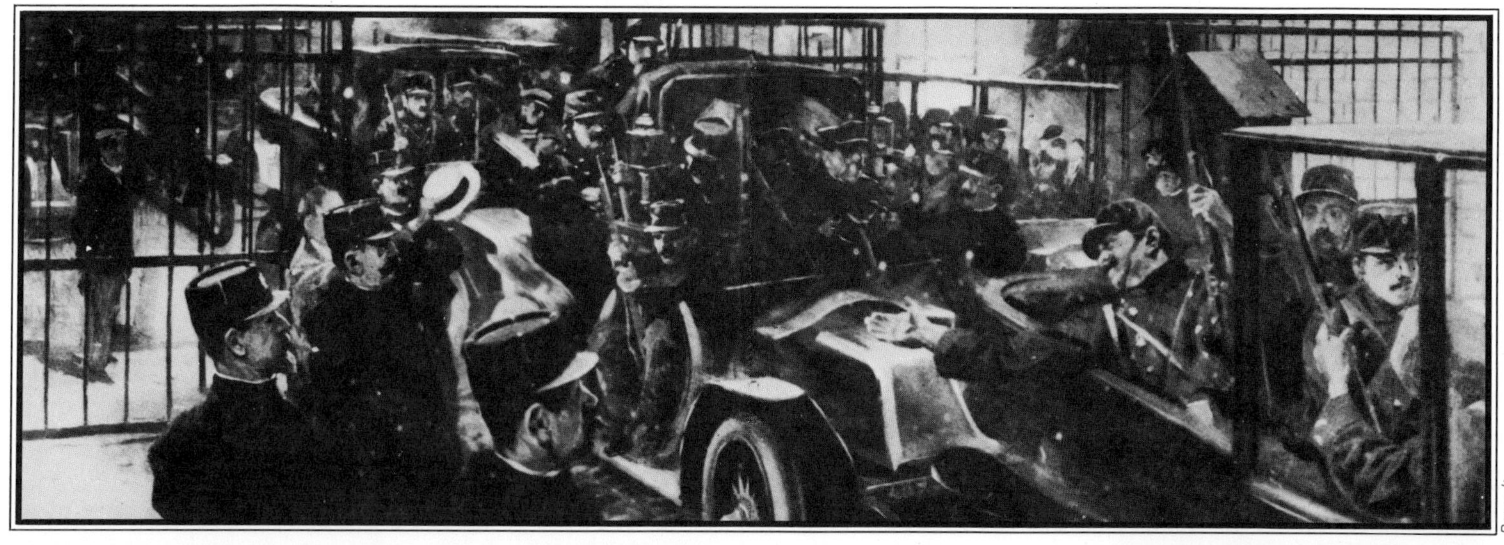

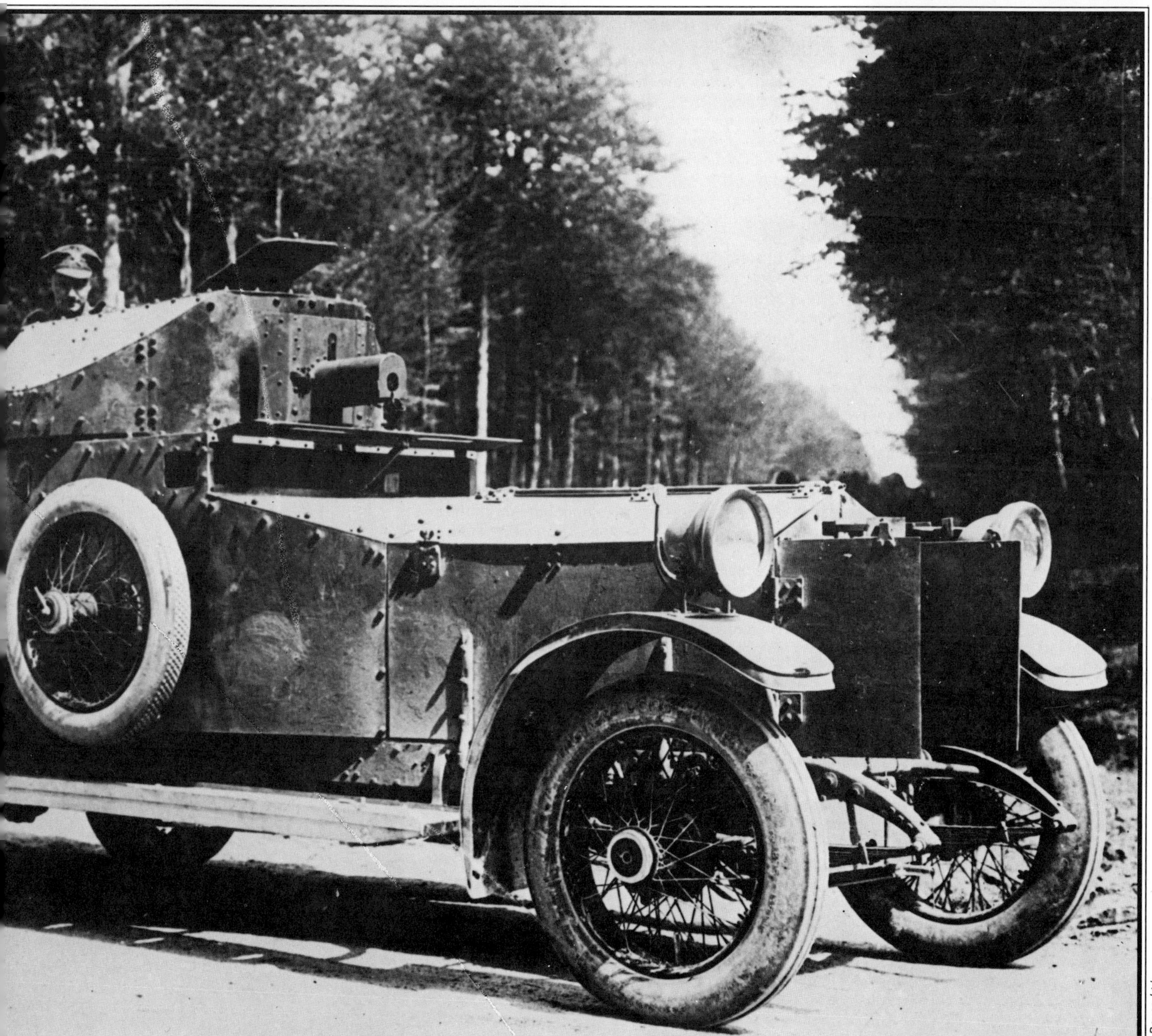

Rolls-Royce Ltd

motor shows were held in 1919 — the Paris Salon in October and the London Show at Olympia in November — the public swarmed to see (and hopefully to buy) the new models. In all the 80 years' history of motor exhibitions, very few could compare with the two of 1919 for sheer euphoria, optimism and excitement. Although less than a year had elapsed since the Armistice, designers fettered for four long years to martial needs really let themselves go. Superb new luxury cars, enterprising new sports cars, new family models, a new clutch of cyclecars and some way-out non-conformist designs all appeared, even if many were hastily completed prototypes, some with 'engines' of wood, or locked bonnets to hide their complete absence!

'The super-luxe Salon'

In reaction to prolonged austerity, Paris 1919 brought an inordinate number of new, 'expense no object' super-luxury cars. Famous aircraft or aero-engine makers seemed set on showing the world their mastery of high-precision, sophisticated engineering, whether on wheels or wings. The French themselves called it 'the *super-luxe* Salon', and one British periodical remarked that just the exquisite aluminium scuttle and dash of one model cost as much as a pre-1914 small British car! Hispano-Suiza, Isotta-Fraschini, Farman, Voisin, Renault and Gnome-Rhone — all famous names in the War — plus Lancia of Italy and Excelsior of Belgium, presented fascinatingly opulent automobiles to awed Parisians.

Hispano-Suiza's new 37.2hp six is usually acclaimed as the greatest design at that historic Salon. Certainly it was outstanding for its superb execution, but it was a pity that the creator, Marc Birkigt, chose the in-line six-cylinder engine layout after designing one of the Allies' finest aero-engines, the Hispano-Suiza 180hp ohc watercooled V8. This unit was so successful that 14 different firms in France, and 7 others in Britain, Italy and the USA built over 50 000 examples between them. Yet when Birkigt planned his post-war car he adapted one cylinder bank of a later 270hp V12 aero-engine design rather than employ the V8 layout with its compact dimensions, fine torque and excellent balance.

Yet the Hispano-Suiza six-cylinder car engine undeniably eclipsed all other efforts. It had a 7-bearing crankshaft, aluminium alloy block with fixed head and steel cylinder liners, shaft-driven overhead camshaft operating 12 vertical valves, aluminium pistons, a twin-choke carburettor and Delco coil ignition. Bore and stroke were 100×140 mm (6597cc), giving a reliable 134bhp at 2750rpm. The 3-speed gearbox was in unit with this engine, and embodied a drum-type brake servo operating excellent four-wheel brakes. The chassis was conventional with semi-elliptic leaf springs all round, but light alloys helped to keep its weight down to 23cwt. A 12ft 1¼in wheelbase gave many famous coachbuilders full rein in practising their craft, encouraged by the elegant long bonnet and a radiator of superb proportions. Birkigt's car easily outmoded and outperformed the Rolls-Royce, and by achieving equal reliability proved a worthy challenger in those elite markets where quality came first.

Hispano's Italian counterparts were Isotta-Fraschini, who had also built aero-engines in quantity during the war. Their new Tipo 8, seen at the Salon, was remarkable in having the first straight-eight engine to be produced commercially anywhere. This was a long 85×130mm, 5880cc aluminium unit with pushrod ohv. Isottas had long enjoyed a lucrative market in the USA, and the Tipo 8 continued the tradition, many Hollywood film stars using them. With its engine giving a gentle 80bhp at 2200rpm it had no sporting pretensions, but it propelled this very large and weighty car with silent ease. Steering and handling were rather heavy, but as virtually all Isotta-Fraschinis were chauffeur-driven, their owners seldom complained!

Of other *super-luxe* Salon' exhibits, the Farman, Gnome-Rhone, Excelsior and Renault were all big sixes. The famous

Right: A balcony view of the 1919 Olympia Show, where over 260 different makes of car were on view. Among several aviation factories which took up car manufacture after the Great War was the famous French firm of Farman with this sporty-looking 6½-litre model (far right).

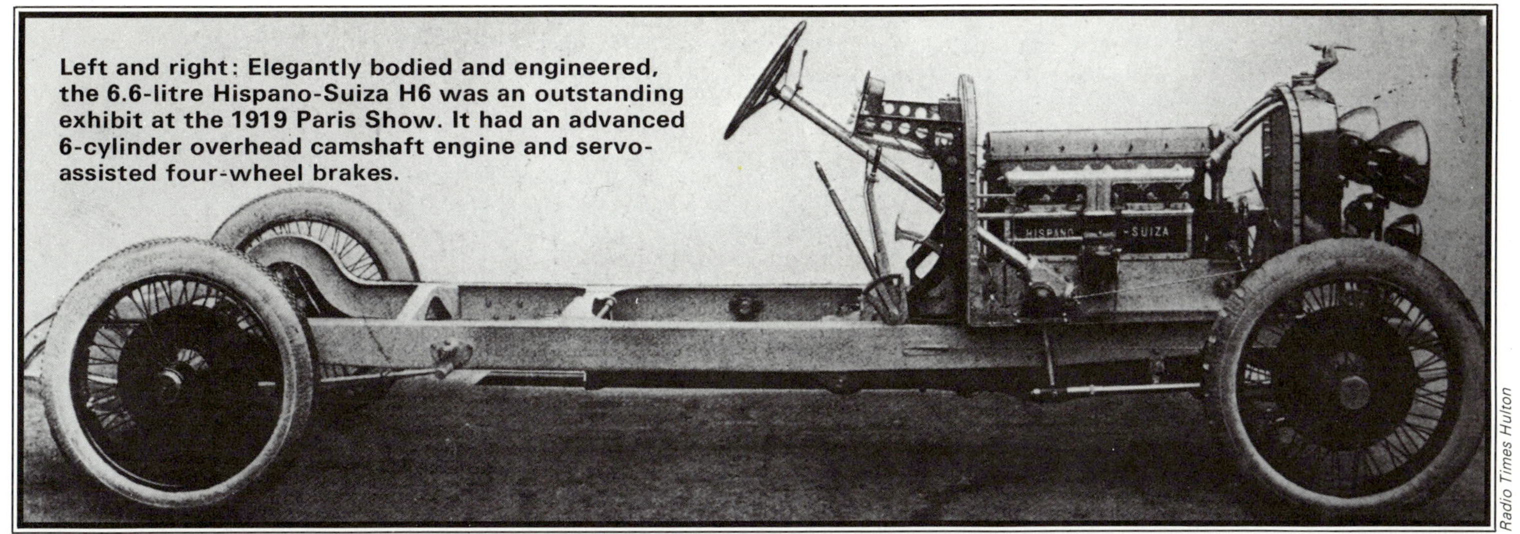

Left and right: Elegantly bodied and engineered, the 6.6-litre Hispano-Suiza H6 was an outstanding exhibit at the 1919 Paris Show. It had an advanced 6-cylinder overhead camshaft engine and servo-assisted four-wheel brakes.

Radio Times Hulton

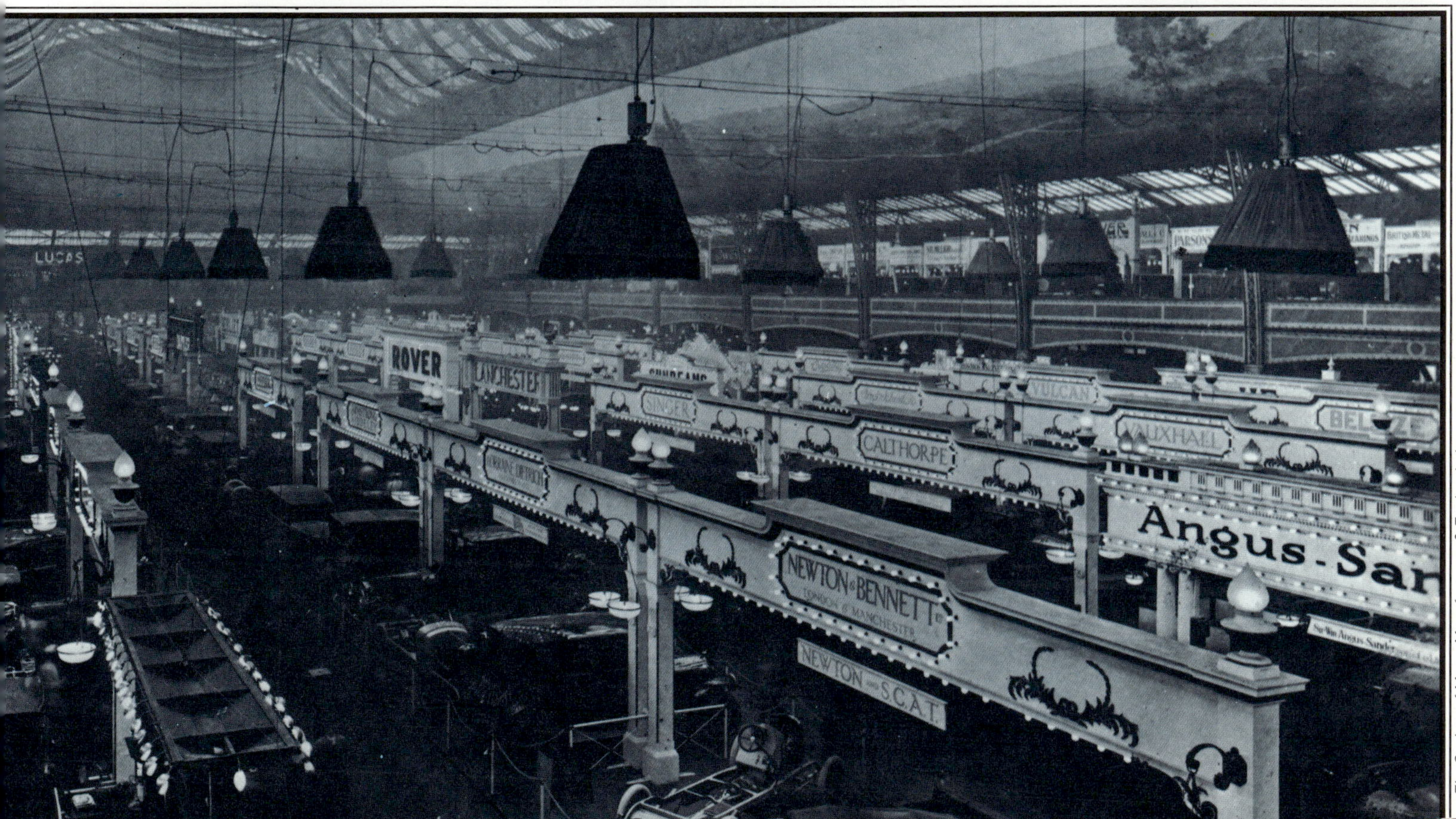

The Society of Motor Manufacturers & Traders Ltd.

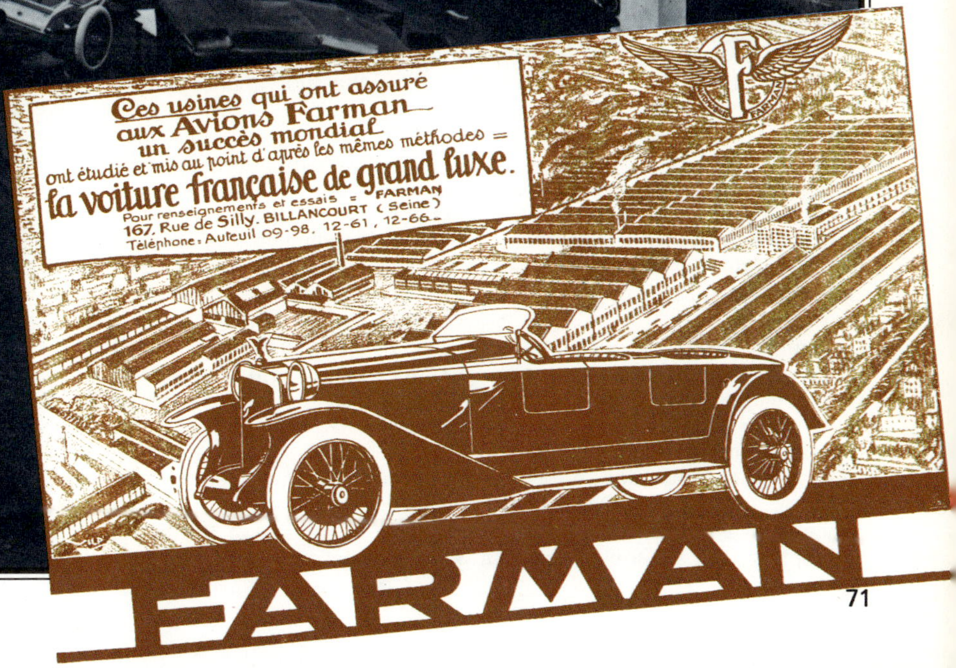

pioneer aviators, Maurice and Henry Farman, had become major aircraft makers during the war, switching to cars when the war ended. A sophisticated 6½-litre ohc engine and good body aerodynamics including a full-length undershield were natural legacies from an air-minded concern, but although film actress Pearl White and air ace Nungesser owned Farmans, they never really broke into the *très snob* Rolls-Hispano-Isotta domains.

Louis Renault's contribution, the '40', was frankly primitive, having a vast and very pre-war side-valve engine in two blocks of three cylinders, fixed head and a capacity of no less than 9.1 litres. Turning at a lazy 1800rpm this coped easily with a road weight of around 2½ tons, and with Renault's traditional reliability this monster sold well throughout the '20s. In contrast, Belgium's Excelsior Adex, with single-cam engine and servo-assisted four-wheel brakes, was much in the Hispano-Suiza idiom and became one of Europe's best luxury cars as the 5.4-litre 'Albert 1'. Outdoing all in Paris for engine novelty was a 6½-litre 12-cylinder ohv Lancia, with all its cylinders in a single casting containing two banks of six at only 22° to each other. The car bore most attractive open 'torpedo' bodywork, but like the Gnome-Rhone its design proved uneconomic to produce; its monobloc narrow-angle vee engine principle was to figure, however, in important subsequent Lancia models.

Citroen makes an impact

Moving down the capacity scale, the new 4-litre Voisin by yet another notable aircraft manufacturer made great impact. Its engine was a smooth-running five-bearing four-cylinder with Knight double sleeve valves and alloy pistons, the two-wheel braking was augmented by duplicated sets of brake shoes, and the bodywork was of aluminium. This model was built for over 10 years, forming the staple product of a marque which also aspired to the Hispano-Suiza class with big sixes and 12-cylinder models, always of original if sometimes eccentric design. At the lower end of the market an outstanding newcomer was the Citroen. Breaking directly into Renault and Peugeot territory, this was designed from the start for mass production in the American style by André Citroen. This remarkable son of a Dutch father and Jewish mother was works manager at the Mors car factory before the war, then launched a gear-cutting firm specializing in helical-tooth pinions from which he derived his famous 'chevron' trade mark. When hostilities began he turned out shells in massive quantities for the Allied artillery, and in 1919 he formed Automobiles Citroen in a factory on the Quai Javel in Paris.

Here the first Type A 1½-litre model took shape — a strong, simple, monobloc sv four with ¼-elliptic springs all round, rear brakes only, rather heavy-looking disc wheels just introduced by Michelin, and quite a shapely four-seater touring body. André Citroen was a 'go-getter'. He had 50 demonstration cars available at all times outside the Salon, and the factory was already turning out 35 cars per day when the Show opened. And although the bargain price of 7500 francs, *including* full equipment, soon rose to over 12 000 francs, more than 20 000 orders were placed within days of the car's unveiling.

The mood at the Olympia Show in London a month later was equally cheerful. Never had there been so many cars — 134 British makes alone (today there are 25!) and over 130 foreigners. Never such variety — with engines from one to 12 cylinders, including 3 and 5! And never such crowds — the overall attendance was 285 837, over 65 000 above the 1913 record. In the profusion of makes and models were many 'warmed-up' 1914 types, offset by bright new ventures, some with solid backing, others financially precarious but hopeful. A new arrival in the Morris 'value for money' class was the Bean, built by a consortium of Midland concerns. Amongst new quantity-production medium-sized cars were the Angus-Sanderson and the Cubitt. The Guy company, famous as lorry builders, introduced the first British V8, and Wolseley, inspired after building Hispano-Suiza aero-engines during the War, employed an ohc on a promising new Ten. Rover showed a new 8hp 'Runabout' with 998cc aircooled flat-twin motor, and AC had a clean, advanced 2-litre six-cylinder ohc engine with 'wet' cylinder liners in an aluminium block — a unit destined for a distinguished career lasting 45 years.

A handsome sporting newcomer from a famous rotary aero-engine designer was the Bentley, with 3-litre four-cylinder ohc 16-valve engine and a promising power-to-weight ratio. New, too, was the Alvis, a well-engineered 1½-litre four with four speeds and a lively performance. The august 7.4-litre Rolls-Royce 'Silver Ghost', elegantly rebodied but still very 'pre-war' underneath, retained that indefinable 'something' despite advanced new rivals. These included a fine 6-litre six-cylinder Lanchester '40' with skew-driven ohc and 3-speed epicyclic transmission, a 6.8-litre Ensign six, and a new 6.2-litre ohc Napier 40/50, not forgetting the challenging Hispano-Suiza, Isotta-Fraschini, Lancia V12, Renault 40 and the Farman, all sent over from Paris.

Radical designs

There were several 'radicals' to enliven the Show. Aero-engine designer Roy Fedden built the CAR 'Cosmos', with 3-cylinder radial power unit and bell crank-operated compression-type springing. Aircraft designer Claude Grahame-White presented a Dorman-engined car with friction drive and a primitive 'buckboard' with single-cylinder engine. Enfield-Allday exhibited a most ingenious car called the 'Bullet', with 5-cylinder sleeve-valved radial engine in a triangulated tubular chassis, while Duplex exhibited a strange opposed-piston, sleeve-valved 1½-litre 8-cylinder model.

It was all highly stimulating. If just 12 months' peace could bring so much mechanical enterprise and novelty, what might the next two or three years produce? For many of the 'hopefuls' it was as well that they could not see into the future.

Right: Release from the pressures of war inevitably brought several 'ideal' designs, including the British Cosmos with three-cylinder radial engine and unusual suspension by bell cranks and coil springs, by the Bristol aero-engine designer, Roy Fedden. Left: André Citroen, the far-seeing industrialist who brought mass production to Europe in 1919 in emulation of Henry Ford. Below: A test shop scene at the Citroen factory at Quai Javel, Paris, with several $1\frac{1}{2}$-litre Type A tourers in evidence.

National Motor Museum

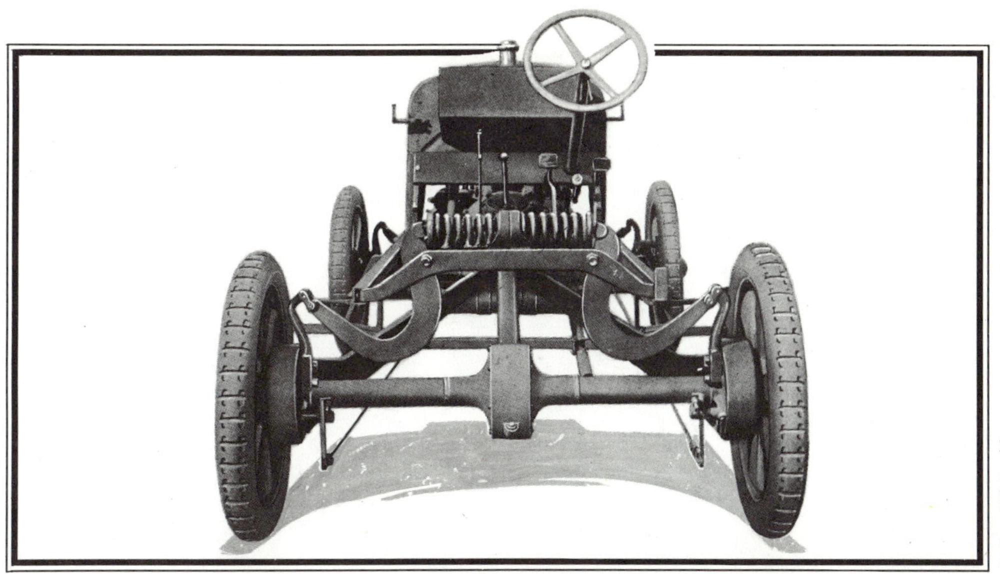

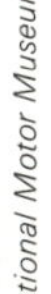

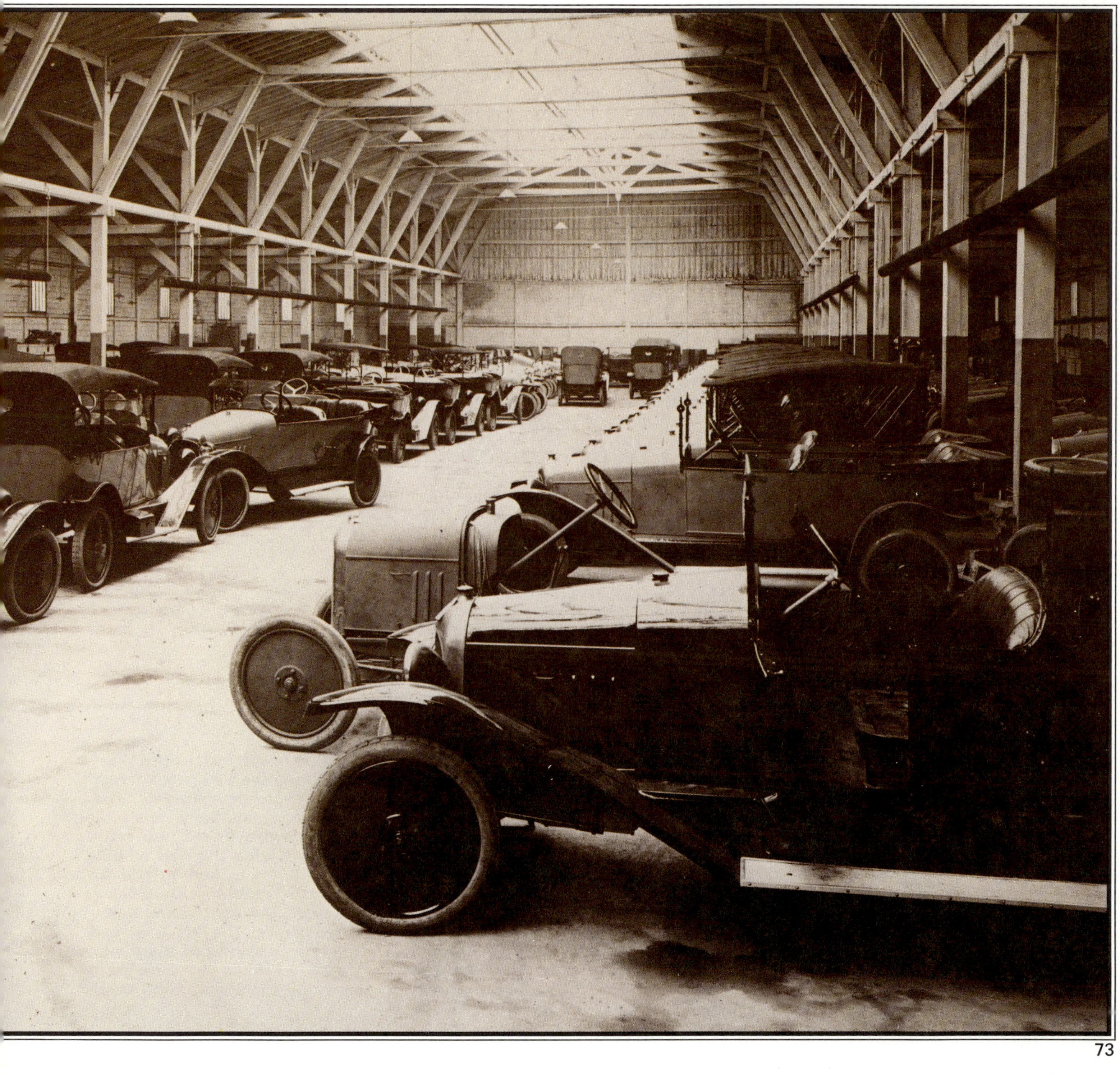

SLUMP

In recording the excitements of the 1919 Olympia Show, *The Autocar* weekly magazine commented sombrely that they feared 'many months would pass' before the record number of orders taken could be fulfilled. How right they were. A world geared up to all-out war for four years needed time to get back on a peaceful footing. Supplies of almost everything — coal, iron, steel, castings, forgings, pressings, wire and so on were erratic, and the situation was seriously aggravated by labour troubles and unemployment. Men back from fighting a war which cost over 10 million lives were naturally bewildered that work could not be found, or that wages could not meet living costs, and registered their protest by striking. There was a big railway strike in Britain, another in the mines, and yet another in the iron-moulding industry, directly affecting car production. Moreover, prices rose persistently, sabotaging everyone's economy and increasing unrest. Even while the Olympia Show was still on, the first price rises were announced, including £100 on the £195 aircooled ABC, and £275 on the £1575 Rolls-Royce chassis.

The post-war 'Utopia' everyone dreamed of was proving highly elusive. The French were badly off with most of their industrial areas disrupted by the war and with little coal, current or heating. Ravaged Belgium had lost much of her engineering potential, Italy was in the throes of inflation and political upheavals, while defeated Germany fought dire economic problems for survival. Serious strikes and shortages even affected the USA, although car production never actually stopped during the 17 months they were at war, 1918 output totalling 943 436 cars against 1 745 792 in 1917, and rising to 1 651 625 in 1919. Thus American cars continued to alleviate the European transport famine until Britain, France and Italy achieved some mastery over their problems and car production at last got under way. It then became necessary to protect home sales and employment; France imposed a 45% customs barrier on all foreign car imports, while Britain had the McKenna duties to hide behind, and the ever-mounting price of petrol. This had rocketed from 1s 8d (8½p) per gallon in 1914 to around 4s 3d (21p) by the autumn of 1920 — modest-sounding by modern standards, perhaps — except that in those days £2–£3 was a good week's wage!

America's boom days in Europe thus came to a gradual close, even though Ford had the advantage of a factory in Manchester, where Model Ts were built largely from British materials by British labour on British soil, thereby escaping the McKenna tax. Yet as 1920 advanced, and factories at last began to catch up on orders, the once eager purchasers found they were expected to pay far more than the sums quoted at Olympia the previous year. Costs all round had risen so sharply that by October 1920 car prices had practically doubled, together with garage services, tires, spares, petrol and oil. Many would-be motorists had to cancel their orders; others were saved the trouble when the makers closed down. The bewildered inheritors of 'a land fit for heroes' found themselves faced instead with a sudden trade recession and over a million unemployed. The Continent and America were similarly affected, and in a few months scores of motor businesses went bankrupt.

The French cancelled their 1920 Paris Salon, but the British persevered with their second post-war motor show in November, 1920, and were rewarded with a record display of 292 different makes of car! 149 were British, the remainder coming from France, Belgium, Holland, Italy and America. The show had to be split between Olympia and the White City, and despite their profusion the exhibits reflected current economic conditions. There were more economical small cars and a fresh outbreak of cheap, rickety cyclecars. Cheapest of all at £100 was the engaging little Carden, with twin-cylinder 2-stroke engine geared to the rear axle. King Alfonso of Spain ordered one on the spot when visiting Olympia, prompting a jest that he proposed slinging it between davits on his Hispano-Suiza as a 'lifeboat'! The AV Monocar at £179 had centre-pivot steering by wire cables, like an urchin's go-cart, and the Tamplin at £165 had front engine, belt drive and tandem seating. Even Bleriot, famous in aviation, joined the cyclecar market, while the best of all was the British GN, with overhead valve twin-cylinder engine, chain drive and a vigorous performance.

Wheels for all: After the War there followed a spate of small, cheap cyclecars. Top left: The Carden, which had a rear-mounted 707cc twin-cylinder two-stroke engine driving the rear wheels through gears. Above: The tandem 2-seater Tamplin with 980cc twin-cylinder JAP engine and belt drive. Right, The GN, best and longest surviving of them all, with its lusty 1100cc vee-twin engine and chain drive giving three speeds.

AND RECOVERY

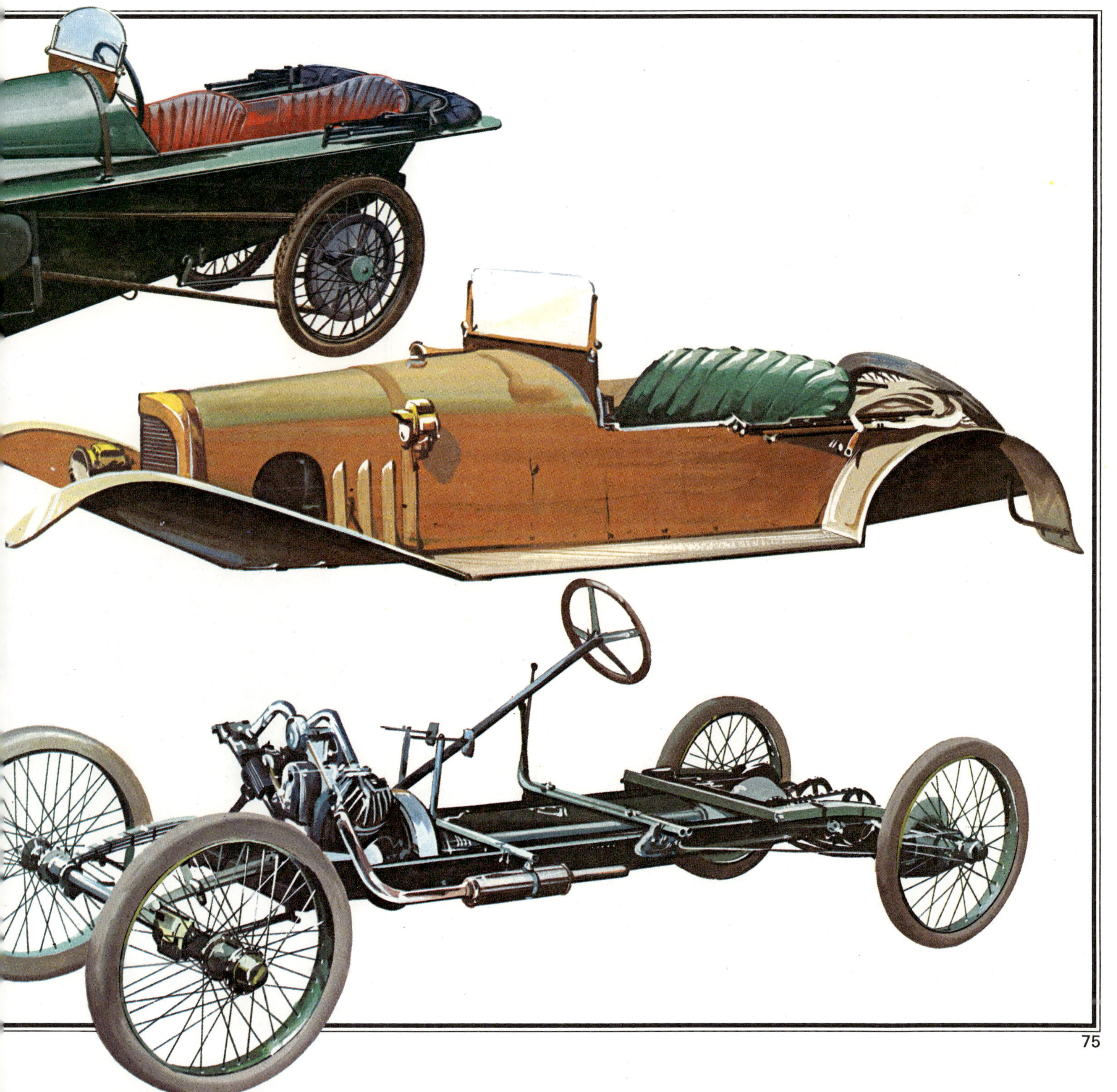

The eccentrics and the exotics of 1919 had diminished, but Britain produced a *super-luxe* in the Leyland Eight. This name today encompasses the controversial group which controls 10 British makes (Austin, Morris, Daimler, Jaguar, Rover, Triumph, MG, Mini, Vanden Plas and Princess) and has been responsible for killing off two classic marques in Wolseley and Riley. In 1920 Leyland were famous for their lorries, and their first private car, designed by J. G. Parry Thomas, seemed aimed directly at deposing Rolls-Royce from their throne. Technologically it was certainly far superior, having a superb 115bhp, 89×140mm, 7967cc straight-eight engine (Britain's first), with single ohc driven by silent eccentrics. Other bold features were leaf-type valve return springs, vacuum servo-assisted rear wheel brakes, leaf spring suspension embodying torsion bars for roll resistance, and a final drive with twin bevels permitting angled half-shafts and hence slight camber of the wheels for extra stability.

'The Lion of Olympia'

In the taut 1920 economic atmosphere this technical *tour de force* seemed highly unrealistic. It was hailed as 'The Lion of Olympia', but its chassis price was daunting at £2500, £400 more than Rolls-Royce's. America contributed a new contender for the 'Croesus class' that year, called the Duesenberg Straight Eight or Model A. It was the first of countless straight-eights to go into production in the USA, and although the prototype had horizontal valves the manufacturers, Fred and August Duesenberg of New Jersey had an ohc head ready by 1921.

Backed by a fine pedigree from marine and aero-engine manufacturers as well as much motor racing, the Duesenberg was very expensive but superlatively made. Its 4260cc engine gave an impressive 98bhp at 3600rpm — a high engine speed for the time — the 3-speed gearbox was in unit with the engine, and the A type was the first production model in the world to employ hydraulically-operated four-wheel brakes. These used a mixture of glycerine and water rather than the special oil we have now-adays, and the 16in diameter front brake drums, like those on the contemporary Hispano-Suiza, were beautifully finned for cooling. Weight with roadster bodywork was just under 30cwt, and engine torque was outstanding, permitting top gear starts without protest. Sales of this fine car were not helped by rather uninspiring coachwork in the top-quality markets where such things counted, but over 600 were built between 1921 and 1926.

Sales of even that great mechanical 'workhorse', the Model T Ford, began to flag in the 1920 summer of depression. Their normal daily output then was an awe-inspiring 3800 cars per 8-hour day, but high costs of living and materials cut into world markets. The answer, simple but drastic, was to reduce car prices and encourage sales that way. Henry Ford acted decisively. In September 1920 he cut the price of the T Runabout from $550 to $395 — a figure actually below the current cost of production. He continued at full output until December, when he closed his Detroit factories for a drastic six-week purge on production methods and costs. His company ended the year with a terrifying $50 million loss, but by delivering unsold cars to his agents and securing immediate payment, Ford emerged solvent without needing help from the banks he disliked so much.

In Britain, Bean and Swift were first to get the message that September, announcing respective cuts of £105 and £55 on their most popular models. Citroen, Singer, Hillman, Jowett, ABC and others followed suit during the autumn, but some makers hung fire. Star, Deemster and a few others unwisely guaranteed buyers against reductions, but by the New Year the writing was clear on the wall, and prices began to tumble. In February 1921 William Morris made a dramatic £100 cut from £525 to £425 on the popular Morris-Cowley 4-seater, and brought the 2-seater down from £465 to £375. In June, Henry Ford reduced the Model T to $370, and proudly told the world that their output had topped the 5 million mark. In July Morris lopped another £81 off the Cowley, and in September Ford cut the basic Model T price still further to $325!

The world had to follow suit, the depression lifted, and sales resumed a healthy level. The short, sharp slump had been a salutary experience all round, and reviving motor industries planned their future production warily, with the emphasis on economical family transport, economically built. The opening phase of retrenchment thus produced a crop of dull if worthy motor cars, but as the economy cheered up, so design enterprise again blossomed.

Surprise from Berlin

This was the true age of the Vintage car. In earlier years, termed the Veteran (1885–1904) and Edwardian (1905–1916) eras in Britain, the car had advanced through its birth pangs and formative stages to full fruition. In the '20s it reached a peak in individual character and quality of workmanship unequalled in later years when mass production dominated. It was admiration for the more sporting cars of the time, such as the Bentley, Aston Martin, Vauxhall, Alvis, Salmson, Amilcar, Alfa Romeo etc. which brought the enthusiastic Vintage Sports Car Club into being. They chose the apt term 'Vintage', referring to 'a season in which wine reaches an exceptionally high standard', to cover cars built between January 1st, 1919 and December 31st, 1930, and these dates now have world-wide acceptance as representing the Vintage era.

An extra 1921 surprise was the staging of a Berlin Motor Show in the suburb of Charlottenburg. It was promoted in an urgent bid by German industry to secure overseas trade. Since the Armistice, the Germans had suffered tremendous privations through political and economic chaos, massive unemployment and near-starvation. Private cars could only run with a permit, and petrol and tires were both prohibitively

Challenging the best: New post-war contenders in the world super-luxury car class included Leyland of Great Britain and Duesenberg of the USA. Left: J. G. Parry Thomas, designer of the 8-litre straight-8 Leyland, was also a famous racing driver. Right: The two Duesenberg brothers, August and Frederick, builders of the straight-8 Model A Duesenberg.

Indianapolis Motor Speedway Corporation

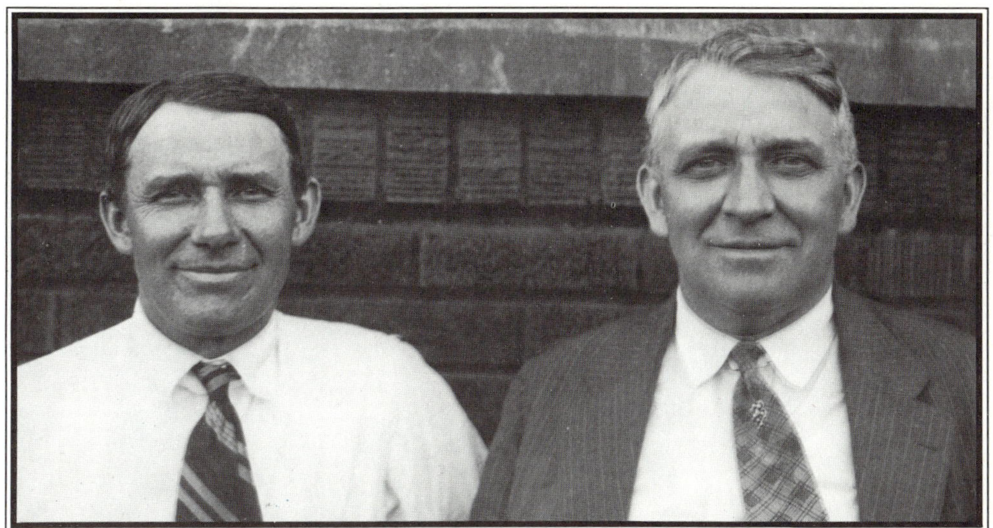

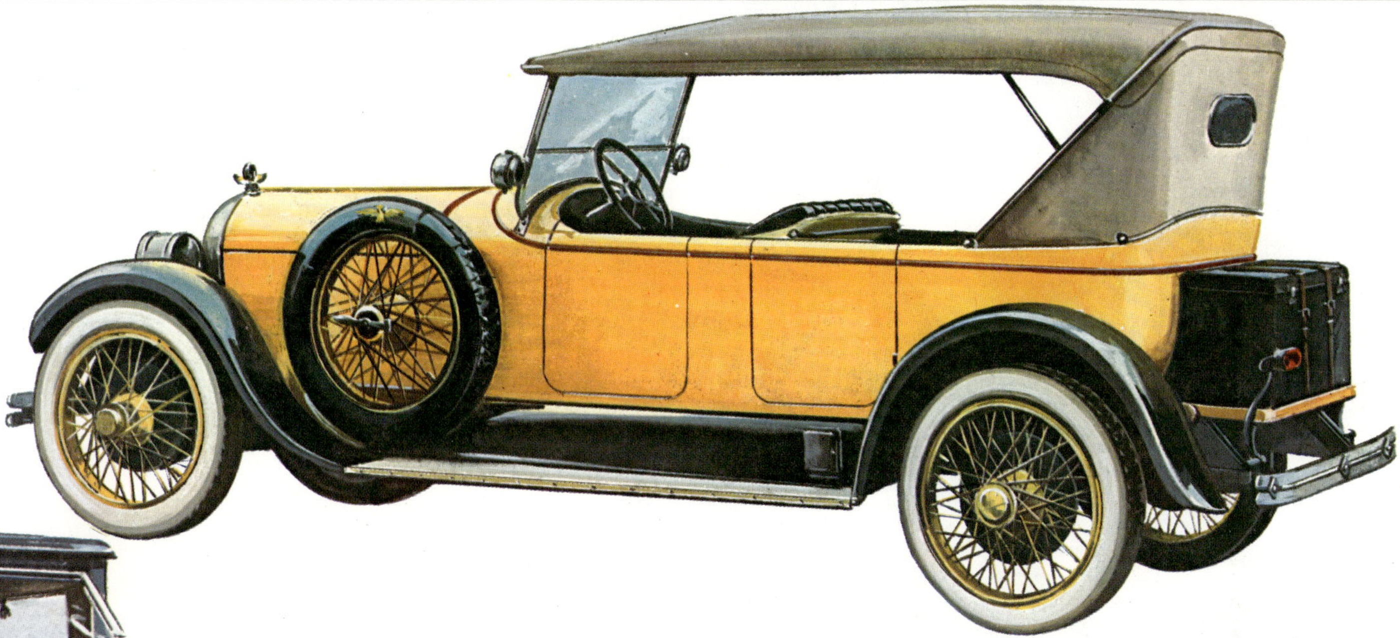

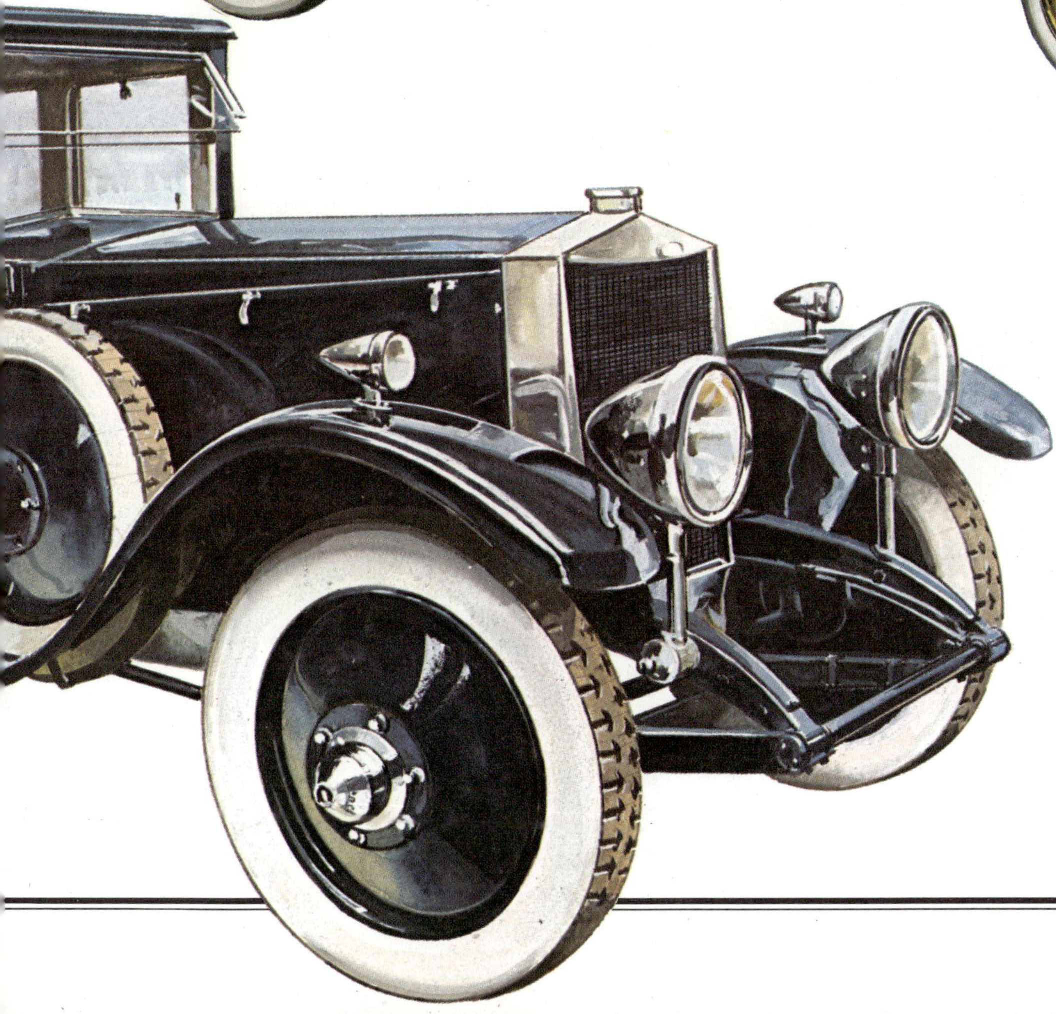

Above: The conventional appearance of the 4.26-litre Duesenberg concealed top-quality workmanship and an advanced design including America's first straight-8 engine and hydraulic four-wheel brakes. Left: A 1921 Leyland Eight with elegant Van den Plas limousine coachwork. Problems involved in the manufacture of this superb but ultra-expensive car forced it off the market after only 18 had been built.

expensive and in short supply. Realizing that recovery depended greatly on exports, their Government gave priority in coal, iron and other supplies to car and truck factories and other vital industries. Such materials were so limited, however, that it was a 'bricks without straw' challenge for German makers to produce new models, and actually to stage a motor show within two years of the war was remarkable.

Only German cars were shown. German products were specifically excluded from other post-war motor shows, so no foreign makes were invited to Berlin. Despite this, the organisers drummed up a comprehensive variety of makes and models from no less than 46 home factories. The Show broadly followed the pattern of Olympia and the Paris Salon; there were the usual 1914 models 'warmed up' by established

Left: Publicity for the unique 'broad arrow' rear-engined boat-like Rumpler from Germany was as bold as the car itself.
Below: One of Britain's best light cars of the early '20s, the Rover Eight with its front-mounted flat-twin aircooled engine brought reliable motoring to thousands. It was even built under licence as the Peter-und-Moritz in Germany.

fabriken such as Benz, Adler, Mercedes, Opel, Hansa, Dixi and NAG – sound, solid Teutonic designs which sold well in Eastern Europe, Scandinavia, Spain, Portugal and South America. Benz also managed to produce a neat new 1½-litre ohv sporting model, and there was a 960cc sports Apollo with independent front suspension.

Other bright new designs employing light alloys and overhead valves came from Dinos, Szawe, Steiger, Pilot and others, and there were the inevitable cyclecars and cheap small cars such as the ingenious chassis-less Grade, the Bob, Omega, Eos, Koco and the Peter-und-Moritz, which turned out to be the British flat-twin Rover Eight built under licence. With aircraft and armaments manufacture strictly forbidden by the peace terms, many concerns famous in these fields turned to cars. Among them were Mauser of pistol fame, who exhibited a notably eccentric 'single-track' small car with support-wheels on each side, Maybach as a new *super-luxe* contender, and Rumpler as a way-out non-conformist.

The Maybach was a well-engineered 5.8-litre sv six designed by Karl, the son of Wilhelm Maybach, who had been Gottlieb Daimler's right-hand man back at the birth of the motor car. Called the W3, it had a clutchless 2-speed preselector transmission with pedal operation like the Model T Ford, and four-wheel brakes. The Rumpler was the brainchild of Dr Edmund Rumpler, formerly with Adler and designer of the Rumpler *Taube*, a famous WW1 observation plane. His car embodied a rear-mounted 2.6-litre engine made by Siemens & Halske, having its six cylinders in three pairs, in inverted broad arrow fashion. The chassis was a fabricated hull of sheet steel, its shape conforming to the 'teardrop' body-work in which the driving compartment resembled an aircraft cabin. Rear suspension was by independent swing axles, the mudguards were swept horizontal strips, two headlights were mounted centrally, one above the other, and the spare wheel was housed under the floor. Weight must have impeded performance, and although the unorthodox engine later gave way to an in-line four, the Rumpler never emerged from the experimental stages.

Although some Rumpler features were unpractical, some of its ideas later became commonplace. Much other design ingenuity seen at Charlottenberg was to founder and perish through subsequent financial crises. Galloping inflation hit the new republic in 1922, a man's lifetime

Tandem two-seater: Peugeot of France began production of their Quadrilette economy car immediately after the war. It had a neat little 760cc four-cylinder engine and 3-speed gearbox, a track of only 3ft 10in and a body with the two seats one behind the other. It could reach 37mph, and about 3000 were built between 1919 and 1922, when the makers switched the seating to the more conventional side-by-side arrangement.

Above: The pretty 1100cc four-cylinder side-valve Amilcar 2-seater was a versatile French sports car which served admirably on the road and in all forms of competition. Below: The famous 7hp Citroen 'Cloverleaf', with 856cc four-cylinder side-valve engine was mass-produced in Paris and became a common sight on European roads for many years.

Above: Outstanding in the early '20s for its fine roadholding, good handling and vigorous performance was the four-cylinder 1½-litre ohc 16-valve type 22 Bugatti 'Brescia'.

savings came to represent the price of one meal, and a newspaper or tram ticket cost hundreds of thousands of marks. At the peak of the crisis the mark was worthless — 43 000 000 000 000 representing £1 sterling — and before the German Government got their currency under control again many fortunes had crashed and countless companies collapsed, giving little hope for enterprising but under-financed automobile projects. Only the strongest, such as Benz, Mercedes and Opel, survived to regain international status.

The Paris Salon which opened a week later was dubbed 'the 12hp Show'. Frugal small and medium-sized cars were in the majority, most important of them being a new, smaller Citroen to supplement the Model A. This was the 856cc 5CV, or 7hp as models imported into Britain were called. It had a cheeky 2-seater open body with turned-up tail and was initially produced only in yellow with dark-painted mudguards. There were also some interesting new offerings in the thriving, sometimes hilarious, 'cyclecar' class which, under French law, was limited to two seats, an up to 1100cc engine, and an unladen weight of under 350kg (6.9cwt). It being a French national sport to outwit officialdom, these requirements were often met by leaving off vital fitments such as shock absorbers, spare wheel or proper lighting, and offering them as 'optional extras'!

The class certainly stimulated imaginative weight-saving designs, and out of the scores of devices concocted in backyard workshops in Paris and elsewhere, two competitive marques emerged. They were Salmson and Amilcar, one based at Billancourt, the other at St. Denis. Salmson were yet another of those firms which had earned fame and fortune by building aeroplanes and aero-engines for the war, and when peace returned they took to building the excellent British GN cyclecar under licence. They produced about 1600 before making their own car with four-cylinder watercooled engine, in a chassis of GN derivation, retaining similar quarter-elliptic springing at front and rear. The new engine measured 1087cc, had an aluminium crankcase and an efficient cylinder head shape with 68° inclined ohv, each pair ingeniously operated by a single pushrod and rocker. With about 18hp under foot in a car weighing about 7cwt, performance proved distinctly lively.

The Amilcar was simpler, having a 903cc splash-lubricated sv engine, but it, too, had springing by quarter-elliptics, while both makes had very pretty racing-style 2-seater open bodies. They became immediate rivals for 1100cc supremacy, the battle starting with the 1922 Bol d'Or 24 Hours race where an Amilcar beat two Salmsons. Salmson retorted by beating an Amilcar in the Le Mans 24 Hours the following year. Both makes were exported in appreciable numbers, creating a fine international reputation for small French sports cars. Other sporting models at the Salon by Bignan, Ballot, Bugatti, Chenard-Walcker etc. brought similar prestige for France in the 1½-, 2- and 3-litre categories. Bugatti's ohc

Above: Britain's outstanding Vintage sports car was the 3-litre Bentley. With its rugged long-stroke 16-valve engine and sturdy chassis, it withstood all manner of competition work from trials, seen here, to 24-hour endurance races. Many still survive today. The most popular car on Vintage British roads was the 'Bull-nose' (left) the 1½-litre Morris Cowley, which offered cheap, dependable motoring backed by good servicing. Right: The makers of the AC called it 'the Rolls-Royce of light cars'. Their 2-litre overhead camshaft Six certainly set high standards in smoothness and elegance. Seen here is a 1923 two-seater.

$1\frac{1}{2}$-litre 16-valve four-cylinder Type 22, called the 'Brescia' after a sweeping 1921 race victory there, was a notably nimble performer, and at the Salon it was joined by a new 2-litre straight-eight, the Type 30, which was unusual in having hydraulic front brakes but mechanical operation at the rear. It was not the best Bugatti, but it was the harbinger of more brilliant things.

No French show was complete without some extravaganza in the 'Croesus class', even in times of austere economy, and 1921 brought a breath-taking trio. One was an all-alloy 7.2-litre sleeve-valve V12 Voisin with four-wheel brakes worked by compressed air (as on modern commercial vehicles), electro-magnetic clutch and 2-speed gearbox. Another was a mammoth 8-litre straight-eight from Spain, the Elizalde Type 48 with bronze cylinder heads, combined cantilever and semi-elliptic rear springing, and an overall length exceeding 22ft. The third was a new Italian V12, the Super-Fiat 520. This had a beautifully clean 6.8-litre engine with cylinders at 60° and a central camshaft working ohv through pushrods, but its elegant long bonnet and coupé de ville coachwork were offset by somewhat prosaic Sankey steel artillery wheels. It is believed the car was aimed at the competitive American market, but presumably the makers decided that production would be uneconomical, for the Super-Fiat never went beyond the prototype stage.

British buoyancy

Britain at that time showed spirit and buoyancy and when the third post-war Motor Show came up in November 1921, it was again divided between Olympia and the White City, with an all-day coach service between the two halls. Listed makes had dropped to 110, but if several ventures had died in the 1920 slump, others came bravely forward. One was the Rhode, which had its own pleasing little ohc 1100cc engine but economized initially by dispensing with a differential and starter, and fitting stark, unappealing coachwork; the makers soon learned their mistake and refined the design. Another excellent new light car, the Talbot 8/18, came from the big new Anglo-French combine formed after the war,

called Sunbeam-Talbot-Darracq (STD). First evolved in France, this neat little ohv two-seater possessed that particular Gallic charm endowed by a light chassis, lively engine and good handling and braking. Enlarged into the 10/23 by Talbot, it became one of the outstanding Vintage tourers.

Since the war, Austin of Longbridge had concentrated their efforts on one model, the big 3.6-litre four-cylinder Twenty, which gave yeoman service for years and years as a 'Hackney carriage' or hire car. The 1920 depression forced the Company into a brief receivership, but they quickly recovered and announced a smaller four-cylinder model in 1921. Broadly following its bigger brother in pattern, the Twelve's great virtues lay in its strength and dependability rather than any technical sophistication. The 1650cc engine had side valves, magneto ignition, a sturdy five-bearing crankshaft and thorough lubrication. The entire design was produced in only three months, yet it proved immensely successful. The basic model endured right up to 1936, and a further ten years or so beyond that in taxicab form.

Meanwhile Morris, the marque destined to become Austin's greatest rival, were going from strength to strength. Although he is often falsely credited with pioneering the price-cutting measures which overcame the 1920 slump, William R. Morris undoubtedly set the pace for the British motor industry in the Vintage period. Production at the Oxford works showed his progress. He built 337 of his famous 'Bullnose' Oxfords and Cowleys in 1919, 1932 in 1920, 3077 in 1921, 5166 in 1922, and 15 987 in 1923. His business philosophy was that of a British 'Henry Ford' but without the ruthlessness. In 1913 he had visited the USA and arranged to buy $1\frac{1}{2}$-litre side-valve Continental 'Red Seal' engines and other components at highly competitive prices, for use in the Morris Cowley 4-seater he launched in 1915.

The McKenna $33\frac{1}{3}$% duty on imports made such purchases uneconomic after the war, so Bill Morris bought the 'Red Seal' design outright from Continental and arranged for the Coventry engines branch of the French Hotchkiss company to produce the former American unit in quantity. These Hotchkiss-built engines powered

both the post-war Cowley, which was the cheaper, more austere model with 'pegamoid' upholstery instead of leather, thin tires and no self-starter, and the more comprehensively equipped Oxford. Morris had already bought a radiator plant in 1919; he acquired the Hotchkiss engine factory outright in 1922, and subsequently took over the Wrigley concern who supplied his axles, steering gear etc., Hollick & Pratt, the coachbuilders, and the SU Carburettor company, thus being able to control supplies of major components under one organizational 'roof'. By such means could Morris Motors Ltd. produce sound, reliable cars in greater quantities and at lower cost than most of the opposition.

A determined newcomer

Inevitably in a fast recovering market, rivals multiplied. Standard, Swift, Calcott, Singer, Hillman, Seabrook, Phoenix, Cluley, Enfield-Allday, Albert, Dawson, Bean and Calthorpe were just some of the British makers in the $1\frac{1}{2}$-litre class, but few could compete directly with the 'Bullnoses' on price. A determined newcomer, however, was the Clyno, a '10.8' with 1386cc sv Coventry Climax engine, introduced in 1922 by a former motorcycle manufacturing firm from Wolverhampton. Though under-capitalized and lacking modern factory equipment, Clyno kept a close second to Morris on sales, turning out a pleasant-handling and reliable car by cutting costs and profits to the bone.

Despite the cost of the war, Britain was still wealthy enough not to worry about the export market, as she had to later on. In 1921, for instance, only 3800 cars were exported, comparing strikingly with 368 737 in 1951, and the 721 094 of 1971! 1921 had brought a more expensive and unpopular new form of car taxation at £1 per RAC or 'Treasury' horsepower. This rating system, first introduced in 1910, was misguidedly based on the bore but not the stroke of an engine, and British makers naturally 'tax-dodged' by prescribing as narrow a bore as possible, coupled with a longer stroke. The tax certainly helped reduce the ever-present menace on the UK market of the Model T Ford and other cheap but largish-engined American cars such as

the rival Chevrolet, but it also militated against British small-bored cars on overseas markets where ample power was needed. The result was that the typical British Vintage car remained very much a domestic vehicle.

Yet there were some small-engined European cars so good that they challenged British cars in their home market. The Citroen and Renault from France became familiar on British roads, their ruggedness backed by sound spares and servicing facilities; another popular Continental car was the Fiat 501, first announced in 1919. The famous Turin concern had built a huge new 5-storey factory at Lingotto with a test track with banked corners laid out on its roof. Planned from the outset for flow line production, it was completed in three years. The first car off the line was the 501, which seemed broadly similar to any British 1½-litre of the time with its four-cylinder sv engine and conventional chassis, but had a 4-speed gearbox with ratios bred for hilly Italian conditions, and hence rather low for British conditions. It was dearer, too, than the run-of-the-mill British counterpart, but its flexibility, good suspension and handling had wide appeal, while time revealed its unusual toughness. It was mass-produced up to 1926, many thousands being exported to Britain (as the 10-15) Belgium, Denmark, Spain, Portugal, Switzerland, Australia, Argentina and even Japan, where the influence of the motor car was slowly but surely bringing Nippon into the 20th century.

A rival for Fiat

Interesting opposition to Fiat came from the giant Ansaldo steel, hydro-electric engineering, shipbuilding and aircraft concern, who converted their Corso Peschiera factory in Turin for mass production of a mass appeal car designated the 4C. It was a 1.8-litre four with clean, sturdy ohc engine, three speeds and a rather American appearance. Selling at a very keen price, it intruded somewhat on the 501 home market, but Fiat 'know-how' always kept them a jump ahead, and the Ansaldo car disappeared a decade or so later. Another Italian 'newborn', the Alfa Romeo, lives on strongly, however. The pre-war Alfa company

(Anonima Lombarda Fabbrica Automobili), formed in 1909 from a Darracq assembly plant in Milan, had been taken over in 1915 by an industrialist named Nicola Romeo. With the coming of peace the new marque was launched, quickly acquiring a unique sporting image thanks to numerous racing successes, and epitomized by the 3-litre six-cylinder pushrod ohv RL series of 1922. These cars, with their distinctive sweeping lines and handsome vee radiators, were the first of a long line of thoroughbreds which actually inspired Henry Ford to declare: 'Every time I see an Alfa Romeo pass by, I raise my hat'.

Ford moves up

Tightened purse-strings had their effect in all classes. Packard produced a smaller six-cylinder sister to their illustrious V12 Twin Six. With its 3.9-litre sv engine, three speeds and Delco coil ignition, the Single Six was typically American. More surprisingly so was a new, smaller Rolls-Royce which broke the famous 'one model' tradition established back in 1907. The new Twenty had a 3.1-litre pushrod ohv six-cylinder engine, coil ignition, 3-speed gearbox in unit, and central gearchange, while its classic Grecian radiator was marred by horizontal shutters, as also used on the humble Detroit-built Essex, a smaller-engined line from the Hudson factory. Indeed, the entire concept followed American practice closely, but the design execution was to the usual superlative Rolls-Royce standards.

Henry Ford, of course, had to be different. If Rolls-Royce and Packard could take a step down, then he could take several steps up and enter the *super-luxe* class. Henry M. Leland, former Cadillac designer, had founded the Lincoln make two years earlier. The depression caught them short of capital and forced them into receivership, whereupon Ford acquired the Lincoln Motor Company for $8 million. The car was a fine 5.8-litre V8, and Henry and his son Edsel soon set it back on the road to prosperity, fitting aluminium pistons and four-wheel brakes. They had the privilege, in 1924, of supplying one to the United States President, and Lincoln cars have graced the White House scene ever since.

Turin Giant: The Fiat concern in Italy
went from strength to strength in the
1920s, although their ambitious Type
520 12-cylinder Super-Fiat of 1921,
seen on the left with d'Orsay coupé
de ville body, did not go into
production. Right: The strong, lively
Type 501, with 4-speed gearbox, was
built in many thousands from 1919 to
1926 in Fiat's huge new 5-storey
factory at Lingotto, Turin. Below: The
roof at the Lingotto factory served as
a test track for production model
Fiats.

David Burgess Wise

THE

Once the 1920 slump was over, the motor industries of the world could at last settle down to the business of making and selling cars, with reasonable hopes of stable currencies, economies and labour conditions. The 'quantity' makers were mass-producing on conveyor belt methods, the 'quality' were still hand-fitting and finishing, while lesser concerns were muddling along somehow with out-dated equipment. The aspirations of 1919 were at last becoming reality by 1923. But it should be remembered that the sector of public in Europe who could then afford a car, when the average 10 or 12hp four-seater cost £300 or more, and the most basic cyclecar about £170, was much smaller than now. With wages averaging perhaps £3 per week for a professional man, £300 was a large sum, even when broken down into hire purchase payments.

In Britain the motorist-to-be was not required to wear L-plates, or undergo a test before getting a driving licence — he simply applied for it and paid 5 shillings, while insurance cover was voluntary. Roads were narrower and often in poor condition, and cars travelled more slowly. A ridiculous 20mph speed limit still prevailed, although 30mph was tolerated by all but the most diligent 'bobbies'.

The average car

The typical car being driven in Britain then was of around 12hp RAC rating, or 1500cc, having a four-cylinder engine, generally with side valves, a 3- or 4-speed gearbox, often still separate from the engine, and harsh semi- or quarter-elliptic, or canti-lever non-independent springing with prim-itive friction dampers and rigid axles. Wheels were of detachable steel artillery or disc type (the wire-spoked wheel figured more often on better class or more sporting vehicles, or, in very spidery form, on cyclecars), with thin high-pressure tires. Brakes were internal expanding on the rear wheels only, and there were separate mudguards and side running boards which generally carried a 2-gallon petrol can and sometimes a spare wheel on one side and a battery on the other. Bodywork was usually of open 'touring' pattern, with two or four seats. Saloon body-work, or 'interior drive' as they termed it, was a luxury costing £100 or more extra, so the average motorist bought a tourer, encum-bered with rather ugly folding canvas hood with support irons, and clumsy, vulnerable celluloid side-screens, which slotted or clipped on to the doors and bodysides.

Electric lighting and starters were stand-ard by then, except on the very cheapest models, although many drivers would still preserve the battery by swinging the starting handle with which every car was equipped then. Resistance to the cheap but sensible American-type central gearchange was sur-prisingly fierce in Britain, many diehard makes sticking to right-hand gear gates and hand-brake levers, but eventually logic won the day. Synchromesh gears had yet to be invented, so every gearbox was of 'crash' type, and double-declutching was the rule to avoid the grating of pinions. From the mechanic's angle, detachable cylinder heads were becoming more popular, the magneto still outweighed that other invention from America, coil ignition, and the cone clutch of prewar days was still around although the single-plate type was muscling in. Propellor shaft transmission with fabric flexible joints and spiral bevel final drive was largely favoured, except in the starker cyclecars where chains were still used.

The motoring niceties which we now take for granted were mere dreams in 1923. Some designers still expected drivers to open the bonnet and flood the carburettor when the engine was cold, but the 'strangler' as they called the choke then, was fortunately catching on fast. The screenwiper, vacuum-operated from the inlet manifold, was an optional extra, although Trico of the USA had just introduced the first electric wipers. For most people rainy weather meant a periodic screen wipe with a chamois leather, or a potato-half rubbed over it. There were also chemical preparations such as 'Mystic', which claimed to merge raindrops into a transparent film, or hand or cable-operated

Right: A Paris traffic scene over 50 years ago — the vehicles look old-fashioned but the jams were the same. Top left: Petrol pumps were also becoming a more common sight on roadsides — at first they were operated by hand but later by electricity.

TRAFFIC BUILDS UP

'squeegee' wipers (''just one stroke of the hand''). Short of one or the other of these aids, the unhappy driver had to open his screen and take the rain in his face in order to see. Car heating, too, was a rarity except on expensive cars; the Americans by-passed exhaust gases to the vicinity of the passengers' feet, but usually people just had to suffer the cold.

Oiling and greasing the mechanism was a frequent and tiresome chore, with dozens of lubrication points requiring attention, some as often as every 200 miles. Headlamp 'dippers' and 'dimmers', adjustable front seats, wind-up windows and spotlights were still luxury extras, while luggage was carried on an exposed, folding metal grid at the rear. Road-side petrol pumps and filling stations were on the increase, although most garages still stocked 2-gallon cans of what was then termed 'motor spirit'. The new-fangled 'wireless' could be fitted in a car at considerable expense – but if you wanted to listen to it, you had to stop the car, hang your aerial on the nearest tree or post and don the earphones. The Marconi company were experimenting with a real 'mobile' receiver on a Daimler, which carried a huge pentagonal aerial on its roof, but reception was marred by interference from the magnetos of nearby cars, while passing tramcars drowned the broadcast.

Twins and fours

The British motoring scene changed noticeably as 1923 advanced. In the smaller, cheaper class there was much dissension on design. The twin-cylinder engine, either horizontally-opposed (i.e. flat) or vee, and air or watercooled, was popular for its simplicity and compactness if not for its roughness and noise. The Rover Eight was probably the most successful example of the breed, but Jowett, Ariel, Lea-Francis and Wolseley also built economy flat-twins, while Belsize, Crouch, Stoneleigh, Buckingham, Princess and BSA opted for the vee layout. All were noisy and most of them vibrated excessively, but the alternative, the miniature watercooled four, cost a lot more to build except in large quantities.

Citroen and Peugeot of France managed this successfully, however, the former with their 856cc 5CV, the latter with the 680cc sv Quadrilette, its tiny crankshaft running in ball bearings. A 3-speed gearbox was combined with a differential-less back axle, springing was by transverse leaf front and quarter-elliptic rears, and this pretty little car's austere nature was emphasized on early models by hand starting and acetylene lighting. Manufacture of Germany's pre-war Wanderer *Püppchen* ('Doll') small four was also resumed, but none of these cars made the tremendous impact of Sir Herbert Austin's new Seven.

Sir Herbert Austin was particularly appalled by the general untidy design of the motorcycle-and-sidecar which many family men then rode in preference to the fragile and almost equally exposed cyclecar. He believed it was possible to build a miniature car for around the same price, which would occupy no more space in the garage or drive, but offer many more comforts. His 'Twenty' and

Motoring niceties such as we know them today were non-existent in the early '20s but designers were beginning to think in terms of the comfort and convenience of the motorist. Left: A hand-operated screenwiper of 1923. Right: A 1923 11.9hp Bean with front, rear and side screens to shield passengers from the wind – a constant problem when most cars were still open. By 1922 you could take a wireless with you in your car but if you wanted to listen to it you had to stop the car and clamp a tall aerial on to the car, as seen below, or attach it to the nearest tree.

'Twelve' were good models but not selling well enough, so he resolved to produce a car for 'the man in the street'. Not all his shareholders agreed with him, so Sir Herbert and a draughtsman quietly worked out the design at his home at Lickey Grange near Birmingham, the billiard table serving as a drawing board.

The prototype Seven, shown to an astonished press at Claridges Hotel, London, in July 1922, and later to the public at Olympia, had everything that a 'real' car had — a four-cylinder, watercooled sv engine in unit with a 3-speed gearbox, single dry-plate clutch, spiral bevel final drive, four seats, and even four-wheel brakes, all within dimensions of 8ft 8in long by 3ft 10in wide. Its engine measured a miniscule 54×75.2mm bore and stroke (697cc), its tiny crankshaft ran in two main bearings, and output was 10bhp at 2400rpm. The frame was the simplest possible channel steel structure in the form of an A, with radiator and engine at the narrow top end. Suspension followed the Peugeot Quadrilette style, which itself took after the Model T Ford — i.e. a transverse leaf spring at the front, aided by radius arms, and quarter-elliptics at the rear, projecting rearwards from the two legs of the A.

Three-stud wire wheels were fitted, and the 'Chummy' touring body contained two nominal rear seats, into which two or three children or equivalent luggage could be crammed. When production was under way in 1923 the engine had grown to 56×76mm (747cc), and weight to 9cwt, while fuel consumption was around 45mpg. An electric starter now featured, and the price, including dynamo lighting, 'all weather' equipment and spare wheel, was down in the 'cyclecar' bracket at £165. Sir Herbert Austin's prodigy had instant appeal; it set his company well on its feet again, and was in production, basically unaltered, right up to 1937. During its career, manufacturing licences were sold to Dixi (later BMW) of Germany, Rosengart of France, Bantam of the USA, and Datsun of Japan, while rights to build the engine, modified to take three main bearings, were acquired by the Reliant company for use in their 3-wheeled cars and vans right up to 1963, making an impressive life span of 40 years.

Austin's racing success

Like Ford's Model T, the 'baby' Austin was the butt of countless jokes, but it was one of the most important cars in British motoring history. Also, like the T, it was exceptionally durable, and it belied its seemingly frail and utilitarian design by scoring many racing successes. In its very first year of production, 1923, Herbert Austin's son-in-law Arthur Waite drove a tuned roadster down from Birmingham to Brooklands for the Easter meeting, won his race after lapping at 62.4mph, then drove back again. A week or two later the same car was shipped to Italy, where Waite then won the Monza 750cc Cyclecar Grand Prix! Yet the Austin Seven was anything but a cyclecar — indeed, it rendered that precarious cross between a motorbike and a car totally redundant, and brought about a considerable revolution on British roads.

British Leyland

Radio Times Hulton

Left: Sir Herbert Austin, whose remarkable 'baby' car, the 4-cylinder, 4-seater, 4-wheel brake Seven (below) revolutionized economy motoring.
Top right: The Bradford-built 907cc flat-twin Jowett rivalled the Austin Seven for seat room and long service.
Middle right: 'Slow but sure' was the philosophy behind the unconventional 2-stroke chain-drive 1½-litre Trojan.
Bottom: Renault of France challenged the economy market with the 8.3hp, 951cc 4-cylinder 4-seater model KJ, with characteristic radiator behind the bonnet.

Further small fours introduced in 1923 hastened the end of the cyclecar. Humber of Coventry produced a well-engineered 8/18 with 982cc engine; intended for a somewhat wealthier clientele than the Austin, it had more generous dimensions and cost twice as much. Mathis of Strasbourg built a frugal 628cc sv four which was much in demand, Chapuis-Dornier marketed a proprietary 898cc sv four which several makers employed, while Renault, stung to reprisal by the success of Citroen's 5CV, introduced the 951cc four-cylinder Model KJ with side valves, three speeds and remarkable longevity.

One by one the twin-cylinder models died out — with the notable exception of the Jowett. Bred in the Yorkshire hills, this tough little utilitarian with its strong, flexible 907cc watercooled flat-twin aptly called 'the little engine with the big pull', flourished well into the '30s, and served for a further twenty years in the Bradford van, thus sharing long-service honours with the Austin Seven.

The incredible Trojan

The final nails in the cyclecar's coffin were driven home by an even more surprising British light car than the Austin Seven. This was the Trojan, another 1922 Olympia debutant which was displayed alongside the most expensive 'exotic' at the Show, the Leyland Eight, commanding £1875 for the chassis alone. The complete Trojan four-seater cost less than a tenth of that sum at a mere £175, yet incredibly, it, too, was a Leyland product, built at Kingston-on-Thames. Its designer was Leslie Hounsfield, a great individualist whose concept departed in almost every way from convention. Beneath a square, uncomely exterior, the Trojan had a steel, punt-type chassis with long cantilever springs running fore and aft, and a 1½-litre watercooled, four-piston 2-cylinder 2-stroke engine, installed horizontally together with the 2-speed epicyclic transmission under the front seats.

There was a long, single, silent chain driving a fixed rear axle, and the tires were solid rubber. The engine managed 11bhp at a leisurely 1000rpm, with remarkable low-speed torque similar to that of a steam engine. Starting was by a hand lever next to the driver's seat, and though roomier than the Austin Seven, the Trojan was equally economical at 45mpg. Its forward progress was slow but sure, with 38mph its modest maximum, but the car could tackle almost any gradient, albeit very slowly, while mechanically it was virtually indestructible. Its 2-stroke engine emitted a soothing 'bumbling' noise, and its simple handling made it popular with women drivers and the clergy, and Leyland actually advertised their 'ugly duckling' in *The Church Times*. The solid tires resulted in jokes about owners getting caught in the tramlines and ending up at the terminus, and pneumatics soon became an optional extra. Its eccentricity probably weighed against it, for although built up to 1929, Hounsfield's design never made the international impact of the Austin Seven.

One of the delights of the Vintage era was its variety. There were cars for the

Left: A great favourite among early post-war sporting motorists, the lively 4½-litre Vauxhall 30/98 4-seater tourer. Below: A popular 'quality' 1½-litre sports, the Alvis 12/50 with famous aluminium 'duck's back' body, seen here climbing a rocky section in a Land's End trial. Right: Walter Owen Bentley, creator of the most famous of all British Vintage sports cars, was also a successful racing driver. Far right: The 4½-litre Bentley was virtually an enlargement of the earlier 3-litre model in a sturdier chassis with 4-wheel brakes.

million and for the millionaire, some built merely to be functional, others to give pleasure and good performance. In such a decade the sports car came into its own, epitomized by long, slender, sweeping mudguards, wire wheels with 'knock-off' eared hubcaps, rakish open bodies in polished aluminium, and big exhaust tailpipes emitting a throaty roar. The 30/98 Vauxhall, which virtually initiated the sporting breed in Britain just before the Great War, became highly popular after it. Its 4½-litre sv big four engine and wide-ratio 4-speed gearbox gave an exhilarating performance and 85mph in a good-handling if somewhat under-braked chassis. In 1922 an ohv head and slightly reduced stroke made the 30/98 a smoother performer, but regrettably, although the car scored in countless sprints, hill-climbs and short Brooklands races, it

never took part in the major international long-distance sports car races which contributed so much towards developing and maturing design. The 30/98's younger, smaller-engined rival, the Bentley, eclipsed it, and Vauxhall's sporting image faded soon after the Company was taken over by the American General Motors Corporation late in 1925.

Although first shown at Olympia in 1919, no 3-litre Bentleys were delivered until late 1921. Before then, however, the little factory at Cricklewood were forcing design development by racing; they scored a couple of race wins at Brooklands, and then ventured a three-car entry for the 1922 Isle of Man TT. They did extremely well to place 2nd, 4th and 5th, winning the team prize, even though this hard race stressed their need for four-wheel brakes. Then one of the

first private owners of a Bentley, John Duff, drove it into 4th place in the very first Le Mans 24 Hours race in 1923. Encouraged, the Company fitted Duff's car with four-wheel brakes for the 1924 event, and this time he won by 90 miles from a Lorraine-Dietrich, scoring the first of five rousing Bentley victories in the French endurance classic. The British marque, with its handsome vee radiator, 'British green' paintwork, and big Rudge-Whitworth wire wheels became pre-eminent as a high speed long-distance runner of prodigious stamina. Such was W. O. Bentley's confidence in his 3-litre that every car was delivered with a 5-year guarantee, its durability impressively borne out by the fact that, of 1620 examples built up to 1928, over 400 are still running today, many being raced on British circuits by members of the Bentley Drivers' Club.

Left: First of a long line of sports cars — the 1924 MG 14/24 tourer based on the Morris Oxford.
Below: Cecil Kimber, the man behind the MG.

A parallel to Bentley in the 1½-litre class was the Coventry-built Alvis, a durable, 'rev-happy' 4-speed sv four which graduated from a 10/30 in 1919, through 11/40 and 12/40 stages to the ohv 12/50 of 1923, which perfectly epitomized the classic Vintage sports car. The aluminium-bodied 'duck's back' two-seater was a valiant performer in every branch of competition — trials, sprints, hillclimbs and races, reaching its peak when a modified racing version won the 1923 200 Miles Race at Brooklands at a remarkable 93.29mph. Like the Bentley, the Alvis survival rate speaks volumes for its quality, over 300 still being extremely active. Four and six-cylinder Sunbeams, Talbots, 1½-litre Rileys and Aston Martins, the Lea-Francis, HE and Lagonda — all these makes formed the hardcore of British sports cars in those early days, with new ones eagerly joining in. From the outmoded twin-cylinder GN sprang a vigorous successor, the four-cylinder 1½-litre Anzani-engined Frazer Nash, unique in retaining the GN's famous chain-and-dog 3-speed transmission, and possessing an even better power-to-weight ratio. Another important newcomer, of milder temperament but great customer appeal, was the first MG, a sporting variant of the 1.8-litre 'Bullnose' Morris Oxford called the 14/28, introduced in 1924 by Cecil Kimber — a particularly attractive car with polished aluminium body side panels and disc-covered wheels.

In addition to the 'working', 'luxury' and 'sporting' models around at that time, there was also that rare and fascinating category, the 'ideal' design. All too often the daringly unorthodox solution to mechanical problems was hampered by inadequate materials,

let alone lack of money. Late in 1922, however, a radically new car appeared that was practical enough to survive and teach the conservative automobile world some useful lessons. This was the unforgettable Lancia Lambda. Its designer, Vincenzo Lancia, was a former Fiat engineer, tester and racing driver who founded his own make in 1906. He built sound, conventional cars until 1919, when he produced the abortive V12, then a V8, and then his masterpiece, the V4 Lambda.

Like the 12 and the 8, its engine was a monobloc aluminium casting with four cast-iron cylinder liners set in narrow vee formation at 22°. A three-bearing crankshaft was used, and the whole unit was notably short, compact and rigid. Bore and stroke were 75 ×120mm (2120cc), a single ohc operated the vertical overhead valves, and initial output was 49bhp at 2350rpm although over 3000rpm proved readily attainable. There were further innovations apart from the engine. Instead of an ordinary channel-section chassis, Lancia anticipated modern integral construction by using deep pressed steel side members which also formed the flat-sided open 4-seater 'torpedo' bodywork. There were four shallow doors to avoid frame weakness, a tapered stern, and a tubular truss framework at the fore-end carrying independent front suspension. This was of sliding pillar type, much the same as used since 1910 on the British Morgan 3-wheeler, but with the coil springs damped by co-axial telescopic hydraulic shock-absorbers.

The Lambda was probably the first car with independent front springing in which the advantages to roadholding were really

Continental prophets: Integral chassis/body construction, independent springing and rear-engine location are taken for granted on modern competition cars, but were decidedly unusual over 50 years ago. Below: The Lancia Lambda introduced in 1922 had a chassis with pressed steel side members which also formed the body, independent front suspension and a 2.1-litre overhead camshaft V4 engine formed from one basic aluminium casting. Right: The unique 1924 German 2-litre Benz 'Tropfenwagen' had its six-cylinder twin overhead camshaft engine at the rear, driving through a 3-speed gearbox and independent swing axles.

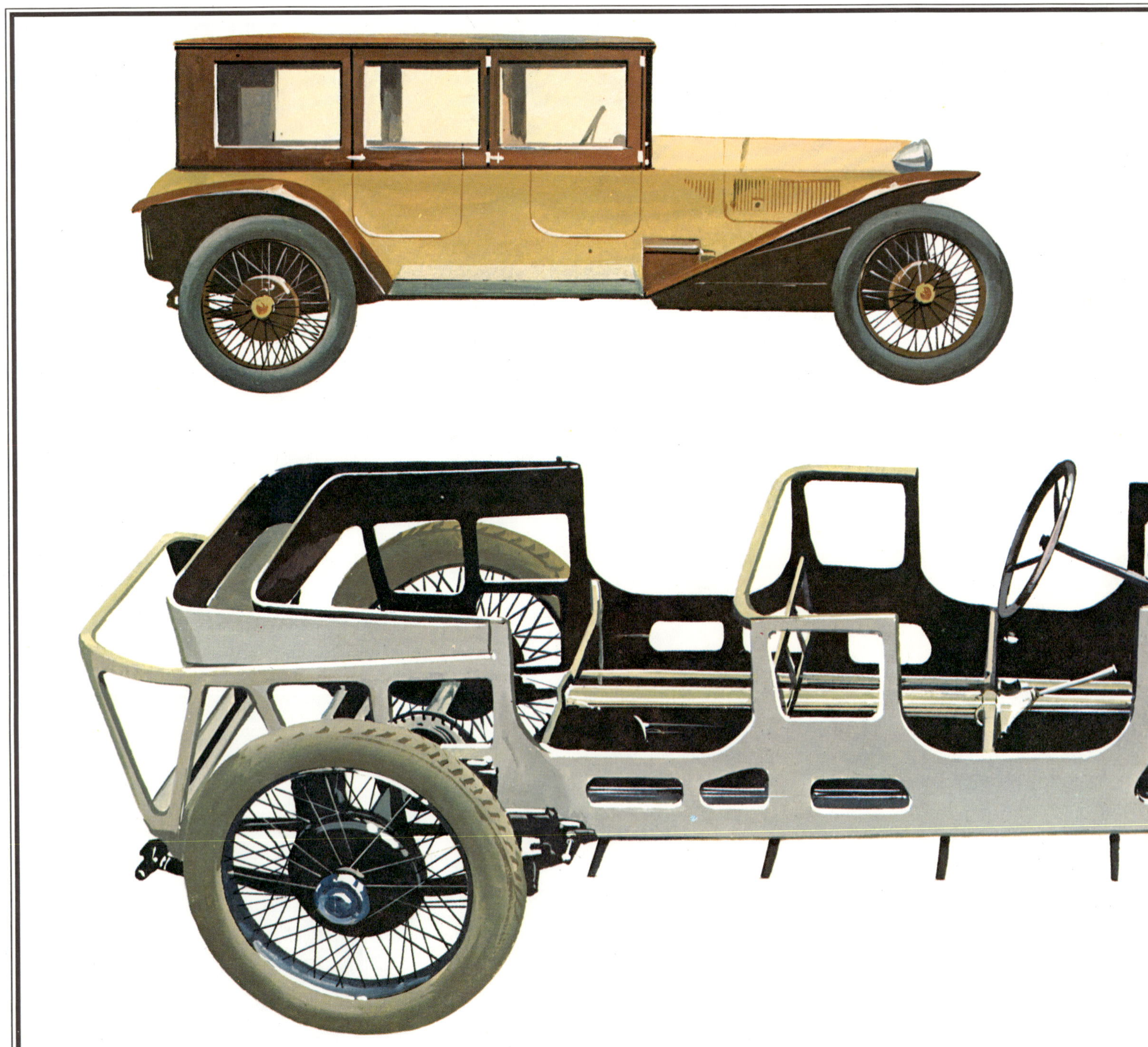

appreciable. Its handling on uneven roads, its cornering power, and its excellent four-wheel braking all drew considerable praise from the experts, and although designed as a touring car, its overall performance rated with the best known Vintage sports models. A 1-2-3 class victory in 1924 in the unique ''Bad Roads Race'' held near Lille, France, over a deliberately neglected, war-torn course of shattering severity was an early pointer to its abilities. Some 13 000 Lambdas in nine series, each embodying detail improvements, were built between 1923 and 1931, and although the integral chassis/body construction was eventually dropped because of coachbuilding problems, the Lancia-type front suspension was employed for many years subsequently.

Other 'idealists' were also preoccupied with independent suspension and abnormal chassis construction. An astonishing British 'one-off' in 1922 was the North-Lucas, with five-cylinder sv aircooled radial engine installed above the rear axle, driving down through three speeds and independent swing axles. The rear brakes were mounted 'inboard', close to the final drive rather than on the wheel hubs – a feature still thought daring over 30 years later – and the front wheels, too, were independently sprung by co-axial coil spring/damper units, as are commonly employed today. Julian S. Brown of Syracuse, New York, was also 'radial-minded', his 1922 engine having six cylinders and overhead valves. It was fitted into a 'backbone' chassis formed from one large-diameter steel tube with cross-pieces attached. The steering and driving seat were central, with passenger seats on both sides.

'Backbone' exponent

Another 'backbone' exponent was the Italian San Giusto, on which the main member was of square section, carrying transverse leaf all-round independent springing with tubular lower wishbones. A tiny 748cc aircooled four-cylinder engine was fitted just ahead of the rear axle, driving through a 4-speed gearbox. Similar mid-engine/transmission arrangements featured on the advanced Benz *Tropfenwagen* (teardrop) sports car, developed from their 1923 Grand Prix racing machine. A 2-litre six-cylinder twin ohc engine drove through a 3-speed gearbox to independently-sprung swing axle final drive, made to Rumpler patents. Unfortunately, the designers' courage failed them when considering the front end, and they played safe with a rigid axle sprung by quarter-elliptics. A crescent-shaped radiator was located directly over the engine, so the nose was neatly closed off, the headlamps were faired elegantly into the body, which carried Rumpler-like horizontal mudwings, and had a shallow vee-wind-screen. This radical sports car gained a few speed hillclimb successes in 1924–25, but its lessons were largely unrealized until the '60s, when the Cooper 'Monaco' and Lotus 23 sports-racing cars came on the scene.

Left: The successful Tatra Typ II from Czechoslovakia, with twin-cylinder aircooled engine and central backbone chassis. Right: Symbol of progress – the red triangle which denoted four-wheel brakes in the '20s, seen on a Morris Oxford. Extreme right: The 1922 Essex 'Coach' from the USA, with all-metal saloon bodywork soon to outmode the tourer. Below: A Citroen 11cv all-steel saloon made to American Budd patents, being welded up in a large assembly jig at the Quai Javel factory. Below right: The Dodge all-steel sedan in contemporary publicity.

More successful commercially was the 1923 backbone-framed Tatra from Czechoslovakia, which had a 1056cc aircooled flat-twin engine installed transversely in front, with the propellor shaft actually passing through the backbone tube to drive the rear swing axles. Endowed in 1925 with front end independence by split axle beam and transverse leaf spring, and also four-wheel brakes, this tough little machine proved admirably suited to rough mid-European roads, and was built and sold for several years.

In an attempt to achieve extra performance, the Mercedes concern of Stuttgart had long been experimenting with supercharging – a method of augmenting power by literally forcing the mixture of petrol and air into the engine by a pump, or *kompressor* as they called it. They had first explored the principle in high-altitude flying during the War, then they tried it out in racing, and next tentatively marketed a supercharged $1\frac{1}{2}$-litre four-cylinder sports model in 1922. This had a vertical Roots-type *kompressor* (i.e. with two 'figure of 8' paddles rotating in a common chamber), which only came into operation when the driver fully depressed the accelerator pedal (like the modern 'kick-down' in automatic transmission), giving extra power boost when required. The additional stresses of compressing brought their own problems, but further experience in racing mastered them, so that by around 1928 supercharging began to enjoy a considerable vogue on sports cars.

Four-wheel brakes

Of far greater importance to the development of the ordinary private car was the ever-increasing adoption of four-wheel brakes. These had been a subject of controversy ever since their first tentative introduction back in 1910. When well-designed, which meant expensively, as on the Isotta-Fraschini and the Hispano-Suiza, they worked well, but some cheaper versions were disastrous. Fierce action at low speeds produced locking wheels, impaired steering and resulted in too many accidents. The Italians and French were well to the fore in their early development, the Perrot and Hallot systems gaining many adherents, though the tiny four-wheel brakes on the

National Motor Museum

American Motors Corporation

Austin Seven, so impressive in the specification, proved of limited value through being uncoupled, the rear pair operated by pedal and the front by hand lever.

Cautious manufacturers stuck to two-wheel braking, but as car performance improved and town traffic increased they could no longer dodge the issue. Established quality designs were borrowed and simplified, and 1924 stands out as 'the 4-wheel brake year', when a distinctive red triangle on the offside rear wing of a car denoted their fitting, and became an increasingly familiar sight on British roads. Daimler, Lanchester, Vauxhall, Bentley, Armstrong-Siddeley, Sunbeam, Alvis, Aston Martin and numerous others all adopted front-wheel brakes. Rolls-Royce, always wary about branching into anything new, acquired a licence to use the Hispano-Suiza servo system, while Allford & Alder marketed a proprietary set costing around £25, which appeared on a number of cheaper cars.

Enclosed motoring

Comfort as well as safety now received further attention, and improved factory techniques soon made the saloon body less of a luxury. Dodge of the USA had introduced the first all-steel welded body back in 1914, and their compatriot rivals, Essex, introduced a 'Coach' model in 1922. This had uncompromisingly square and erect lines (curves in metal costing more) and its price made it an instant best-seller. In France the Weymann-type closed body, with light wooden framework joined by metal strips allowing it to flex, appeared in 1923–24. The outside was covered with 'Zapon' artificial leather, the inside with cloth, and the space in between filled with cotton wool. The seats were bolted to the chassis rather than the body, the structure thus being usefully light and inexpensive to make, and 'Weymann saloons' soon became familiar in France and Britain. Then the ever-enterprising André Citroen secured a licence to build all-steel saloon bodies to the American Budd patents as used by Dodge, and in 1925 began mass-producing a severely square *tout acier* saloon on the 11CV chassis at a highly competitive price. Renault and others countered with welded metal saloons of their own, and enclosed motoring soon be-

Citroen

The Motor

November 6, 1925

GOOD WILL GIVEN A NEW IMPETUS

Dodge Brothers Saloon leaves nothing to be desired in comfort, refinement and dignity of appearance. It is ideal for any occasion where five persons wish to be independent of weather conditions. No expense has been spared in the equipment, which includes a heater, interior lights, gearchange lock and windscreen wiper. The goodwill which always follows the use of Dodge Brothers vehicles will be given a new impetus by this larger and finer vehicle.

£495

came the rule rather than the exception.

With the economic turn of the tide, important new names came forward. In America, the ambitious Walter P. Chrysler, formerly with General Motors and then Willys, gained control of the Maxwell company in 1921, and three years later established his own make, the Chrysler. It was a striking car, powered by a 3.2-litre six-cylinder engine with 7-bearing crankshaft, typically American wood-spoked wheels and drum-type headlamps, and four-wheel hydraulic brakes – a novelty on a car of moderate price. These were of Lockheed external contracting type, as also used by Buick that year. Subsequently, similar Lockheed braking was employed on the 1925 Triumph 13/30, the second model by a new British make springing from the famous motorcycle concern.

It was in the '20s that the now formidable Japanese car industry quietly began taking root. The very first car built in Japan seems to have been a 'one-off' fitted with an American twin-cylinder engine and built by two engineers, Yoshyda and Uchiyama, in Tokyo in 1902. Crown Prince Arisugawa made an extended visit to Europe in 1905, acquiring a Darracq car which he took back to Japan. It was with his encouragement that the Tokyo Jidosha Seisakusho (Tokyo Automobile Works) was founded in 1907, with Uchiyama as chief engineer. They produced a car, the Takuri, which followed European style with four-cylinder engine and chain drive, although only 17 were built in the next few years as the Company was more occupied producing buses and trucks.

Developments in Japan

By 1912 they had a rival in Tokyo, the Kwaishinsha concern founded by three partners named Den, Aoyama and Takeuchi. This trio built a prototype, and two years later produced a high, spidery 12hp model which they called the DAT, after their three initials. Japanese roads then were poor and narrow, and car widths were restricted by law so that the DAT had an unusually narrow track. After the Great War two more marques, Mitsubishi and Gorham, appeared. The 'Mitsu' was a Fiat built under licence, while the Gorham was designed by an American, William R. Gorham, who founded the Jitsuyo Jidosha Seizo in Osaka to build motor trucks. He also constructed a small three-wheeled one-seater vehicle from motorcycle parts for the use of his works manager, who was crippled. It worked encouragingly, and from it they evolved the handlebar-steered 8hp twin-cylinder Gorham three-

wheeled car and a van in 1920.

Being cheap and easy to maintain, many Gorhams were built, and soon a four-wheeler with bigger engine and shaft drive was put into production. In 1923 this was succeeded by the 10hp Lila, with aircooled four-cylinder engine and a very slender chassis which contrived to support four-door closed bodywork. Then, in 1925, Gorham sold out to the DAT partners, who stopped production of the Lila and concentrated on commercial vehicles. Meanwhile another Japanese make, the Otomo, appeared on the scene with air and watercooled light cars, and in 1930 DAT built a tiny 500cc four-cylinder car which they named the Datson (meaning son of DAT). When it was realized that *son* also meant 'loss' in Japanese, a discreet change was made to Datsun, a name which has advanced to world fame today, no less than

Left: Walter P. Chrysler, who introduced a significant new name to American motoring in 1924. Below: The first Chrysler car, with characteristic wood-spoked wheels and 4-wheel hydraulic external-contracting brakes. Right: Japan moved into the motoring age in the early '20s, first with the utilitarian Gorham three-wheeler designed by an American and powered by a Harley-Davidson twin-cylinder motorcycle engine. Below right: This 1923 Japanese 10hp Lila bore four-seater closed bodywork, coyly curtained, on a chassis which was deliberately narrow to comply with local laws.

645 000 private cars being exported in 1975 alone.

While Japanese cars were still totally unknown beyond the Far East, the world's greatest exponents of quantity car production, Ford of Detroit, established a car and truck assembly plant in Japan. That was in 1925, when they also opened factories in Stockholm, Sweden, and Antwerp, Belgium, to assemble still more Model Ts. The omnipresent 'Tin Lizzie' had undergone some much-needed styling refinements in 1923, gaining smoother lines through a raised radiator, lowered body, a new one-man hood and raked windscreen. World-wide demand continued, sales that year exceeding 2 million vehicles for the first time. A year later they added a new 'Tudor' sedan to the range, and celebrated the completion of over 10 million Model Ts!

The first motorway

In addition to the considerable achievements of the 1923–25 period were some important technological developments. They included the introduction of the low-pressure 'balloon' tire, first in the USA and then in Europe; the use of 'Ethyl' leaded fuels which reduced detonation or 'pinking' in an engine; and the first use in US mass production factories of 'Duco' spray-on quick-drying cellulose, developed by the du Pont corporation, and invaluable in cutting the man-hours spent in painting cars. And in Italy, Europe's very first stretch of special motorway, the *autostrada* from Milan to the Lakes, was opened in September 1924, less than 40 years after Karl Benz had driven his first hesitant yards on a Mannheim cart track in the world's first petrol-driven car.

INTO

By the middle of the 1920s even Germany's wildly disrupted economy had recovered some semblance of its equilibrium. The *Deutschmark* was back on the gold standard, and although many under-financed post-1918 'mushroom' makes had vanished, the bigger factories settled down to steady production. America's quantity output philosophy had infiltrated by 1924, when two rival marques, Opel and Hanomag, produced widely contrasting interpretations of the car 'for the man in the street'.

Opel of Russelsheim, guided by the five Opel brothers Carl, Wilhelm, Heinrich, Fritz and Ludwig, decided to emulate Ford, Citroen, Renault and Morris and turn cars out by the thousand on the assembly line. Following an exhaustive visit in 1923 to factories in the USA they completely refitted their factory with American conveyor belt equipment and machine tools. In 1924 they unveiled their new economy model, a simple, sturdy two-seater called the 4/12. Nicknamed the *Laubfrosch* or 'Tree-toad' because of its standard green finish, this car was astonishingly like the famous Citroen 5CV. Its engine was a similar monobloc sv four, measuring 60×90mm (1016cc) to the Citroen's 55×90mm, and the open body with pointed tail, the flared mudguards and disc wheels, and even the nickelled flat-vee radiator were very similar.

The French company sued for licence fees, but Opel convinced the court that they contravened no patents and won the case. Whatever its origin, the *Laubfrosch* was an immediate success on the German market, 4571 examples coming off the line in 1924 at 4500 marks each. This was soon cut to 4000, a four-seater was added, output rose to 125 cars daily, and the price was axed again to 2950 marks. Opel soon augmented their range with larger models, but it was the 'Tree-toad', 39 000 of which were built up to 1927, that established the Russelsheim concern as Germany's first mass producer of cars.

Hanomag's solution to the cheap personal transport problem, the Typ 2/10, was much more original. The Hannoversche Maschinenbau AG were famous as heavy steam locomotive builders from Linden, Hanover, but their first car was a veritable miniature. It had a tiny watercooled 499cc 10bhp

Two 1924 approaches to the economy problem by German makes. Above is the Opel 4/12 or 'Laubfrosch', which closely followed the pattern of the 5CV Citroen, illustrated on pages 80–81. Below: Open and closed variants of the 2/10 Hanomag seen sporting in the snowy hills near Hanover. Nicknamed the 'Kommissbrott', the little car had a 499cc single-cylinder engine between the two seats and the rear axle.

TOP GEAR

single-cylinder ohv engine, mounted between the two seats and the rear axle, which it drove through an integral 3-speed gearbox and enclosed chain. A pontoon-type chassis, largely of thick plywood, carried transverse leaf independent front suspension, and the narrow-tracked rear axle had no differential. The body, semi-integral with the chassis, and made of wood and canvas, pioneered the modern full-width styling with no running boards. Starting was by an awkward handle between the seats, wheelbase was only 6ft $3\frac{1}{2}$in, weight $7\frac{1}{4}$cwt, and speed 40mph. Both open and closed variants were available, with one door only and a single 'cyclops eye' headlamp. This tiny car's unusual shape gained it the nickname *Kommissbrott,* a special military issue loaf well known to hungry Germans, although the makers used the slogan 'Cheaper than a 3rd class railway ticket'. It was certainly cheap at 2300 marks, and nearly 20 000 were built between 1924 and 1927, when a larger and more orthodox Hanomag succeeded it.

German merger

A further important development in Germany was the amalgamation of the two great pioneer marques, Benz and Mercedes, on June 29th, 1926, under the name of Daimler-Benz AG. A merger had long been recognized as a sound means of strengthening the two firms. It was first proposed in 1919 and Benz and Mercedes opened negotiations in 1924. The final agreement combined their formidable designing and engineering talents and the cars they produced thereafter were called Mercedes-Benz. These rate today among the greatest, and some experts consider them worthy contenders for Rolls-Royce's title 'The best car in the world'.

But for the unrelenting engineering standards imposed by Sir Henry Royce, the Rolls-Royce 'Silver Ghost' could never have lasted until 1925. Yet its 7.4-litre 40/50 six-cylinder sv engine, born in 1907, still functioned with velvety smoothness under the elegant R-R bonnet. Many refinements had been made during its lifespan, while as mentioned earlier it acquired a smaller brother, the Twenty, in 1922. It was to the latter that the Silver Ghost's successor, the Phantom 1, owed its overhead valves.

Thoroughness has always been a vital part of the Rolls-Royce image. Unlike lesser firms, they did not rush in with new ideas, but researched and tested them exhaustively to ensure that their products were indisputably 'the best'. Before arriving at a pushrod ohv six-cylinder engine of 7.7 litres for their new Phantom, they designed and built straight-8, V12 and six-cylinder ohc test units – and found them all wanting in some respect or other. If the design they finally chose seemed disappointingly ordinary, it sufficed that it bore the *cachet* of Rolls-Royce's incomparable engineering. The design sophistication of multi-cylinders or overhead camshafts did not concern their clientele, who merely required that the power source behind that august radiator performed with traditional effortlessness, silence and total dependability – which, of course, it did.

New British aristocrats

Unlike the Silver Ghost, which had equal bore and stroke dimensions, the Phantom 1 engine had a longer stroke at 108×140mm, giving 7668cc. On being asked what power output their units produced, it was the Rolls-Royce custom to reply 'sufficient', and the Phantom's circa 105bhp was supremely adequate for propelling 2 tons of luxury car and passengers at speeds of well over 70mph. Its excellent Hispano-Suiza type mechanical servo 4-wheel brakes and light, precise steering enabled the chauffeur to maintain suave control at all speeds. Like the Twenty, the radiator was distinguished by radiator shutters, but these were vertical and enhanced the general elegance.

The American Rolls-Royce factory, opened at Springfield, Mass., in 1920, began building their own Phantom 1s in 1926. These differed from the Derby product in having a central-change 3-speed gearbox, centralized chassis lubrication, 6-volt electrics, dual coil ignition and other typical US features such as left-hand drive, drum-shaped headlights, bumper bars and white side-walled tires. Although 1240 examples were built up to 1931, many American customers insisted on 'the real thing', the British-built Phantom, so that eventually Derby produced a special US export variant.

It was quite by chance that Rolls-Royce encountered an unexpected new rival in the aristocrat class. British makers then habitually tested their new designs in secret on the long, fast, straight roads of France, and one June day in 1924 a Rolls-Royce tester in a prototype Phantom 1 tourer came across a strange Weymann-bodied saloon with British number plates. This was an experimental 4.2-litre six-cylinder Bentley, virtually a 3-litre with two more cylinders, disguised by an ugly, wedge-shaped radiator and registered as a 'Sun'. Its driver was W. O. Bentley himself, and the two cars were soon engaged in a high speed duel which was brought to a halt only when the Rolls driver lost his hat. The encounter was enough, however, for Bentley to realize that his car was short on power, and so he increased the bore from 80 to 100mm, making the capacity 6½ litres. It was in this form that the new luxury touring Bentley was launched in 1926.

The new 100×140mm unit gave 140bhp at 3500rpm – some 35bhp more than the Phantom's 7.7-litre six – enabling the first 6½-litre Bentley to attain an effortless 85mph. Design-wise it was more enterprising than the Rolls-Royce, with single ohc driven by silent triple connecting rods, four valves per cylinder as on the 3-litre, an 8-bearing crankshaft, and twin magneto ignition. Bentleys were always substantially built, and the road weight of a 6½-litre saloon was over 2¼ tons. A longer wheelbase variant with several design refinements came in 1928, and had it not been for the makers' preoccupation with racing the Speed-Six derivative, the superb 6½-litre might well have made greater impact on the world of *super-luxe.*

The new Rolls-Royce and Bentley models were reaching their first lucky customers when the 'grapevine' brought advance news of a third British candidate for this class of car – Daimler of Coventry. New models from this very conservative concern were rare, and their 'Double-Six', Britain's first 12-cylinder, was a big surprise at the 1926 Olympia Show. It was a clever instance of design expediency, combining two cylinder banks from the well-established 81×114 mm, 3567cc 25/85 six at 60° on a massive aluminium crankcase. The Knight double-sleeve valves which Daimler had championed since 1909 naturally remained, and each

Grace and space: The large luxury-type chassis gave specialist coach-builders full scope to practise their art. Here are three superb British examples. Left: A Rolls-Royce 40/50 Phantom 1 of 1927 with Park Ward body. Right: A 6½-litre six-cylinder Bentley with Gurney Nutting fabric coupé coachwork. Below: Daimler's 50hp 12-cylinder Double-Six with limousine body by Hall-Lewis.

David Burgess Wise

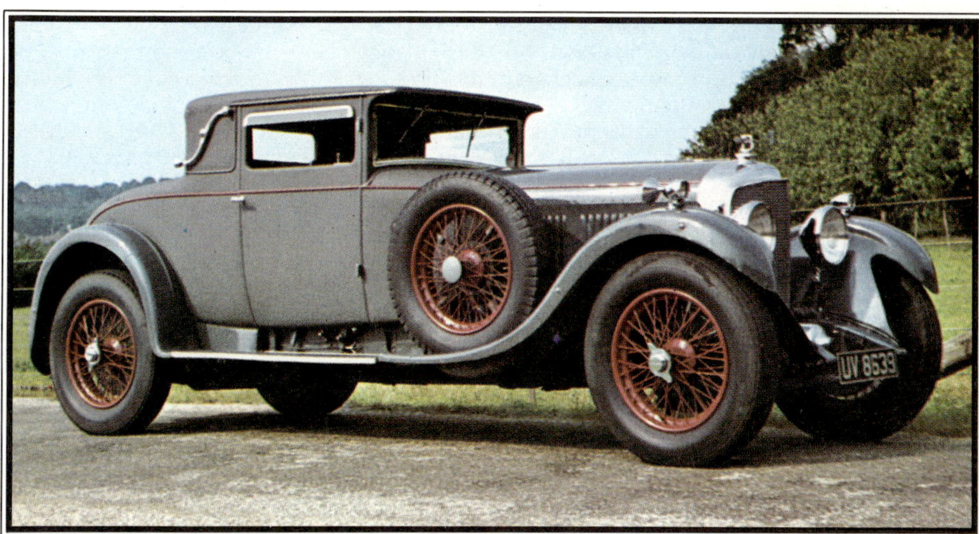

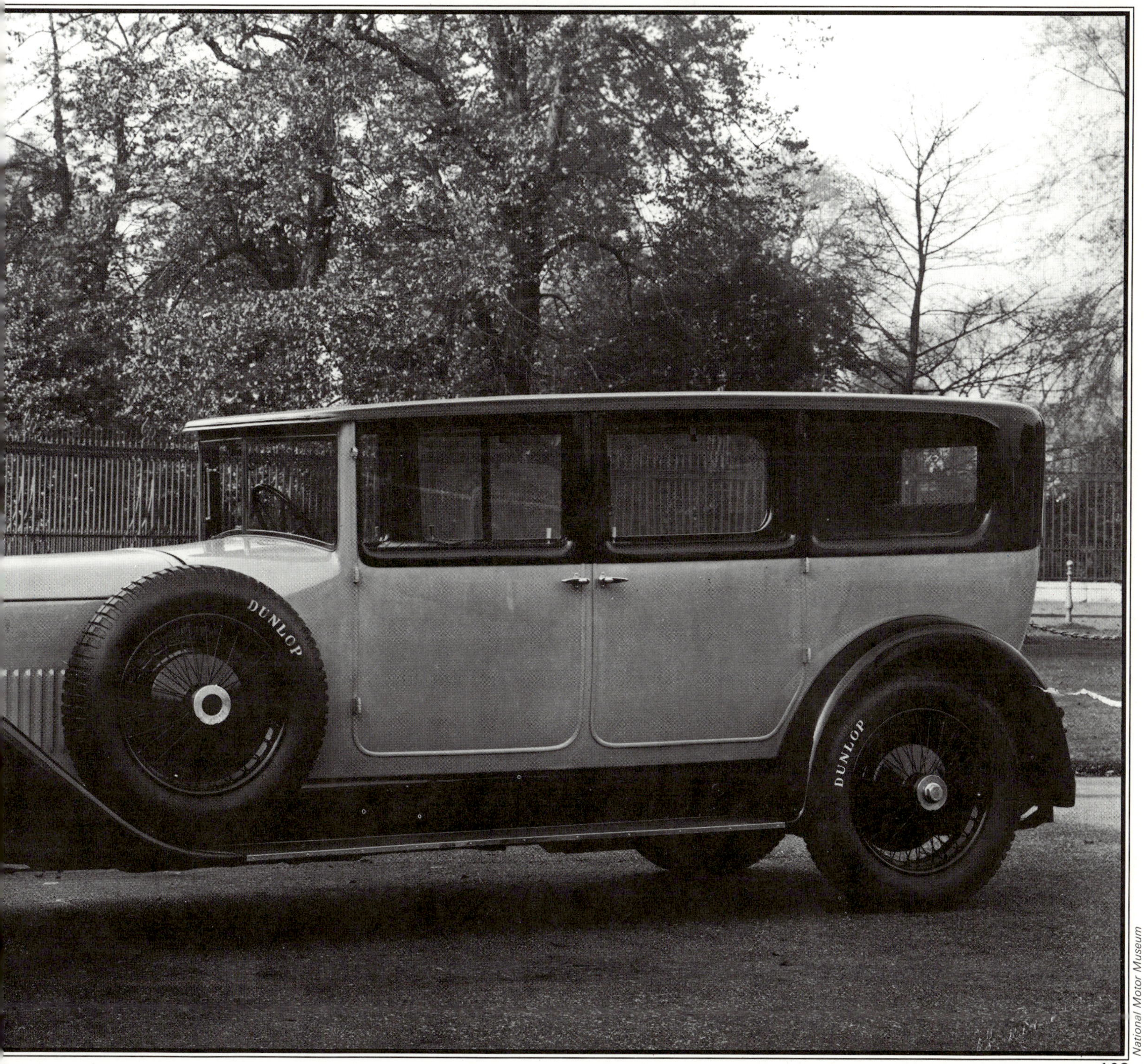

National Motor Museum

set of cylinders had its own 'main services', with separate dual ignition systems by magneto and coil, water pump, silencer and Daimler exhaust-heated carburettor, the latter on the outside, with the exhaust manifolds inside the vee.

Power from this heavy unit was adequate to 'carry a large closed body from walking pace to hurricane speeds with the least possible noise or vibration', as *The Autocar* put it. The Double-Six was a very large car indeed, with a choice of three wheelbases from 12ft 11½in to 13ft 7in, and a weight of 2 tons for the chassis alone. Checking this mass from speeds of over 80mph was in the care of vacuum servo-assisted 4-wheel brakes, and such was the engine torque that the car scarcely needed its four-speed gearbox, being able to proceed in top gear from 2mph without unseemly noise or protest.

Coventry contributed another important design that year, not in the prestige class this time, but in the thriving light car market. The Riley Co. were a very old firm which started business in weaving; they joined the rush to build bicycles in 1890, made their first de Dion-engined motor tricycles and quadricycles in 1899, and their first four-wheeled cars in 1905. By the early '20s their staple product was an 11hp 1½-litre sv four, whose liveliness gave it quite a sporting image, especially in the very attractive 'Redwing' model with polished aluminium body and handsome red-painted, swept wings.

But side valves were becoming outdated by 1925, so Riley set to and designed an advanced new 1100cc, 32bhp ohv four. Its hemispherical cylinder head form was outstanding, with valves inclined at 45°, and operated by twin 'high' camshafts in the

upper reaches of the crankcase, working the valves through short pushrods and rockers. The Pipe car from Belgium had used such valve gear many years earlier, but Riley were the first to commercialize an engine of racing efficiency without the cost and noise of those racing 'musts', twin overhead camshafts. Though intended at first for a touring car, the Riley's potential took it into racing in four and six-cylinder forms, producing three Ulster TT winners and powering the highly successful ERA racing voiturettes in the middle '30s. The first 1926 Nine, called the Monaco, was also outstanding for its dropped chassis frame, giving lower lines, and its rakish fabric saloon coachwork incorporating a neat luggage boot which precipitated the 'stepped' body fashion still employed today. Seasonally improved, the model quickly established itself as one of

Trend-setter from Coventry: The 1926 Riley Nine 'Monaco' fabric saloon set new fashions with its stepped saloon coachwork with built-in luggage boot and high-efficiency overhead valve engine.

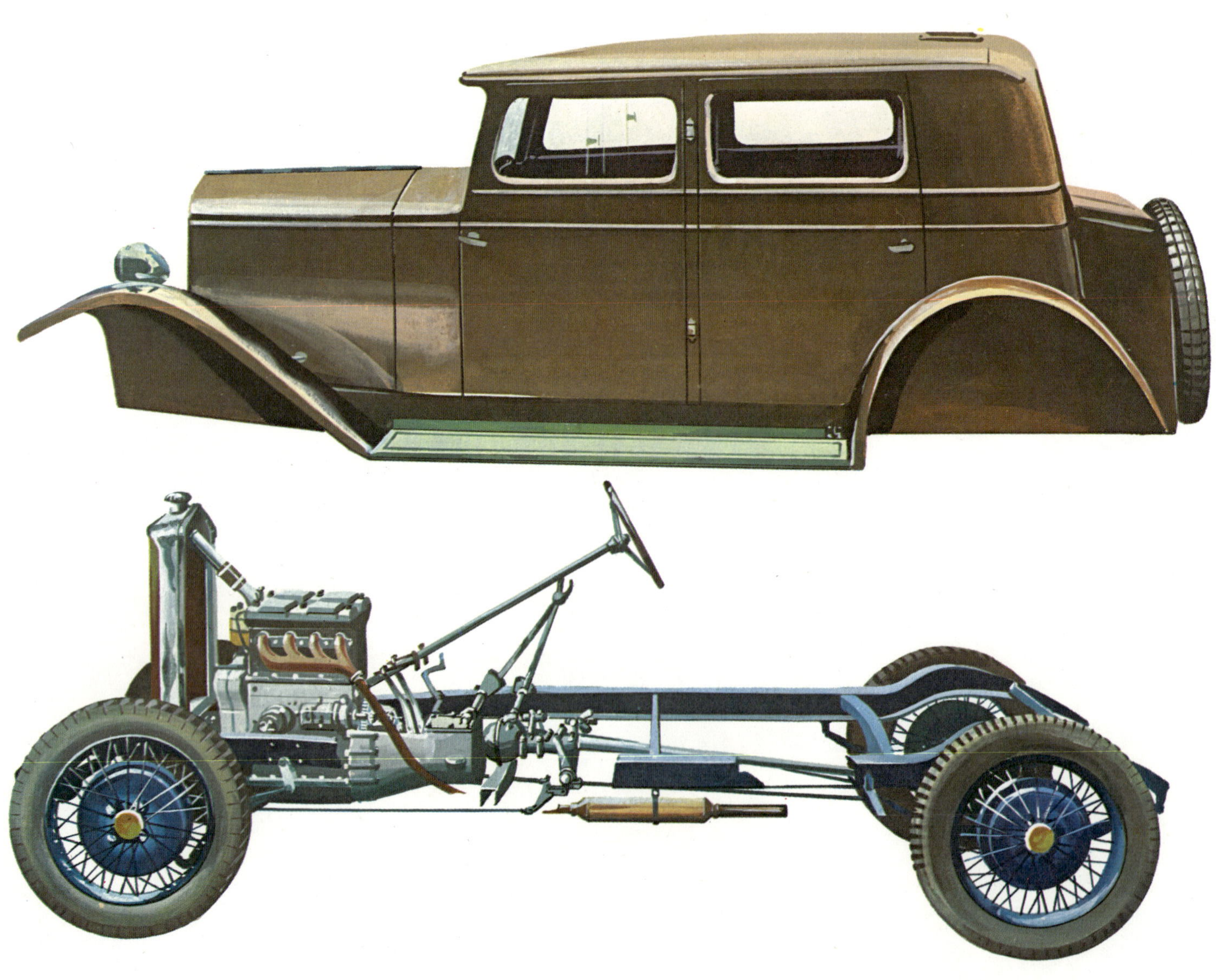

Britain's most popular sporting saloons, and was built right up to 1937.

Another outstanding débutant came from Fiat of Italy. Up till then the smallest-engined Fiat, excluding their very first car of 1899, was the sv 1460cc Tipo 501, but late in 1925 they entered the under-1-litre class with a pleasing little ohc four-cylinder design, the 509. Its 57×97mm, 990cc engine had a two-bearing crankshaft able to turn at 3800rpm and produce 20bhp, and with three speeds geared for Italian conditions this newcomer was a nimble performer despite roomy open or closed four-seater bodywork and an 8ft 4in wheelbase which made the 747cc Austin Seven seem extremely diminutive. The Italian car had servo-aided 4-wheel braking, a flat radiator, and a distinctly American look about its squarish styling, but it was cheap in Italy,

Italian sophistication: In 1925 Fiat introduced the Type 509 car with 990cc overhead camshaft 4-cylinder engine (right), in a neat servo-braked chassis carrying full 4-seater saloon or touring bodywork (below).
Bottom: A distinctive British sports car of the period was the 1½-litre Anzani 4-cylinder engined Frazer Nash, with 4-speed transmission by dog clutches and chains and a high power-weight ratio giving vigorous performance.

eminently practical, pleasing to drive, and dependable. Although the British Wolseley and Rhode were earlier exponents of small-capacity overhead camshaft, Fiat's Tipo 509 was produced in far greater numbers, with over 90 000 satisfied customers by 1929.

In Britain the month of May in 1926 was memorable for the General Strike which paralyzed the country for 10 days. This historic event saw the motor car in yet another role, playing a vital if controversial part in helping to maintain food and other essential supplies. With train, bus and tram services drastically cut, private cars provided lifts for thousands of non-striking workers. Both sides – strikers and Government – published their special newspapers, and the car was invaluable for distributing these, and in performing other transport and communications tasks.

Enter Volvo

In 1927 a new make destined for world fame crept quietly on to the motoring scene – Volvo of Sweden. Scandinavian roads then were loose-surfaced and rugged (many in the Arctic circle still are) to counteract severe frosts, and only the strongest cars could withstand such conditions. Many of those found in Sweden were sturdy German makes, others were cheaper American ones. Scania-Vabis had ceased car production in 1924, so two Swedes named Assar Gabrielsson and Gustaf Larson, both senior executives from the SKF ball and roller bearing company, decided to found a new domestic make. They launched their venture in 1926, choosing the name Volvo (meaning 'I roll' in Latin), and laying down 10 cars to establish that production was feasible.

Manufacture and machining of many components was sub-contracted out to firms such as Bofors (famous for their guns in the 2nd World War) and Husqvarna (famous for their motorcycles), and the first Volvo was very like a scaled-down American car. It had a 75×110mm, 28bhp, 1950cc sv four-cylinder engine, a 3-speed gearbox and rear brakes only, while performance was 'slow but sure' with a maximum of around 40mph. The 4-seater body was covered in imitation leather, American-style wood-spoked wheels were fitted, and the radiator bore the diagonal motif that was to symbol-ize Volvos of 45 years later. They called the car the PV4 or 'Jakob'.

Once their prototypes had been thoroughly tested, Volvo secured financial backing from SKF and took over a factory in Goteberg, beginning production of the Jakob in open and closed forms in 1927. At first they aimed at Scandinavian markets only, building 300 cars in the first year, increasing to 900 in 1928 and 1400 in 1929. They then introduced a bigger and very American 3-litre six-cylinder model, adopted hydraulic brakes, and also began making trucks and buses. Volvo cars were exported in small numbers to Holland, Belgium, Spain and South America, earning a reputation for robust construction, although the name was scarcely known in Britain or the USA until after the 2nd World War.

Still rarer makes came forward. One result of the 1919 Armistice terms was the dissolution of the old Austro-Hungarian monarchy and the creation of Austria, Czechoslovakia and Hungary as separate states. Austria retained her Austro-Daimler and Graf und Stift marques, Czechoslovakia had Nesselsdorf (which became Tatra) and Laurin-Klement (which became Skoda), and Hungary was left with the little known MAG, product of the Magyar Altalanos Gepgyar of Budapest. They turned out a rather dated 1.8-litre four-cylinder car for local needs from 1920, then laid down modern assembly lines for a new 2-litre sv six of broadly Teutonic aspect, called the Magosix. This appeared in 1927, when it was well up-to-date in having hydraulic 4-wheel braking. Many were built as taxis, and were still to be seen in Budapest 25 years later.

Despite Soviet leader Josef Stalin's dismissal of the automobile as 'an affectation of the rich', even Russia found it indispensable, and possibly resented the preponderance of imported German cars. Accordingly, the Nauchnii Avto-Motornii Institut, or NAMI (Scientific Auto-Motor Institute) was founded in Moscow, and students there formed a design group which produced a 1200cc, $18\frac{1}{2}$bhp, aircooled two-cylinder 4-seater model called the NAMI-1. This was a tough all-steel affair capable of over 40mph on rough Russian roads, and some 300 examples were claimed to be built in 1927–28. Ironically, although today Russian-built cars

Swedish débutant: One of the first Volvo 'Jakob' cars to be built (left) coming off the production line at Goteborg in 1927. Right: A glimpse into the motor car works at Mlada Boleslav, Czechoslovakia, where Laurin-Klement cars, which later became Skoda, were manufactured. The Big Strike: Oxford Circus, London (below) during the General Strike of 1926, with an armoured car escorting food convoys to the Hyde Park distribution centre.

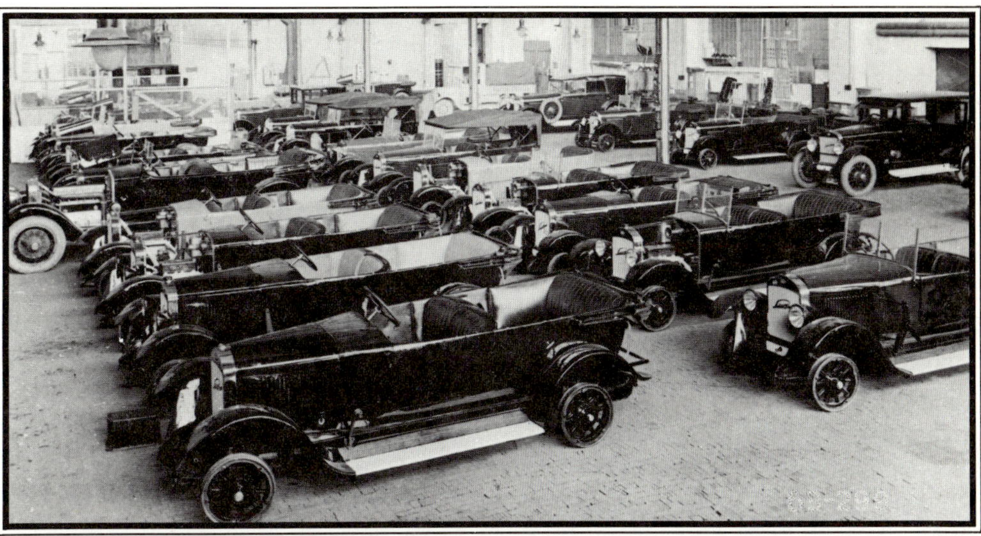

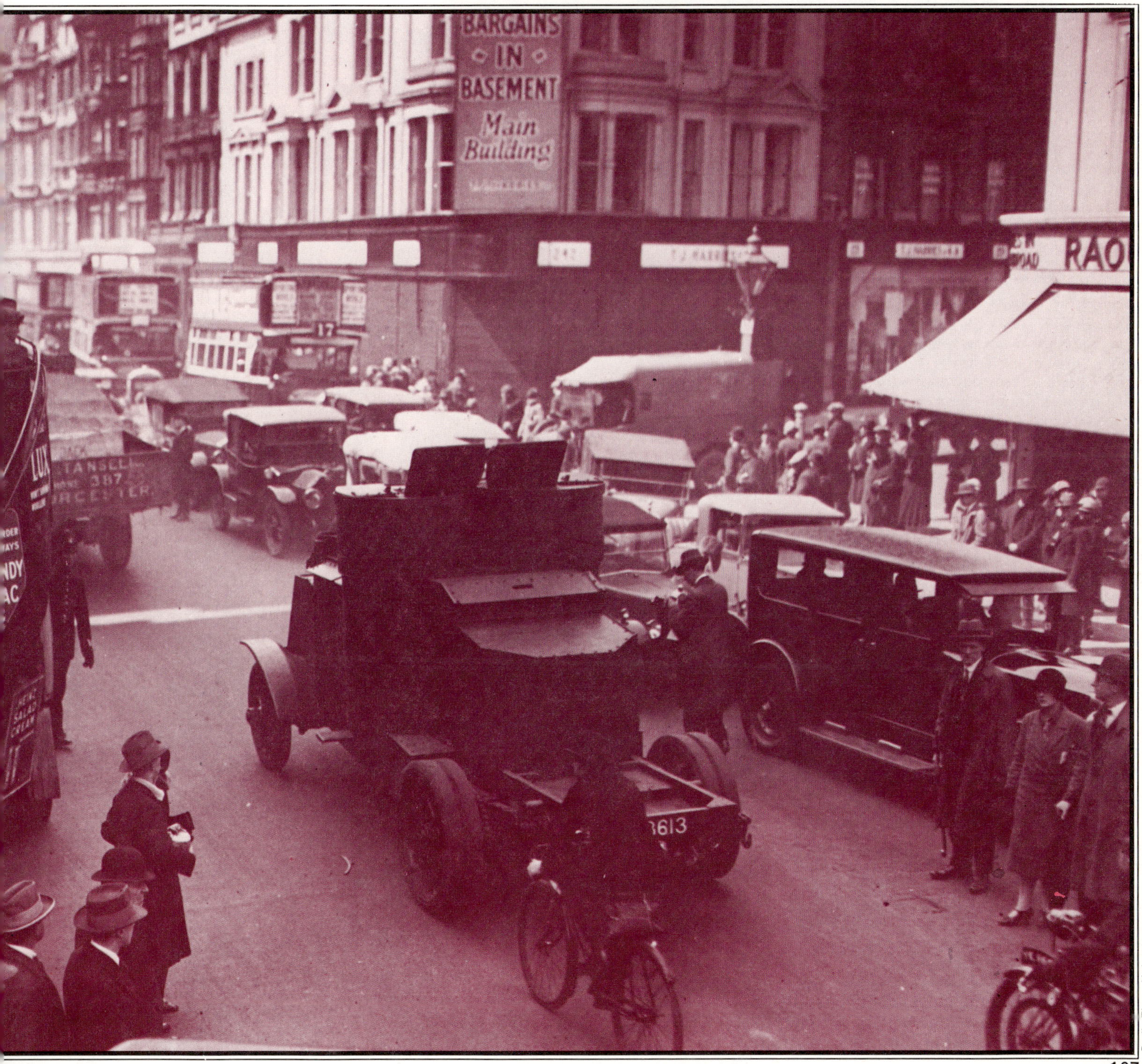

Radio Times Hulton

of Fiat origin are making an important break-through on Western European markets, the Soviet Union learned its first useful lessons about mass production from that arch-capitalist, Henry Ford, after he had launched the world's most important new model of 1928 — the successor to the seemingly immortal Model T.

In a motoring world where new models emerged every 12 months, it was remarkable that two famous makes at opposite ends of the social scale — Rolls-Royce and Ford — could retain their original basic design for so long. Even Rolls-Royce replaced the Silver Ghost with the Phantom after 19 years, whereas Ford's 2.9-litre Model T, given a post-war look in 1923, still came pouring off the lines in staggering quantities. Yet there was an ominous tapering-off after 1923's all-time record output of 2 055 309 vehicles, to 1 991 518 in 1924, 1 966 099 in 1925, and 1 629 184 in 1926, when the car was given another facelift and optional wire wheels.

The truth was that the faithful 'Flivver', born in 1908, was getting old and customers were getting choosey. New and more modern, less spartan rivals were coming forward, notably the Chevrolet from General Motors, which sold nearly 600 000 units in 1926, and the Overland, and in a comfortably prosperous America plenty of clients could find a few more dollars for something a little less utilitarian.

Henry Ford gives in

Having invented 'the universal car' and prospered exceedingly from it, Henry Ford became myopic about the T. His son Edsel, son-in-law Ernest Kranzler, production manager Charles Sorensen and others saw the falling sales graphs and clamoured for a replacement, but Henry wouldn't budge. His one dream project was an X-8 engine, with cylinders disposed like a two-row 4-cylinder radial, planned in 1925 to power a Model T successor. When this engine proved too radical for early production, Ford was all for continuing the T. 'Why kill the goose that lays the golden eggs?' was his attitude, but pressures mounted, his innate business sense finally yielded, and in mid-1926 he gave the go-ahead for a new car.

Speculation about it became almost a national sport. Most authorities, including W. B. Stout of Ford itself, predicted a six-cylinder, but some opted for a 'valve in head' (ohv) four. Not that it could make any difference, for Henry Ford ran his empire like a dictator and directed every aspect. As the new design jelled and tooling-up problems loomed, he did a sensational thing. On May 26th, 1927, he stopped T production altogether, and began a gigantic retooling operation in his plants which lasted almost seven months. In 19 years of uninterrupted production, 15 007 033 Model T Fords had been built, a prodigious total only surpassed by the Volkswagen 'Beetle' in 1972. On December 2nd, 1927, the T's replacement, the Model A, was released.

At first sight it seemed disappointingly ordinary, having a 3.3-litre sv four-cylinder engine in unit with a 3-speed 'crash'-type gearbox, four-wheel brakes and transverse leaf springing. Its plated radiator and body styling suggested a small-scale Lincoln (Ford's small-output prestige car), and some components such as clutch and transmission were indeed 'miniaturized' Lincoln in pattern. The general proportions were pleasing with welded wire spoked wheels to enhance them. Gone were the T's flywheel magneto and hand throttle; instead conventional coil ignition and an accelerator pedal figured. The engine gave 40 rugged horsepower, meaning 65mph, the springs had very effective Houdaille dampers, and there was a safety glass windscreen, wipers as standard, and a choice of several colours — all at about the price of the old 'Flivver', and $100 cheaper than the Chevrolet. The Ford car had become civilized, the public recognized value for money, and the orders poured in. Ford's immediate problem became that of meeting demand, and although the Model A never enjoyed the tremendous life-span of the T (car fashions had begun to change too quickly by then), over $4\frac{1}{2}$ million were built in under five years, reaching all corners of the world, including Soviet Russia.

It was in 1928 that the USSR launched its first Five Year Plan, important items on the agenda being extensive land mechanization and the foundation of a large-scale Russian motor industry. To help achieve these, they sought capitalist mass production 'know how' and approached Henry Ford, who agreed to build and equip a big new plant for manufacturing trucks, tractors and cars at Gorky, 250 miles east of Moscow. The new Molotov or GAZ factory did not attain effective operation until 1931, when the first flow of tractors and lorries was accompanied

The 'New Ford': America's most eagerly awaited car of the late '20s was the Model A Ford, successor to the world-famous T of which over 15 million were built in a period of 19 years. The car had conventional 3-speed transmission, 4-wheel brakes, many refinements and a modern appearance, and it cost about the same as the old model. Right: The Model A's engine was a conventional 3.3 -litre side valve four-cylinder unit with coil ignition. Petrol was gravity-fed from a tank in the scuttle.

British 'babies': The success of the Austin Seven and an increased petrol tax brought several new small cars on to the market in 1928–29. Left: The Clyno Nine 2-door fabric saloon. Below left: The Triumph Super Seven, introduced in 1928, had hydraulic brakes. Right: Eager viewers at Olympia in 1928, crowding round the new overhead camshaft Morris Minor engine. Far right: The Morris Minor car – plain to look at, cheap to buy. Bottom right: A seaside holiday scene featuring a Singer light car.

National Motor Museum

Autocar

by just 15 GAZ-built Model A Ford passenger cars. Output increased under the second Five Year Plan, but quantity car production in the Soviet Union did not come into its own until the '70s.

Although Britain's car production was modest compared with the huge output of the USA (3 083 360 cars built in 1927!), major factories such as Morris and Austin which used diluted forms of mass production were thriving. Singer of Coventry had also expanded their markets in the '20s, and in 1926 they introduced an important new 'baby' car, the Junior. It was noticeably larger and more comfortable than the 747cc Austin Seven, but had a zestful ohc engine only 100cc larger, able to propel a 7ft 6in chassis carrying full four-door touring bodywork at 50mph. With three speeds and two-wheel brakes the cost was only £148, and with seasonal improvements the Junior lasted until 1932.

In 1928 Britain's Chancellor of the Exchequer imposed an extra 28% tax on petrol thus focusing special interest on smaller-engined, less thirsty cars. Two more under-1000cc models swiftly appeared from Triumph and Clyno. The Triumph Super Seven was the obvious retort to the Austin; an enterprising little car with 832cc sv four-cylinder engine, four speeds, worm final drive and Lockheed hydraulic four-wheel brakes – all for £149 10s in touring form. The

Clyno Nine was a 951cc sv four with three speeds and two-door fabric saloon bodywork costing £160. With so much interest in the 'baby' class, rumours began to spread that Morris would soon be joining it, culminating in the spring of 1928 when William Morris officially confirmed that a smaller Morris was on the way.

Birth of the Morris Minor

Once again expediency decided the format of a new car. In 1926 Morris had given their best-selling Oxfords and Cowleys a face-lift, replacing the dated bullnose radiator with a plain, flat one, and also fitting excellent four-wheel brakes. Early in 1927 they acquired the financially ailing Wolseley concern, out-bidding Austin and an American bidder by paying £730 000, thereby acquiring a fine factory, an expert staff, and some excellent overhead camshaft engine designs. These embodied a neat drive by vertical shaft and bevels, inherited from the Hispano-Suiza aero-engines which Wolseley built during the Great War. When asked to produce an engine for the new 'baby' Morris, Wolseley adapted an ohc design they had prepared for a still-born Eight of their own.

It was a clean little unit, measuring 57 × 83 mm (847cc), and the camshaft drive spindle ingeniously performed double duty by also acting as an armature shaft for a vertical

dynamo. The rest of the car was very much a scaled down Cowley, having semi-elliptic springing all round, a similar flat, plated radiator, and four-wheel brakes. With all this, plus really comprehensive instruments and the fashionable new bumpers front and rear, the prices of £125 for a tourer and £135 for a fabric saloon were very attractive. Sliding rather than winding windows featured, and a safety glass windscreen cost £2 extra.

The new car, named the Morris Minor, was released in August 1928, but before that its arrival inadvertently precipitated a tragedy. Following the preliminary announcement, a Morris spokesman had intimated that the coming 'baby' would be 'two-thirds the size of the Cowley, and about two-thirds the price'. The cheapest Cowley then cost £170, yet many inferred from this that Morris was about to launch a £100 car. The rumours reached the Clyno firm, always doughty competitors with Morris, though financially weaker. Their own recently introduced Nine saloon cost £160, and the management panicked. They hastily produced a sadly cheapened open fabric version which they called the Century, but even with the most drastic cost-cutting they could not attain that magic figure, fixing the price at £112 10s, and unveiling the car a month before the Minor. The latter was so complete, and the Century so stark, that Clyno had little chance. They built and sold 300, but they were poorly made, and with tough competition all round the plucky little Wolverhampton company folded in March 1929. William Morris, the most humanitarian of automobile tycoons, was genuinely sorry.

Away from harsh realities of mass production, ingenuity and enthusiasm still abounded. Front wheel drive was now attracting sports car designers, and both Alvis of Britain and Tracta of France tried out the principles in racing, then applied them to catalogue road cars. At the 1927 Paris Salon, Tracta's designer, J. A. Gregoire exhibited a low-built 1100cc front-drive sports Tracta which embodied his company's patent homokinetic drive joints, later employed by other fwd exponents such as Adler, DKW and Rosengart. Alvis showed their front-driver, a potent-looking 1½-litre single-cam four, at Olympia a year later. The

Radio Times Hulton

National Motor Museum

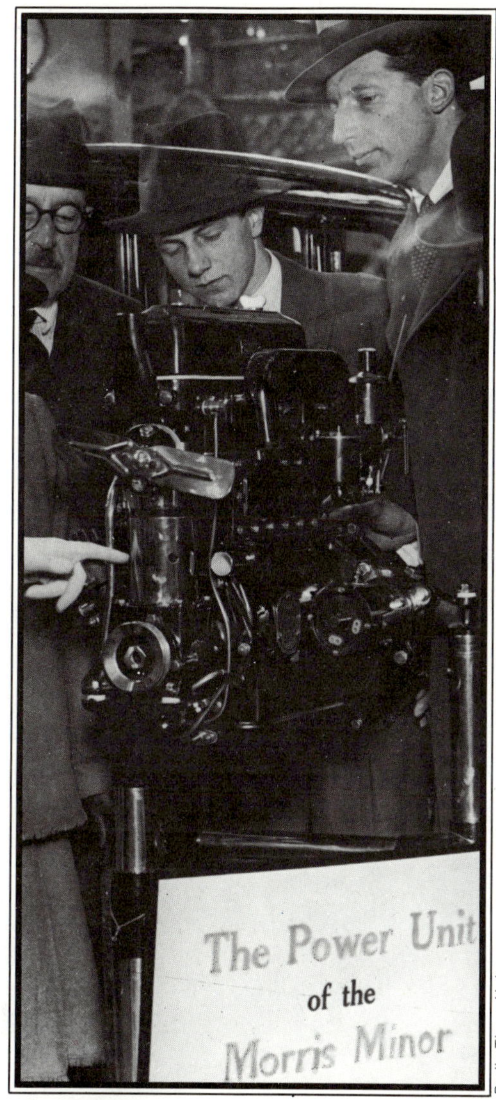

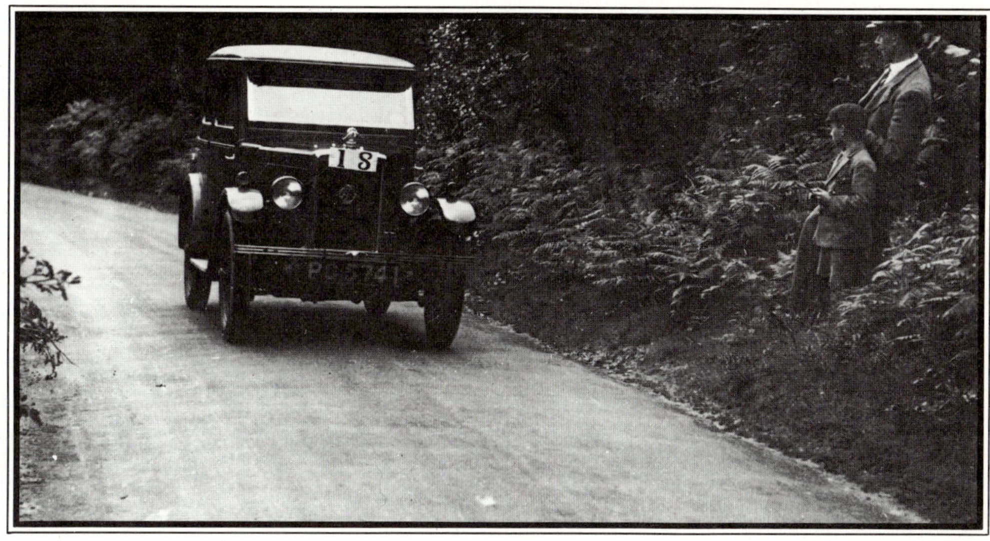

drive was through universally-jointed half-shafts and ball joints, with independent front suspension by four $\frac{1}{4}$-elliptic transverse springs. It was not a success, being noisy, complicated and requiring frequent maintenance, and Alvis dropped production after turning out about 150 cars. Through limitations on material and technical data these French and British designs were short on lock and excessively robust and heavy, but their enterprise in exploring a principle now featuring on a large percentage of European cars was commendable.

Apart from cars as a whole, the 1926–28 period was immensely fruitful in design refinements, most of them coming from the USA. Cadillac introduced the synchromesh (or 'clash-less') gearbox which is universal today; AC-Delco marketed the first electric fuel pump. Bumpers, foot dippers, centralized chassis lubrication, hypoid-bevel 'low-line' final drive, safety glass, and oilless rubber-bushed bearings all appeared, while of world-wide significance was the adoption in late 1927, by several American makes including Studebaker, Oldsmobile and La Salle, of chromium plating – a bright, hard, non-tarnishing electro-deposited finish which instantly outdated the nickel plating process with its need for frequent polishing. And one further event of far-reaching importance was the introduction that year of the 5-day working week, by Henry Ford.

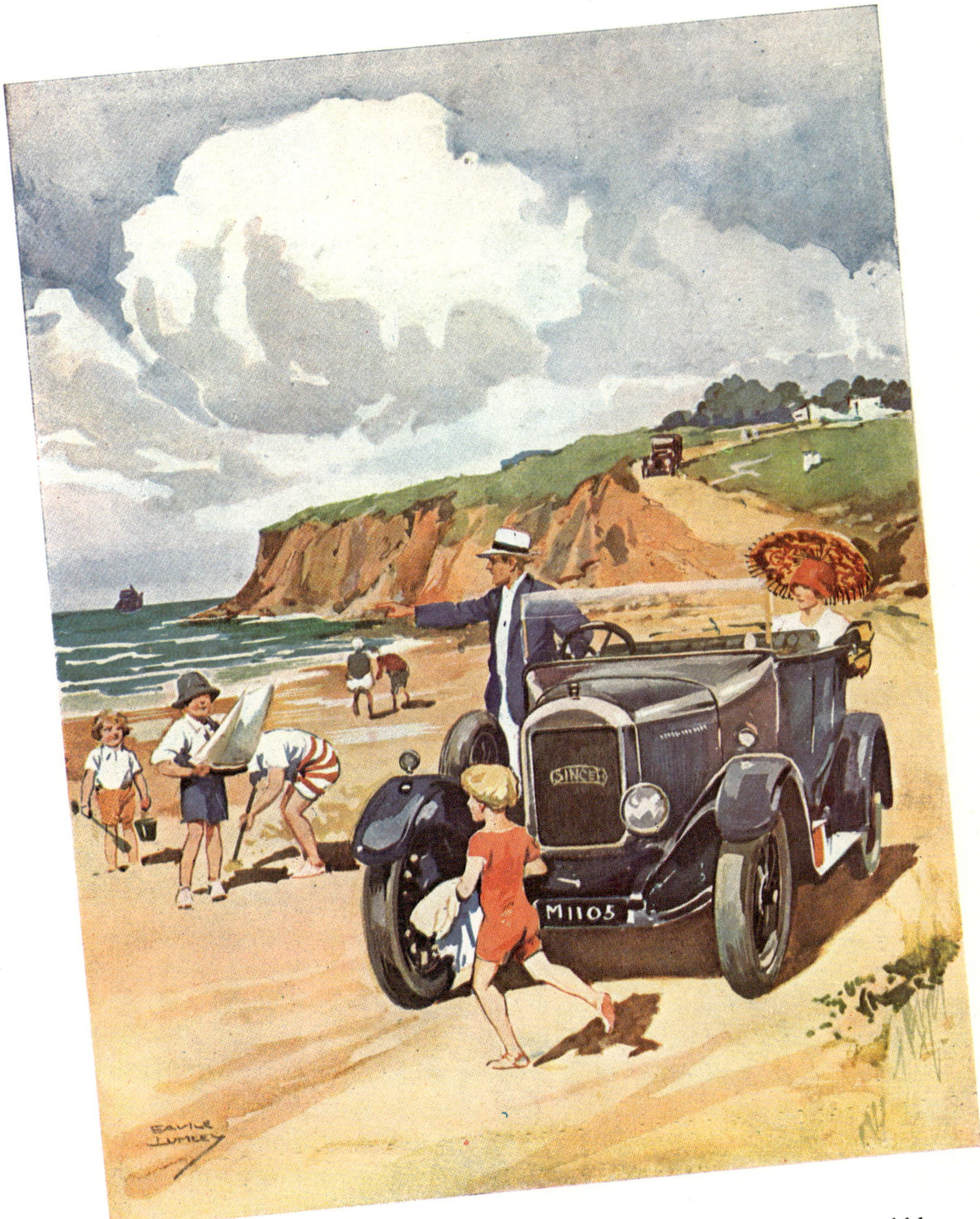

THE END OF AN ERA

The sign on this Chrysler car (left) highlighted a situation which faced thousands in the USA after the Wall Street crash in 1929. Above: Bugatti's 'white elephant' – the huge 12.7-litre 8-cylinder Bugatti 'Royale', of which only six were built.

As 1928 gave way to 1929, only a far-sighted financial wizard could have guessed what lay ahead. To America, everything in the motoring garden looked particularly lovely, with 1928 production up by almost a million cars to a fantastic 4 012 158, and no sign of the boom waning. All over the world there was vigorous competition in every car market, from 'millionaires' row' right down to the humblest motorist.

The rot set in with an unparalleled boom on New York's Wall Street stock exchange in 1928. By 1929 speculation had got out of hand and market prices became inflated beyond all realism. Stock prices rocketed, peaked, then plummeted, and on October 29th, 1929 – 'Black Tuesday' on Wall Street – came the great crash. Share prices collapsed and many banks and finance houses failed; countless investors were ruined, and the crisis sent a shock-wave of apprehension around the world. All continents were affected, and many businesses, car manufacturers among them, were to collapse. The Great Depression had come, and was to hang menacingly over the world for four years.

But none of this could be foreseen by the public, and all looked well in the months beforehand. Indeed, there was a new influx of European and American *super-luxe* automobiles, which outmatched the 1919–20 extravaganzas and threatened to outnumber the royalty, dowagers, maharajahs, film stars, big financiers and other privileged customers who could afford to buy them. France, USA, Britain and Germany all produced new offerings in what are now revered as 'Vintage classics' but were then the very acme of perfection in their makers' eyes.

If sheer size was the criterion for opulence, then the French Bugatti *Royale* took precedence. Ettore Bugatti had long nursed an ambition to build a big luxury car, 'finer than a Hispano-Suiza, or a Rolls-Royce' as he said, and in 1926, with his racing cars on the crest of the wave, he began designing the Type 41. It was the biggest private car ever made, having a wheelbase of 14ft 2in (20in longer than a Rolls-Royce) and an overall length of over 24ft. Its engine was an enormous straight-eight of 125×130mm (12 760cc), with a single overhead camshaft which itself was 4ft 7in long! It operated three valves to each cylinder, and the crankshaft (weighing 7cwt!) ran in nine watercooled bearings.

The gearbox was in unit with the rear axle, and had three speeds. Bottom was for starting only, second was for normal road work up to 90mph, and the 1½:1 'high' for really fast travel. Its actual maximum speed was not known, but Ettore Bugatti himself is said to have attained 120mph with three passengers in tests of the prototype. The vast chassis followed Bugatti practice, with semi-elliptics and a tubular front axle, and reversed ¼-elliptics at the rear. The very finest special coachwork was fitted, and the chassis alone cost about £5000 in 1929 (the equivalent of about £40 000 today). Only six examples of this superb monumental folly were built, and Ettore Bugatti undertook to maintain each car for life free of charge, whimsically presenting every owner with a special radiator cap in the form of a white elephant. The Type 41 engines finally ended up in French railcars, two per train, doing sterling work during the '30s.

Despite its name and the maker's hopes, no *Royale* was ever bought by a king. That arch-motoring enthusiast, King Alfonso of Spain, had wanted one, but in the end ordered a new Duesenberg Model J instead. This was the American luxury car builder's greatest work, a combination of high performance and gracefully balanced proportions, with superbly engineered chassis and mechanicals, and a choice of the finest American and European coachwork. Duesenberg had been taken over in 1926 by Erret L. Cord, who also acquired the Auburn car and Lycoming engine concerns. His brief to the Duesenberg brothers was a replacement for the Model A with no expense spared, and the new J, which appeared at the end of 1928, had a 6.9-litre Lycoming-

113

Radio Times Hulton

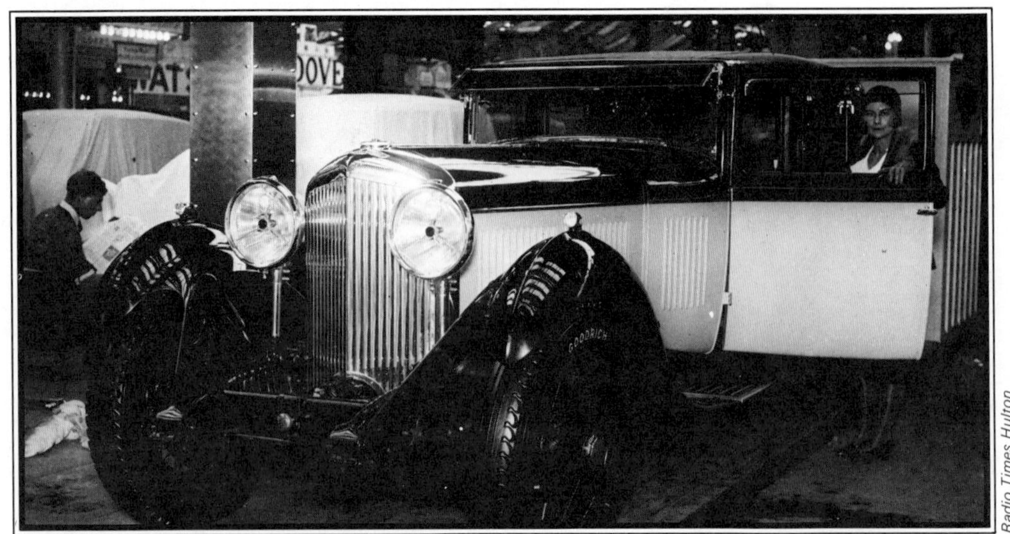

The international 'super-luxe' class: An 8-litre Bentley (left), its elegance concealing a formidable performance and a maximum speed of over 105mph. Right: The 7.7-litre straight-8 'Grosser' Mercedes-Benz, built for Continental heads of state and high-ranking politicians. Below: A superb 6.9-litre straight-8 Duesenberg Model J, with Derham 'Tourster' phaeton coachwork, and film star Gary Cooper at the wheel.

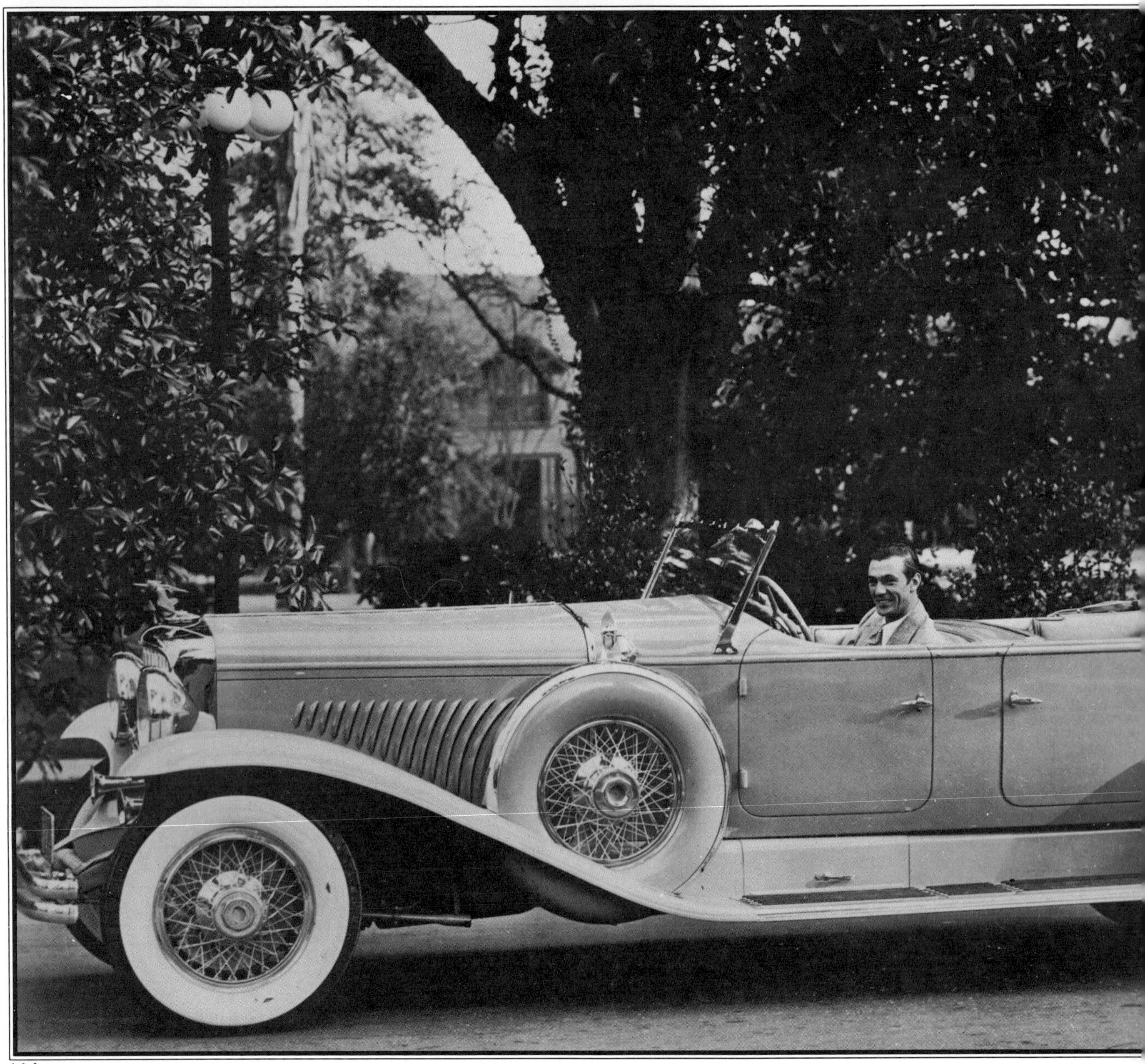

Daimler Benz

built straight-eight power unit with twin ohc (inherited from racing), four valves per cylinder, and an output of well over 200bhp at 4250rpm. Although a complete car scaled $2\frac{1}{2}$ tons or more, the maximum speed was 116mph, with four-wheel hydraulic braking to help control the tremendous performance. Long sweeping lines and a shapely vee-radiator with vertical slats were an invitation to every quality custom coachbuilder, and while some efforts were uninspired and others eccentric, the finest examples gave the Duesenberg an awe-inspiring beauty.

E. L. Cord sprang a second surprise in 1929 with an all-new front wheel drive car named after himself. Designated the Cord L29, its transmission layout was taken from the successful front drive Miller racing car which first appeared in 1925. A 4.9-litre Lycoming sv straight-eight engine was set low and well back in the chassis, driving forward through a 3-speed gearbox and differential to the front wheels. The front brakes were inboard, and suspension was by duplicated $\frac{1}{4}$-elliptics facing forward; with no propellor shaft to dictate floor level, the designer was able to make the car sensationally long and low, with a vee radiator even more elegant than that of the Duesenberg, and a choice of top grade custom coachwork.

At a price of around $2300, the L29 was not everybody's choice, but its demise after over 4000 had been built in four years was due primarily to the Depression. A similar fate awaited another American front-drive enterprise, the $5\frac{1}{2}$-litre 8-cylinder Ruxton. Built by New Era Motors Inc. of New York, this, too, bewitched the 1929 public with its low looks and set-back radiator, but its price and the economic upheaval at the close of the decade killed its chances.

Sixteen cylinders

When the great General Motors Corporation also entered the ranks of the *super-luxe,* their resources gave it a fair chance for survival through the hardest times. The Cadillac V16, first seen at the New York Show late in 1929, deserved to last on technical merit alone, and last it did, right up to 1934. It was powered by a sophisticated vee engine with two banks of eight cylinders at 45°. A single camshaft inside the vee operated ohv through pushrods, capacity was 7.3 litres, and output 165bhp at 3400rpm, with impressive torque throughout the range. A radiator similar in shape to that of the Hispano-Suiza was used, and custom bodywork by Fisher, Fleetwood and other quality US coachbuilders placed the Cadillac 16-cylinder in the highest echelon of prestige cars, even though its price was appreciably less than some.

Cars for the rich

In Britain, more new cars for the rich were forthcoming. By 1929 Rolls-Royce deemed it time to modernize the 7.7-litre Phantom 1, endowing it with an improved engine having an alloy cylinder head and higher compression. This new unit gave notably better performance, delivering the customary Derby 'sufficiency' of silent horsepower via a new unit 4-speed gearbox and a hypoid bevel final drive. In combination with underslung semi-elliptic rear springs replacing the former cantilevers, this lowered the line of the whole car. A special shorter chassis version with higher-performance engine and raised axle ratio, called the Continental, blended sports car vigour with Rolls-Royce velvet, and carried some superb coachwork, making it one of the most coveted among classic cars today.

The Phantom 11 first appeared before the public at the 1929 Olympia Show, there to find an inspiring new rival in the 8-litre Bentley. As usual, this managed to eclipse the Rolls-Royce technologically, and almost in aura; it was virtually an enlarged $6\frac{1}{2}$-litre, the six-cylinder ohc engine having dimensions of 110×140mm (7983cc), which produced no less than 220bhp, making the 8-litre a very fast luxury town carriage indeed, with an easy 105mph gait and remarkable flexibility. It was possible to put the car into top gear at about 4mph, then jump out and walk alongside it. This 8-litre was the final masterpiece of the enterprising Bentley company; 100 examples had been built when, sadly, the Depression killed off this gallant marque, after which, by grim irony, it was acquired by Rolls-Royce.

In Germany Mercedes-Benz, strengthened by the 1926 merger, embarked on the development by Dr Ferdinand Porsche of a series of large cars. These were largely sport-orientated, the 7.1-litre six-cylinder pushrod ohv SS and SSK models proving outstanding in supercharged form, and gaining many racing successes. However, a larger touring car appeared in 1930, designed by Dr Hans Nibel and called the 45/280 *Grosser* Mercedes-Benz. It had a big 95×135mm, 7655cc straight-eight broadly similar to the sixes, with supercharging optional. Transmission could be by 4-speed gearbox or a special Maybach 6-speed which comprised a normal 3-speed unit with auxiliary 2-speed gear; the semi-elliptically sprung chassis weighed 36cwt, and had servo hydraulic brakes and centralized lubrication. The limousine bodywork was rather ponderous and Teutonic, but with supercharger fitted the power was around 200bhp, making the *Grosser* a carriage of formidable performance for kings, heads of state, and top Nazi officials.

Humbler motorists at that time were confronted with an even more bewildering array of worthy vehicles. Several American makers were goaded by the success of the Model A Ford into building cheaper models. General Motors provided greatest opposition with the 3.2-litre 6-cylinder ohv Chevrolet ("a six for the price of a four"), nicknamed the 'Cast Iron Wonder' or the 'Stovebolt Six', a tough, inexpensive motor car of which over a million were sold in 1929 alone. Chrysler brought out the cheaper De Soto six and the even cheaper Plymouth four, Buick launched the Marquette six, Oakland the Pontiac, and Marmon the Roosevelt, 'the first straight-8 for under $1000', and among the first cars to have radio fitted as standard.

Morris expediency

In Britain more expediency by William Morris, now Sir William Morris, had transformed an excellent 1927 6-cylinder ohc Wolseley model into the 2½-litre Morris Six of 1928, and the latter into the new MG 18/80, given individuality by twin carburettors, an improved head and block, a lower chassis, Rudge wire wheels and, of course, sporting bodywork set off by a smart new radiator embodying a central tiebar which was to become highly fashionable. This striking MG came before an approving public at the 1928 Olympia Show, but its thunder was rather stolen by an example of positively inspired expediency by MG's 'kingpin', Cecil Kimber.

On examining prototypes of the new ohc Morris Minor at Oxford, Kimber was quick to see its potential in modified form as a sports car. Only two weeks after the Minor was announced, news came of a new MG, the Midget M-type, using the same 847cc four-cylinder engine in a dropped chassis. It bore attractive open 2-seater fabric bodywork of low build with a pointed tail, while fixed cycle-type wings and louvred side valances completed the sporting picture. With a road weight of only 10cwt, the 20bhp engine gave this perky little newcomer a zestful performance despite having only three speeds. The price was only £175, and such was the demand for the Midget that it soon ousted the bigger 18/80 model from the production line altogether. As time passed, the car was improved in detail, gaining better brakes, a 4-speed gearbox, and metal-panelled bodywork, while much-modified racing versions were very successful in major international handicap events of the early '30s, elevating the MG initials and the famous octagon motif to a world fame which they still enjoy today.

Sir William Morris would have preferred the term 'rationalization' to 'expediency', which his ever-growing group exploited yet again in 1930 with a new small six, the Wolseley Hornet. This was virtually an ohc Morris Minor with two extra cylinders accommodated in a longer bonnet and it cost £175 — the same price as the MG Midget

Sporting Baby: Using the new Morris Minor overhead camshaft engine designed by Wolseley, Cecil Kimber of the MG Car Co. swiftly produced the MG M-type Midget sports car as an open two-seater and closed fabric coupé in 1929.

and £10 less than a Morris Cowley — theoretically just the right sort of car to meet Depression markets. Six cylinders were then still regarded as essential to combat the roughness and vibration in an engine, and that in the Hornet was one of the better parts of the car, together with the excellent Lockheed hydraulic brakes and the new Luvax hydraulic dampers then just coming on the market in place of friction type.

With only the light bodywork of the Morris Minor, this surprising new Wolseley possessed an appreciable power-to-weight ratio, and its potential as a sporting car quickly became apparent. Outside coachbuilders swiftly marketed open sports versions which, in truth, looked faster than they actually were, but gave a lot of pleasure to hundreds of young British motorists at moderate cost in the early '30s. Inevitably the small six motif was copied, Triumph coming up at the 1930 Olympia Show with the Scorpion. This in effect was a Seven with five inches more chassis and a 1.2-litre sv engine. The cult of the tiny six did not last; the engines tended to be heavy on fuel and oil, and limited on power, and the bodies uncomfortably small, so that both increased in size in complement to each other.

1929 was called 'the year of the straight-

British small sixes: The Triumph Scorpion (above), virtually an enlarged Seven with a 1.2-litre six-cylinder side-valve engine squeezed into a lengthened bonnet, was shown at Olympia in 1930. Below: The Wolseley Hornet seen at the same Show used Morris Minor bodywork and running gear, with a 1.3-litre six-cylinder overhead camshaft power unit in an elongated chassis having hydraulic brakes.

8'. America had popularized this type of engine, which, though occupying much bonnet space, gave very smooth, effortless running at not much more cost than a six. In Europe, Sunbeam of Britain and Horch of Germany were among its early converts, joined by their respective compatriots Wolseley and Stoewer in 1928, then Hillman, Lanchester, Arrol-Aster, Delage, Renault and others in 1929, and by Hampton, Minerva, de Dion-Bouton etc. in 1930. For some, the innovation marked their swansong; Hampton, Arrol-Aster and de Dion all collapsed in the Depression, while Lanchester was absorbed by Daimler. But for at least one other marque it heralded a new phase — Renault's new straight-8, the 7.1-litre Reinastella, at last replaced the ancient 40CV six, and was their first model to adopt a normal nose radiator and dispense with the firm's traditional scuttle radiators and 'aligator' bonnet.

The Delage D8 was a compatriot 4-litre ohv straight-8 with a long, low chassis which proved irresistible to the great French *carrossiers* of the day, such as Fernandez-et-Darrin, Henri Chapron, Letourneur-et-Marchand, and others. De Dion-Bouton's dabble in the straight-8 pool was, unfortunately, the last for this great pioneer firm, which finally closed down in 1932, short of direction, modern equipment and orders. Minerva of Antwerp had largely taken over the Belgian *super-luxe* mantle from Excelsior; their 6.6-litre 8-cylinder was a fine car which, together with a smaller 4-litre version, weathered the Depression and was in production until 1935.

On the sporting side of motoring, there were several significant developments. The Swallow Sidecar Co., first of Blackpool and then of Coventry, took up car coachbuilding in the late '20s, fitting particularly graceful sports bodywork to plebeian chassis such as the Austin Seven, Standard, Swift and Fiat. Swallow 'kingpin' and designer was 'Bill' Lyons, later to found the famous Jaguar marque and later still to become Sir William Lyons for his services to the British motor industry. At around the same time, the brothers Alan and Richard Jensen of West Bromwich began building an attractive Bugatti-style pointed-tail sports 2-seater body for a special Standard model called the Avon; later they, too, manufactured

British Leyland

Top far left: This 1929 straight-8 Delage D8 epitomizes sporting fashions of the late '20s, with fixed 'cycle' wings and shallow 'letter box slot' windscreen and rear window. Renault built a straight-8 at around the same time, the 7.1-litre Reinastella (far left), first of the marque to have a normal front-mounted radiator. **Top left:** The 2-litre Lagonda Speed model with fabric bodywork, sometimes known as 'the poor man's Bentley'. **Above:** Before launching the Jaguar car, William Lyons designed and built stylish Swallow bodies on various chassis. **Left:** The highly impressive 4½-litre 100mph Invicta, with big 6-cylinder Meadows engine and all the sporting accoutrements, such as big headlights, clean-cut radiator, rivets on the bonnet and outside exhaust pipes.

their own car, the Jensen. The success of the MG Midget prompted two more British makers, Singer and Triumph, to weigh in with rakish open two-seaters; Singer called theirs the Porlock, and Triumph the Gnat, but neither had quite the zest of the Midget, nor its brilliant future.

Late in the '20s another British make, Lagonda, had renounced their light car image in favour of a handsome 2-litre Speed Model with twin 'high' camshaft engine and optional supercharging, and a 3-litre push-rod ohv six in 1929. Regarded as 'the poor man's Bentley', this car carried particularly pleasing fabric bodywork with swept wings. Another exciting model was a new low-chassis '100mph' Invicta, build at Cobham, Surrey, and propelled by a 4½-litre ohv

Meadows six-cylinder engine. It was first shown at Olympia in 1930, looking extremely impressive with its ultra-low lines, square-cut radiator, stylish wings and beefy outside exhaust pipes. Apart from a fine Monte Carlo Rally win, however, this British sports car never quite lived up to its looks, nor did it ever attain the exalted status enjoyed by Continental machinery such as the French Bugatti and the Italian Alfa Romeo. The latter's high-efficiency twin-cam sixes were winning numerous sports car races and selling well with a stirring choice of coachwork, while the unexpectedly potent sv 6-cylinder OM from Brescia was another agile performer from Italy.

An Olympia surprise in 1929 had been a drastically revised Trojan, in which the lengthy 2-stroke engine had been removed from under the floor and installed vertically in the rear 'boot' of a new coupé called the RE. With wire wheels, fixed cycle-type wings and fabric-covered bodywork, this had a most un-Trojan-like sporting appearance belied by its performance. The old solid tires had long gone, and the cantilever springs gave way to semi-elliptics, but the chain drive remained, as did the leisurely pace and unique 'bumbly' exhaust note. The ingenuity of this rehash was ill-rewarded, and the Trojan faded with the Depression.

Developments in Germany

In Germany there were important but lesser known developments. In 1928 the DKW (Das Klein Wunder — the little wonder) motorcycle concern of Saxony, part-ancestors of today's Audi, marketed their first car, a 584cc twin-cylinder 2-stroke engined economy model with wooden chassis. A sports 2-seater variant, notable for its long empty bonnet with tiny engine at one end, followed, and bigger engines came in 1930. Another famous motorcycle maker, BMW (Bayerische Motoren Werke or Bavarian Motor Works), also entered the car world in 1928 by acquiring the Dixi company, together with their licence to build the British Austin Seven with left-hand drive and German bodywork.

At the same time a farsighted campaigner for independent suspension by swing axles, rear engines and backboned platform frames, Dr Josef Ganz, was laying out the design for a revolutionary car embodying all these features. He persuaded the Ardie motorcycle factory to build a tiny prototype with 175cc engine and chain drive in 1930, and its comfortable ride and nimble performance over rough, slippery roads precipitated further

Italian masterpiece: The glorious Alfa Romeo 1750 2-seater 'Spider' Gran Sport, with its elegant 6-cylinder twin overhead camshaft supercharged engine, designed by Vittorio Jano.

British eccentrics: The rehashed Trojan saloon (above), the RE of 1930, had coachwork 'à la mode' with its 1½-litre 2-stroke engine stowed vertically in the 'luggage' boot. Below: Two Burney 'Streamlines' seen on the Bath Road at Colnbrook. Their engines were in the tail behind the rear wheels, and there was ample room between the axles for seven seats.

experiments with cars built by Adler, Standard, Zündapp and NSU, culminating in the production of the world-famous Volkswagen embodying the Ganz concepts.

Far more adventurous and impractical was a British venture, the Burney Streamline, which staggered the Olympia crowds in 1930 with its inordinate length and grotesque form. It was an attempt by the airship designer, Sir Dennistoun Burney, to apply advanced aerodynamics to an automobile. The engine was placed far to the rear behind the axle, where it impaired stability but allowed a very roomy body with inter-axle seating for seven people. Suspension was independent all round by transverse leaf springs, two spare wheels were carried in the rear doors, and cycle wings were fitted. Engines varied from an unreliable 3-litre twin-cam Beverley-Barnes six to Lycoming and Armstrong-Siddeley units, and the cars were excessively heavy, ill-handling and, inevitably, expensive. Only a dozen were manufactured, one being supplied to the Prince of Wales, before the Depression overwhelmed this bizarre enterprise.

A remarkable feature of the time was the large number of models offered by the big makers. Morris listed 18, Wolseley as many as 33, and even a quality producer such as Alvis offered a choice of four distinct types with wide variations in bodywork. But repercussions from the Wall Street crash were making themselves distinctly felt by the summer of 1930. Sales in Britain and on the Continent fell markedly, while American production for the year, after a euphoric 4 794 898 in 1929, was a comparatively abysmal 2 910 187. The ranks began to thin as the weaker firms dropped out; model ranges were rationalized and prices were cut right back. Even the quality firm of Rover 'went cheap' during the slump, only reverting to its former status when the worst was over.

New styling trends

The end of the decade brought new styling fashions, many initiated by America. Directly inspired by the sleek Duesenberg and Cord, Chrysler became the trend-setters with a range of striking saloons having handsome vee radiators, sweeping wings and clean lines. Most US and European rivals were a year behind or more and still using the narrow-edge 'ribbon' radiator worn by Chrysler in 1929. This was hailed as an innovation on several models at Olympia in 1930, often in conjunction with a new 'gimmick', the central vertical tie-bar on the radiator, as sported by Daimler on their Double-Six in 1928 and by MG in 1929.

Wire wheels with large-diameter hubs, complete with chromed hubcaps enclosing the wheel nuts were also fashionable among the 'majority' class of cars. More important from the safety aspect was the growing popularity of bumpers at front and rear, and of the rear-mounted petrol tank, made easier by the availability of electric fuel pumps. A 'new' feature popular with US makers was the 'silent 3rd' transmission, although this had appeared on the 1926 Riley Nine and also on the original Rolls-Royce Silver Ghost in 1907! Another 'novelty' was flexible rubber engine mounting, — although Gottlieb

121

Daimler had used rubber engine packings on his original car of 1886! America also adopted the freewheel, which permitted easier gear-changes and saved on fuel at the expense of valuable engine braking power.

In Europe, Vauxhall had tried out a new transmission option, the Wilson self-change preselector epicyclic gearbox, in 1927, and a year later Armstrong Siddeley adopted the system. In 1930 Daimler employed it in conjunction with a 'fluid flywheel', on an improved Double-Six, and later on other models. The fluid flywheel acted as an automatic hydraulic clutch, the required gear being selected by a tiny lever on the steering column, and the change effected by a quick dab on the clutch pedal; this was half-way towards the modern automatic system, being heavy and costly but working well.

At a time when costs had to be kept low, it was plucky of Singer to start a trend in 4-speed gearboxes on small cars, in place of the cheaper 3-speed, on their 1930 Junior model. More indicative of hard times at Olympia that year was another new 'baby', the Swift Cadet, with an 847cc sv engine, three speeds and a neat two-door coachbuilt saloon. It was priced rather high compared with its rivals at £185, with an open 2-seater at £160, and unhappily it could not save Swift from becoming another Depression victim and closing down the following year. Perhaps the news most eloquent of those difficult days came in the last fortnight of 1930. Sir William Morris at last announced the £100 Morris Minor. It was an open two-seater version with simpler sv engine instead of overhead camshaft, very basic trim and lighting, and a no-option grey finish with black-painted rather than chromed radiator, bumpers' and lights. Thus did the motor industry emerge from a brilliant Vintage decade with suitable austerity.

Signs of the times: The ever-popular Austin Seven was built under licence in Germany, France, the USA and Japan. This is the German version (above) built by Dixiwerke which became the first BMW car in 1929. Above right: Sir William Morris seated in the £100 Morris Minor which was announced late in 1930. Its austere specification included black-painted radiator and headlamps, open 2-seater body work, and no bumpers. Below: Germany's even starker DKW Typ P had a 584cc twin-cylinder 2-stroke engine and reinforced wooden chassis/body construction.

PRE-PETROL PIONEERS

Ca 3500 BC First recorded use of the wheel on Sumerian chariots.

Ca 500 BC 'Sicilian' surface oil (petroleum) used for lighting by Romans.

308 BC Demetrios (Greece) builds an enclosed 'war wagon' occupied by two men, one steering, the other treadling a wheel driving the rear wheels.

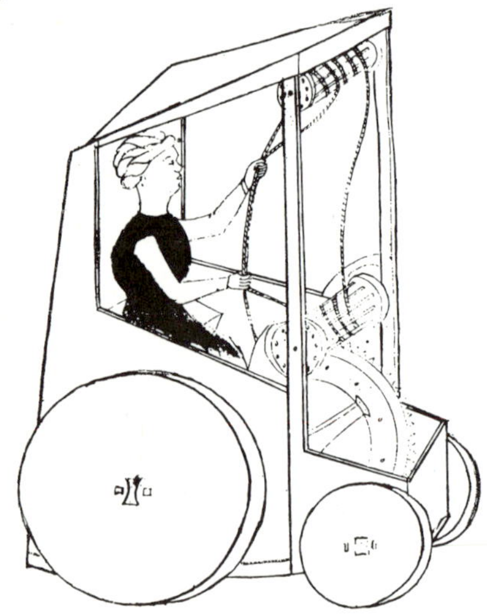

1420 Giovanni Fontana (Italy) builds one-seater four-wheeled 'sedan', propelled by occupant pulling on endless rope working a drum and gears (pictured above).

1649–63 Hans Hautsch (Germany) builds 'wonder' horseless carriages, operated by men concealed within, working cranks.

1673 Christiaan Huygens of Holland demonstrates possibilities of internal combustion by exploding gunpowder in a cylinder, thereby raising a piston and causing a vacuum, atmospheric pressure then forcing piston down and lifting a weight.

1689 Legless cripple Stefan Farffler of Altdorf, Germany, builds hand-operated three-wheeler 'for going to church'.

1694 Elie Richard (France) proposes a carriage treadled by a footman behind passenger's seat.

1771 Nicolas Cugnot (Lorraine) builds working three-wheeled high-pressure steam powered gun tractor.

1784 James Watt (Britain) patents specification for steam road carriage with three-speed variable transmission.

1784 William Murdoch (Britain) builds working model steam vehicle.

1787 Oliver Evans (USA) patents a high-pressure steam wagon.

1788 Pistons on articulated connecting rods first prescribed in an engine by Robert Fourness in a steam engine design.

1791 Nathan Read (USA) projects a twin-engined, rack-driven steam car.

1801 Richard Trevithick (Britain) builds full-scale working high-pressure steam road vehicle.

1803 Charles Dallery (France) patents four-wheeled steam car with change-speed gears.

1807 Isaac de Rivaz (Switzerland) makes a working vehicle propelled by gas electrically fired in a cylinder.

1815 Josef Bozek (Bohemia) builds Watt low-pressure steam-powered four-wheeler.

1823 Samuel Brown (Britain) successfully climbs Shooter's Hill, London, with two-cylinder 'gas-vacuum'-powered four-wheeler.

1825–ca 1840 First steam carriage era brings working vehicles by Gurney, Burstall & Hill, Hancock, Nasmyth, Napier, James, Fraser, Ogle & Summers, Heaton, Macerone, Scott Russell and others of Britain; Dietz (France); Bordino (Italy); Fisher (USA) and others.

1828 Onésiphore Pecqueur (France) patents four-wheeled steam wagon with differential drive.

1885·1904
THE VETERAN ERA

1858 Thomas Rickett (Britain) builds first of several light passenger-carrying steam carriages, one being used to tour the Scottish Highlands by Earl of Caithness.
1863 J-J Etienne Lenoir (Luxembourg) builds and runs a three-wheeled 'break' on coal gas.
1873 Amédée Bollée Snr (France) completes 'L'Obéissante', first of several practical, working steam carriages, driving it 135 miles to Paris without mechanical mishap two years later.
1858–1885 Second steam carriage era: vehicles built by Yarrow, Cooke, Tangye, Thompson, Carrett & Marshall, Inshaw, Prew, Mackenzie, Todd, Blackburn, Grenville and others of Britain; Dudgeon (his vehicle is pictured left), Roper, Reed, War, Carhart, Copeland and others of USA; Ravel, Bollée, De Dion-Bouton and Trépardoux of France; Nussberger of Sweden.
1876 Nicolaus Otto (Germany) patents four-stroke cycle, only to lose rights ten years later on grounds that principle was propounded in 1862 by Alphonse Beau de Rochas (France).
1881 Jeantaud (France) builds and runs electric car powered by 21 Fulmen batteries.

1885 Benz builds first practical petrol-powered tricar; single-cylinder, single speed; belt drive.
1886 Daimler builds first 4-wheeled petrol car with fast-turning single-cylinder engine, two speeds, and belt-cum-gear drive.
1888 Frau Berta Benz and two sons complete first extended motor drive (125 miles).
1889 Daimler introduces twin-cylinder engine and sliding-pinion four-speed transmission.
Panhard and Levassor acquire licence to manufacture Daimler engines.
1890 First Peugeot and Panhard-Levassor cars, both Daimler-engined.
1891 Peugeot car covers 1280 miles, following the Paris–Brest–Paris cycle race.
1892 Panhard-Levassor build the first front-engined petrol car.
Wilhelm Maybach of Daimler introduces constant-level float type jet carburettor.
1893 First four-wheeled Benz car, the Viktoria, is introduced.
1894 Panhard-Levassor and Peugeot share first prize in Paris–Rouen 'Concours', the world's first motoring contest.
Panhard introduce countershaft sliding gear system.
Frank and Charles Duryea found first American motor manufacturing company at Peoria, Illinois.

1895 Emile Levassor in a Panhard-Levassor with 1.2-litre Daimler 'Phénix' in-line twin-cylinder engine and enclosed gearbox wins world's first motor race, the 732-mile Paris–Bordeaux–Paris.
First pneumatic tires used on a car by Michelin brothers.
Rudolf Egg of Switzerland develops lever-controlled gearless variable transmission.
1896 De Dion-Bouton market proprietary aircooled, single-cylinder 1500rpm engines from 1hp upwards for use in light two-, three- and four-wheeled vehicles.
Léon-Bollée produce 650cc tandem-seated three-wheeled voiturette.
First four-cylinder engine built by Daimler for Panhard-Levassor.
British Daimler Motor Company founded at Coventry.
Henry Ford builds first experimental car.
1897 First petrol-engined car with two-speed epicyclic gearbox and shaft final drive to live axle made by F. W. Lanchester.
Mors of Paris produce 45 deg. V4 air-cum-watercooled car with low tension coil and dynamo ignition.
First front-wheel-drive car built by Graf und Stift in Vienna, using De Dion engine.

1905-1918 THE INTERIM YEARS

Low tension magneto introduced by Bosch in collaboration with F. R. Simms.

Benz introduce 5hp 'Kontra' horizontally-opposed twin-cylinder engine.

1898 Louis Renault builds prototype small car with front-mounted De Dion engine, direct drive top gear and universally-jointed shaft final drive.

Decauville 'Voiturelle' has independent front suspension by transverse leaf spring.

Daimler-designed four-cylinder engine used in touring Panhard-Levassor.

1899 Four-cylinder German Daimler 'Phoenix' has honeycomb-type radiator, pressed steel frame and gate-type gearchange.

First monobloc four-cylinder engine made by Amédée Bollée Jnr.

Automatic advance and retard ignition control used by Hiram Maxim and Packard in USA.

1900 Acetylene (carbide) lighting supplements oil and kerosene.

1901 Daimler's first Mercedes car has throttle-controlled engine, improved honeycomb radiator, twin side camshafts operating inlet and exhaust valves, and gate gearchange.

Oldsmobile 'Curved Dash' is America's first car to go into high quantity production.

1902 Bosch introduce high-tension magneto.

Spyker of Holland build six-cylinder four-wheel-drive car.

First straight-eight engined car (two 4-cylinder units coupled together) with single-speed gearbox built by CGV of Paris.

Truffault of Paris introduce friction-type shock absorber.

Disc brake patented by F. W. Lanchester of Britain.

Single overhead camshaft engine with pressurized lubrication marketed by Maudslay in Britain.

1903 Ader of Paris build V8-engined car.

1904 Napier of Britain market first successful six-cylinder car.

Sturtevant of Boston, USA, market first car with automatic 3-speed transmission.

Engine and gearbox in one unit on French Motobloc and American Stevens-Duryea cars.

Riley of Coventry introduce detachable centre-lock wire wheels.

Introduction of Schrader needle-type tire valve.

1905 Moseley of Britain produce detachable wheel rim for easier tire changing.

Renault of France patent a hydraulic shock damper.

Pipe of Belgium make twin high-camshaft engine with inclined overhead valves.

The first Rolls-Royce, the in-line twin-cylinder 10hp, is marketed.

First car by Rover of Coventry has cast aluminium backbone frame embodying engine, clutch housing and gearbox.

Simms-Welbeck car is fitted with pneumatic rubber front bumpers.

1906 Front-wheel brakes fitted experimentally to a Mercedes.

Michelin introduce 'press on' tire gauge.

Rudge-Whitworth market detachable wire wheel.

Electric lighting by accumulator becomes an optional extra.

1907 Rolls-Royce adopt one-model policy with 40/50 six-cylinder 'Silver Ghost'.

Chadwick of Pittsburgh, USA, introduce supercharged sporting model.

1908 Ford Model T ('The Universal Car') is introduced (over 15 million built by 1927).

First coil-and-distributor system of ignition introduced by Delco, USA.

First V12 engine by Schebler, USA.

Car heating by exhaust (USA).

Formation of General Motors, USA, the world's first big motor combine.

Sankey of Britain market steel artillery wheel.

1909 Aquila-Italiana introduce aluminium pistons on sporting models.

Isotta-Fraschini standardize front-wheel brakes.

Christie of USA build transverse-engined, front-drive taxi with independent front suspension (the Mini layout).

First dipping device by Bleriot, France, for acetylene lamps.

1910 Hydraulic tappets patented by Amédée Bollée Jnr.

1911 De Dion V8-engined car marketed.

Delahaye V6-engined car marketed.

1919-1930
THE VINTAGE ERA

1912 Cadillac of USA standardize coil ignition, electric starting and electric lighting.

Hupmobile and Oakland (USA) produce all-steel bodywork.

Triplex introduce splinterproof glass in France.

1913 William Morris (later Lord Nuffield) markets Morris Oxford, using proprietary engine and other major components.

Reo of USA employ centrally-positioned gearchange.

Lagonda of Britain employ unitary construction of chassis and body.

Cable-operated direction indicators introduced in USA.

1914 Loughead of USA (later Lockheed) develop hydraulic braking system.

Adjustable driving seats offered in France and USA.

1915 Cadillac market first American series-production V8-engined car.

Packard of USA market world's first production V12-engined car, the 'Twin-Six'.

Dipping headlights and suction-operated windscreen wipers introduced in USA.

1916 Brake stoplights introduced in USA.

1917 First use of torsion bars in suspension on the Spanish Diaz-y-Grillo car.

1919 Hispano-Suiza of France and Spain pioneer use of servo-assisted 4-wheel brakes. Isotta-Fraschini of Italy market world's first in-line 8-cylinder (straight-8) engined car.

Citroen of France introduce American-type mass production methods to Europe.

New Bentley 3-litre sports car is announced.

1920 Duesenberg of USA employ hydraulically-operated 4-wheel brakes.

Leyland Motors of Britain announce new 7.2-litre straight-8 luxury model.

1922 Integral chassis/body construction, vertical coil independent front suspension and narrow-angle monobloc V4 engine in new Italian Lancia Lambda car.

British prototype North-Lucas car has all-independent suspension by swinging arms, coil springs and coaxial hydraulic dampers.

First British 4-cylinder, 4-seater, 4-wheel braked 'Baby' car, the Austin Seven, is introduced.

Trico of USA produce first electrically-operated screen wipers.

Mercedes of Germany market first European supercharged sports car.

1923 Pratts 'Ethyl' leaded fuel introduced in USA to reduce engine detonation (i.e. 'pinking').

1924 Japan takes up motor manufacture with the 10hp aircooled Lila light car.

The first MG sports car, based on the Morris Oxford, is marketed in Britain.

Introduction of the low-pressure balloon tire by Goodyear, USA.

'Duco' quick-drying cellulose car finish pioneered by du Pont, USA.

1925 Electric direction indicators marketed by Bosch of Germany.

General adoption in USA of front and rear bumper bars.

1926 Two major German makes, Mercedes and Benz, combine to form Mercedes-Benz. Silentbloc oilless rubber bushes are introduced in USA.

1927 Ford USA replace Model T after 19 years' production with the Model A.

World's largest production road car, the 12.8-litre Bugatti Royale with 14 ft 2 in wheelbase and weight of 2½ tons, is announced.

Epicyclic preselector 'self-change' gearbox developed by Wilson of Great Britain.

Triplex of Great Britain market laminated safety glass.

Tracta of France market 1100cc front-wheel-drive sports car.

1928 Widespread adoption by US manufacturers of chromium plating for bright parts in place of nickel.

Cadillac adopt the synchromesh gearbox.

New Morris Minor 'baby' car with overhead camshaft engine is announced in Britain.

The first MG Midget, using the Morris Minor engine, is introduced.

Foot headlight dipping introduced in USA.

1929 Car radios offered as optional extras in USA.

1930 Shell-type quickly replaceable 'thin wall' engine bearings developed by Cleveland Graphite, USA.

World's first production V16-engined car by Cadillac, USA.

'Fluid flywheel' hydraulic clutch and epicyclic gearbox adopted by Daimler of Britain.

Wolseley Hornet 'Light 6' using Morris Minor bodywork is announced.

British rear-engined Burney 'Streamline' all-independently sprung car developed by designer of R101 airship.

Britain's first quantity-production £100 car, the Morris Minor, is introduced.